CRITICAL ACCLAIM FOR
HOLLAND BAY

"Jim Winter has written a novel that like a fine whiskey, just gets better and better with time."

—Ken Bruen, bestselling author
of the Jack Taylor series

"Drug dealers, cops, departmental politics in a beaten-down city. Fans of *The Wire* will love *Holland Bay*."

—Dana King, two-time Shamus Award nominee
and author of the Penns River crime series

HOLLAND BAY

BOOKS BY JIM WINTER

The Nick Kepler Series
Northcoast Shakedown
Second Hand Goods
Bad Religion

Road Rules
Holland Bay

JIM WINTER

HOLLAND BAY

A HOLLAND BAY THRILLER

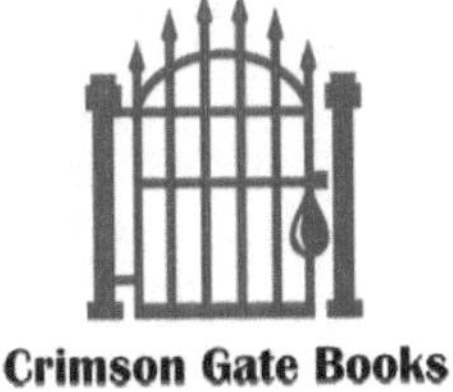

Crimson Gate Books

For Candy Jo
4 feet 11 inches of happiness

CHAPTER 1

Five people tried to hire Armand Cole to drive them home on the night he made his first kill. His employers gave him an old Ford Fusion, spray-painted yellow, a bogus number stenciled on the side, and a pizza-car sign on top with all the decals scraped off. Armand kept the sign unplugged to appear off-duty. That did not matter. With temperatures plunging, the only thing people saw was a yellow car with its motor running.

It never occurred to Armand that "off-duty" cabs only sat idling downtown near the hotels off Gotham Square. His only instructions had been to "blend in" while he waited outside Skip's, a bar in Huron Junction, for the Super Bowl to end.

So, while he waited, he turned down would-be fares, patiently explaining to them that his car was not available, while slipping in questions about the old man. The fourth guy, a fat black guy in a Steelers jacket, said the old man regularly drank at Skip's. Armand didn't know much about Huron Junction, but he knew Skip's was the only bar in the neighborhood with a gringo name.

The old man would be inside on his usual stool. All Armand had to do was wait for the game to end and watch for the old man to come out. Too bad, he thought, that the Steelers were up by six with just over two minutes to play. With the ball on Chicago's twelve-yard-line, people were already streaming out of Skip's and the other nearby bars, but Raul Carcinira was not one of them. The old man would wait until the very end, and maybe even beyond.

Then it happened. Pittsburgh's quarterback, their overhyped rookie out of Rutgers, threw an interception in Chicago's end zone, which Chicago ran back eighty-four yards. Risking his cover, Armand shouted "Go! Go! Go!" while beating the steering wheel. The Bears got the ball down to the Steelers's sixteen-yard-line. They would come out of the two-minute warning running a no-huddle offense. Armand knew he had less than ten minutes.

Armand took the little .22 out of his pocket and checked the magazine. He slipped the gun into the door well and settled back in his seat. The old man would be out soon, long enough to finish his beer after the Bears put this one away. Somebody knocked on his window.

"Hey, man," said a Hispanic man whose face was obscured by his parka, "You take me down to Serievo?"

"Off duty," said Armand, glad he'd slipped the gun into the door well.

"I'll give you twenty bucks, man. Had too many shots to drive myself."

"Sorry," said Armand. "My boss says no fares until the game ends." When it was clear the man in the parka was going to push him on it, he added, "Bears have the ball on Pittsburgh's sixteen with a minute to play."

"Really?" The man staggered back across the street to Skip's, nearly getting clipped by a MORT bus lumbering down Carnegie Avenue. The snow began as the game resumed. Chicago's quarter-back faked a handoff to the running back, found a hole in the Steelers's secondary and ran the ball in. They were now up by two. Chicago decided to run the ball again for the conversion. Chris Collinsworth was freaking out, unusual for that white boy to lose his cool. Armand wished he was home watching it.

The Steelers began a half-hearted drive to get into field-goal range, but from the sound of the crowd and the commentators' defeated voices, it was over. The Steelers had snatched defeat from the jaws of victory. Armand watched the door to Skip's while mentally counting the cash he'd just won for betting on Chicago.

Five minutes later, the bar started to empty. Half the patrons would stick around, but not Raul Carcinira. His boy had arranged to pick him up within five minutes of the end of the game. The younger Carcinira was nowhere in sight. Right now, he was in a meeting with Armand's boss, and Armand would provide the father's transportation.

The old man emerged, dressed just as his son had told them—a dirty Ford cap on his head and a Cleveland Browns jacket that was too light for the Arctic temperatures outside. The snow had really started to come down now. Armand turned on the pizza topper light and made a U-turn in the middle of Carnegie.

The old man wandered along the sidewalk, looking for his son. Armand rolled up in an open spot and lowered the passenger-side window. "Hey, man, you need a ride?"

"I'm looking for my son," said the old man, his Mexican accent thick. "He's supposed to give me a ride."

His eyes were unfocused. He did not beat his arms or fold them against the cold. He only shuffled around, looking for a car that wasn't there.

"Your son Josè?" asked Armand.

"You know Josè?"

"Sure, man. He sent me. He had to meet a guy. I take you home."

The man looked around for his absent son.

"Get in, man," said Armand. "You gonna freeze your ass off out there." The old man did not move. Armand reached across and opened the passenger door. "Get in, man. Heat's good in here."

Actually, the car's heater probably hadn't run right since Obama took office. It barely kept the cold outside at bay. Nonetheless, the old man got into the car and slumped into his seat. Armand pulled out into traffic.

After a couple of lights, Carnegie turned into St. Jakob, a winding series of switchbacks that descended into the river valley. Through the snow ahead, the lights of Monticello's industrial district glowed orange. For now, the Fusion handled the slickening roads well enough. The city had salted the hell out of the streets and freeways. If all went well, Armand would be down on Pier 9 in fifteen minutes.

At the bottom of the hill, Armand jumped onto the freeway, took the next exit, and began climbing a huge yellow-arched bridge dubbed "The Big Mac Bridge" by locals. Officially, it was Francis Rooney Bridge, but it looked like a pair of golden arches spanning the Musgrave River.

"Where are we going?" said the old man, his head lolling from side-to-side now. "Why we going to Vodrey Heights?"

"We not," said Armand. "We gonna see Josè. He down by the docks."

"I want to go home."

Armand ignored him and took the northbound exit to I-73, Monticello's main interstate.

"Why?" asked the old man.

"Why what?"

"Why is Josè down by the docks?"

Armand said nothing. The snow had started to stick, despite the salt. He felt the car slide a few times, hitting ice patches. About halfway to the old port facility, the snow became blinding. He came up on Studebaker Avenue, a service road that crossed the Musgrave River to a warehouse district servicing the auto plants. The car was sliding regularly now. He was never going to make the piers intact.

"You work for Ralph," the old man mumbled, "don't you?"

"Yeah," said Armand. It was now or never. "Josè gonna miss you." He pulled the .22 out and shot the old man in the forehead.

Reaching across, Armand popped the passenger door open and shoved Raul Carcinira out. The car began sliding again as Armand pulled the door shut.

A full bladder woke Jessica Branson around one a.m. She

stretched out and realized she was on the wrong side of the bed. She always slept on the left, even when she had a man over. The snoring next to her told her she had, indeed, spent the night with someone, but...

She moved her legs and noticed she was naked from the waist down. Sitting up, it became clear her bra had disappeared, though her Steelers jersey remained. As her eyes adjusted, her companion came into focus.

"Shit," she said under her breath. Now she remembered. She and Jerry had made a bet. If the Steelers won, Jerry would never hit on her again. If they lost...

She did not remember the sex, but it surprised her that she'd kept on her oversized jersey. They had drunk a lot of beer and several shots of vodka, which was too bad. She would have liked to know what Jerry was like.

In the bathroom, the hangover kicked in, a slight headache and a sour stomach. Branson wished she could call off tomorrow with the freak snowstorm blowing in across Lake Erie. It had been unusually warm in Monticello the past two weeks. Then a very wet front came up from Louisiana only to collide with an Arctic high-pressure system crossing the lake from Canada. So Monticello would have a blizzard and a cold snap at the same time. Jerry, being a web developer, could work from home tomorrow in his boxers and a T-shirt. Branson had to drive all the way down to Holland Bay Station. You couldn't do police work from your couch, even in a useless unit like Special Investigations.

When she finished peeing, she took a look in the mirror. Her honey blonde hair flew wildly about her head. A disheveled woman with bags under her eyes and no clothes except for a thin football jersey stared back at her. Why was she here? Why would she even go into work tomorrow? She needed to leave town, move someplace warm, and start over again.

Right. She had given herself that talk every other night for the past four years. At least she knew Jerry. At least she wouldn't be ashamed of sleeping with him. But when had she stopped even caring what she did and who she did it with?

"What the hell am I doing to myself?" she said into the mirror.

On her way back to the bedroom, she saw the snow piling up outside. She'd have to get up early if she wanted to get in at a tolerable hour. She dressed and went out to sleep on Jerry's couch. Hopefully, she'd wake up around five-thirty and not be hung over when she headed up I-73.

Pier 9 had once been the busiest pier in the Port of Monticello. Before the city's last remaining steel mill built its own loading facility on the Musgrave River, tons of coiled steel and finished ingots arrived by semi in an almost orderly procession, bound for nearby Cleveland and Toledo, up to Detroit, or back up Lake Erie and onto the auto plants of Milwaukee, Chicago, and Kalamazoo. Those were the days of Wolcott Steel beginning in the 1820s, started by one of the city's founding fathers shortly after the Musgrave River War. In those days, other steel companies fought for dominance in the Foundry District, but Monticello looked upon them as interlopers.

Now they all had vanished, even Wolcott Steel, replaced by a single modern mill owned by some company from Luxembourg. Pier 9 had fallen silent, its remaining traffic rerouted to a new facility at Port Jones on the far side of the island opposite the pier. Only two cars remained, a current-model Lexus with its engine running and an early millennium Buick Park Avenue with fading paint and shattered windows. A man sat in the driver's seat. The holes in his temple and forehead had stopped bleeding some time ago.

Around both cars, the snow had piled up. The snow almost obscured the lights of the George V. Voinovich Suspension Bridge, which spanned the sound between Holland Bay and Holland Island. True, these were only construction lights, but the veil of snow made them look something like UFOs hovering in formation above this little strip of Lake Erie.

In the Lexus sat two men, both black. One wore a London Fog overcoat and looked like James Bond—if Bond had been played by Anthony Mackie. He leaned back with his eyes closed while classical music from the stereo softly washed over him. The other man had piled on layers under his Yankees jacket. His face sported a layer of stubble that might disappear every three or four days if he remembered to shave. He often didn't. He was too busy.

"That boy let me down, Rufus," said the man in the Yankees jacket. "He was supposed to bring Raul here so he can see what we did to his boy."

Rufus opened his eyes and stared straight-ahead, his eyes fixed on the Voinovich Bridge. "Be cool. The snow probably held him up."

"Uh-huh. We should have planned for that shit."

That made Rufus laugh. "Monticello may have to bow to the great Ralph Smithers, but you and I and even our tiny-dicked president are all Mother Nature's bitches."

It was Ralph's turn to laugh. "That's 'cuz Mother Nature ain't ever had this." He pointed to himself, dropping his hands down the length of his torso. "One night with me, she never blow another hurricane again."

Rufus pressed his lips thin and went back to staring at the bridge.

"You still thinking that bridge gonna make you some money?" asked Ralph. "Like some Home Depot crap gonna make those properties of yours into gold mines?"

"It's the future," said Rufus. "We can't be bangers forever. I've been telling you that for years."

"Yeah," said Ralph. "Only reason I'm listening is you holding my wallet. But you gonna have to show me before I hand those corners over to Rey and Miguel. Shit, them motherfuckers'll kill the dope trade in Monticello in six months."

"Uh-huh." Rufus did not say anything more. He looked tired

after listening to Ralph's dismissal of his plans.

Ralph's phone buzzed. He took out a cheap phone available at any shack or storefront place in Monticello's finer rundown neighborhoods. The screen had a text message. "Done. Left on Inbound. A."

"Raul dead," said Ralph, not even showing Rufus the phone. "The boy left him on the Inbound."

Rufus opened his door. "Let's do this, then." He triggered the trunk before getting out. Each man went back and took out two cans of gasoline. The snow worked its way into their shoes as they trudged over to the Buick and began dousing it and the corpse inside. When they finished, Rufus took out a copy of *The Wall Street Journal*, leaned over, and lit it with a silver Zippo lighter. The snow threatened to put out the flames before they could catch, but the newspaper finally lit. Rufus tossed it into the dead man's lap. They backed away as it caught, then watched the flames engulf the car.

"Come on, Roof," said Ralph. "A nigger catch his death out here."

They trudged back to the Lexus. Once moving, the car slid, and its wheels spun as it struggled to gain traction in the new-fallen snow. When the car turned onto Lake Road and salted pavement, the Buick's gas tank exploded behind them. The burning car melted a crater in the surrounding snow as the fire destroyed it.

Johnny Cash warbled "Cocaine Blues" as Drew Sherwood blew past the interchange for the airport freeway, entering what most people considered Monticello proper. In reality, I-73 crossed into Monticello at the northern border of Milan (pronounced "My-lan" by the locals, thank you very much), but that part of the city remained scattered, former exurbs and undeveloped tracts of vacant land. None of it mattered. Sherwood planned to stay in his nice warm cab until he reached the port, leaving only long enough to hand off his paperwork and get his return load.

A freak snowstorm had blown into Monticello overnight, but it was nothing Sherwood couldn't handle. He'd been making the run up from Greensboro, North Carolina, twice a week for four years now—even on Christmas. All he needed was a steady supply of No-Doze, coffee, and the occasional other pills available at any truck stop to keep him going. His Peterbilt took good care of him. He didn't even need a motel, though he would stop south of Columbus to crash in the arms of a truck-stop waitress he'd known for years.

He'd reached the point on I-73 where the freeway started its long, winding path downhill toward Lake Erie and the old Port of Monticello. They had promised for years that the new extension to Holland Island would open soon. Yet every time he reached the war zone the locals called Holland Bay, he'd find himself shunted off to the old port, ten crumbling piers, more of them going idle every year, surrounded by urban decay. If he had to go to the new port, the Cleveland Shoreway would take him downtown and over to the Island. Things were beautiful on the Island, except maybe for the landfill on the eastern side. Yeah, things were good on Holland *Island*. In Holland *Bay*...

There was a reason Sherwood liked to stay in his truck as much as possible until he left Monticello.

The State of Ohio had been thorough in plowing and salting the roads. As Sherwood whipped his semi around a salt truck, however, he realized that Mother Nature had also been thorough. He nearly lost the truck. He felt the back wheels of the Peterbilt slide a little, nearly taking the semi back into the salt truck's lane. Sherwood suspected one of Monticello's infamous Freeway Troopers would be waiting for him on the way back later. He could handle it. He'd been pulled over for far worse and gotten off with a warning.

Just inside the Studebaker Avenue interchange, halfway between the airport spur and the port, he ran into real trouble. Something that looked like a deer had tumbled out of the snowbank that another plow had thrown up on the shoulder. He cringed, knowing that hitting it might cause him to lose control momentarily, but stopping would lose him his load.

It wasn't a deer. It was a man.

The Peterbilt skidded, jackknifed, and spun completely around twice before coming to rest against the concrete barrier in the median. Sherwood, clad in little more than a Carolina Panthers jacket and a T-shirt, climbed out of his truck, saw that he'd missed the body, and allowed himself to vomit onto the far-left lane of I-73 North, aka "The Inbound."

Patrolman Greg Murdoch, Monticello Port Police, had spent most of his shift in the Big Boy on Lake Road near Pier 4. Normally, it was his job to patrol all the piers, but the five operating piers had all shut down during the storm while the other five had been abandoned over the past four years, a combination of the economy and the construction of a new port farther out in Lake Erie.

Murdoch debated spending the shift in the station, heading out for emergencies whenever a squeal came through. Unfortunately, Gingham was Port's desk sergeant that night. The last thing Murdoch wanted was to listen to Gingham talk about how Mrs. Murdoch was the finest white girl in the city and how Murdoch should share her. Gingham had not been with a white woman without paying since when he was in Midtown Division, picking up whores and shaking them down for freebies out by the old Locomotive Plant.

Murdoch had grown used to comments about his wife. She was, in fact, the finest white woman in Monticello, and with a sexy English accent to boot. The comments didn't bother him. Gingham did. He was a dumbass who had exploited quotas to get his stripes. Murdoch could probably have done the same, but he liked to think he was a real cop.

Even if port duty was shit duty, at least he wasn't in Special Investigations.

Around six a.m., a squeal had come over his shoulder rig. A

semi had jackknifed on I-73 Inbound at Studebaker, closing the highway. Even with the snow keeping most Monticellans home for the day, the Inbound would be a parking lot by six-thirty.

Murdoch felt sorry for that unknown Freeway Trooper, but not too sorry. His uneventful shift ended at seven. Since the plows had been out, Murdoch had to at least make a token sweep of the piers. He thanked Louise, the overnight manager at Big Boy, for letting him park in a booth, then drove over to Pier 1 where the tankers all docked. Port security would have things under control.

Chances were the crew of any ship that had docked over night or the previous day would stay on board until sunup. It was the abandoned piers that worried him. The homeless liked to hole up in some of the sheds. Murdoch had found more than one frozen to death in the two winters he'd worked for the Port Division, and a few during the past summer dead from heat exposure or worse, someone setting them on fire. This morning, he would pull onto the abandoned piers long enough to see if any faint light came from within the blockhouses or smoke from the sheds. He'd shine his spot over the rest of the pier, looking for stranded motorists or abandoned cars, then head back to the station for a quick end-of-shift report.

That was the plan until he hit Pier 9. For whatever reason, Pier 9 had become the execution gallows for gangs in Monticello. The murders were never solved, but somehow, leaving a body on Pier 9 became a message. Homicide, Narcotics, and even poor pathetic Special Investigations knew who was doing it. They just had no evidence. Harbortown, the borough command over the Holland Bay area, had tried using video surveillance only to find they were supplying junkies with scrap to fund their habits.

So it was with some trepidation that, around six-forty a.m., Greg Murdoch did his cursory sweep of Pier 9, expecting nothing more than smoke from one of the sheds. Hell, it was minus-three outside. He'd probably just leave the poor bastard squatting in the shed alone.

No smoke came from any of the structures near the land end of the pier. A dark shape, probably once a car, sat in a crater in the snow. Murdoch grumbled to himself, called it into Holland Bay Station, and nosed his cruiser into the deep drifts covering the pier.

Eventually, the spot brought the shape into focus. It was indeed a car, most likely a 2000 Buick, that had been completely incinerated. The spot swept across the missing windshield and shined upon...

A charred skull grinned back at Murdoch. With fifteen minutes to go in his shift, he had a homicide on his hands. He pounded the steering wheel.

"Fuck me!"

CHAPTER 2

Branson screamed as she hit a patch of ice. The Pathfinder spun around twice, sliding across three lanes of traffic before stopping against the snow piled up in the shoulder of I-73. It took her a few moments to catch her breath and get her heart to stop pounding its way out of her chest. Once she calmed down, she realized she now faced south into northbound traffic.

She saw brake lights flash in her rearview as morning commuters approached the interchange for the Big Mac Bridge. Her phone rang, blaring out the Imperial March from the *Star Wars* movies. She ignored it. They already knew she was late. No reason for this morning to be any different.

She restarted the Pathfinder, hoping the car was not seriously damaged. That was another thing she did not want to deal with this morning. It was bad enough that Jerry had whined for her to stay in for the day.

Last night had been special for Jerry. Last night, he got to be intimate with a crush who considered him nothing more than a friend. Last night left Branson wondering if she had absorbed an oversexed male twin *in utero*, leaving only his libido intact.

A Freeway Police cruiser pulled to the side directly in front of her. The flashing lights threatened to bring back her hangover until the trooper, as the MPD called its Freeway Division officers, switched them to rear only. The officer climbed out of the cruiser, clad in an official MPD parka and cap with the appropriate insignias for the Freeway Division. When the trooper reached her passenger door, Branson reached over and opened it before he could rap on the window with his Maglite. "Get in, Trooper," she said, holding out her badge. "It's too damn cold out there, even for that parka."

The trooper took her invitation and climbed in. He pulled down his hood revealing a young black male, probably in his late twenties. His shaved head and sharp eyes suggested military. *Bet he's all lean muscle under that parka, six-pack abs, and...*

She mentally slapped herself. *Why can't I just be an alcoholic like every other screwed up cop?* "I hit a patch of ice."

"I saw that," said the trooper, whose nametag read Jones. "Normally, I'd question you and have my ticket pad out, Detective, but I ran your plate as I pulled up. Did you know there's an APB out on you?"

Branson let out a long sigh.

"Sergeant Petrocelli of Special Investigations is trying to reach you. Says he's been trying to call you for the last half hour."

"My phone's turned off."

They both looked down at the Android lying in the cup holder between them. It said, "5 missed calls" and gave two numbers: Jerry's and Holland Bay Station.

"I can see that," said Jones. "Nonetheless, I'm to inform you that you need to contact your sergeant immediately. Something urgent has come up."

Branson could not help but laugh. "You're kidding, right? Do you know which detectives inhabit Holland Bay Station?"

"Special Investigations," said Jones.

"And do you know which cops get sent to Special Investigations?"

Jones tactfully said nothing.

"Whatever it is, it can wait," said Branson.

It did not wait. The Imperial march began playing again, the words "Holland Bay Station" clearly visible on the screen.

"You gonna get that?" asked Jones.

"I have voicemail."

The little voicemail icon was visible on her screen.

"So, you do," said Jones. "I'm only delivering the message." He made no move to leave.

Branson smiled. "You've done your duty, Trooper." When Jones did not move to leave, she added, "You married, Jones?"

Jones let out a nervous chuckle. "No, Detective, but I don't date cops."

"So, you're still here because you don't want to hike back to your cruiser until absolutely necessary. I'll bet you don't write many tickets today if you can help it."

"You've done this before."

"Two years in Freeway, right out of the Academy. I jumped at the chance to go plainclothes in Vodrey Heights. Hated patrolling I-73 and the Inland Parkway in the winter."

Jones chuckled again, this time sounding more relaxed. "Thanks for understanding, Detective."

"Thanks for putting up with this hump's bad luck."

Jones studied her face for a moment. "I've heard your story, Detective. I don't think you're a hump. I think you just got screwed by the brass."

"I'll call my sergeant on the way in. I promise."

"Then I'll let you get turned around." He climbed out of the Pathfinder and headed back to his cruiser.

Branson rocked the Pathfinder out of the snowbank and worked it back into a north-facing direction. Once back in traffic, she saw that the freeway was a solid mass of red lights beyond the Big Mac Bridge's entrance ramps. She called Sgt. Petrocelli.

"Where the hell have you been?" said a man as soon as the desk sergeant put her through. "I've been trying to get a hold of you all morning."

"I lost a bet," said Branson.

"Aw, Jess..."

"Save it. What's so urgent that we have to treat like a homicide?"

"Funny you should say that. Have you reached the Big Mac yet?"

"No, but it looks like the Inbound is a parking lot beyond it. Why?"

"Take the Big Mac over to the Inland Parkway and come back over through downtown. I need you on Pier Nine A-S-A-P."

Branson didn't need to hear any more. She knew she'd caught a body.

Nobody was happy about a semi jackknifing on I-73 Inbound, least of all the first responders. The first police officers on the scene had to force their way down the snow-packed shoulders of the highway. Once at the accident scene, they had to block the highway to stop angry commuters from trying to work their way around Drew Sherwood's rig or hitting the body he had swerved to miss. The ambulance crew could come up I-73 by going the wrong way up the closed lanes. That part did not bother the EMTs. The nearly zero-degree temperatures did.

The medical examiner, sent to pronounce the old man lying by the side of the road officially dead, really hated going out there. No one told him the highway at Studebaker had been backed up, and it took yet another police cruiser to get him to the accident scene.

A small man with a low tolerance for cold, he found his teeth chattering as he knelt beside the man who had fallen out of the snow drift and caused a southern truck driver to spin out against the opposite concrete barrier.

As the police photographer finished getting pictures of the corpse, the ME leaned over and checked the man for identification. He found the wallet, which contained a driver's license, debit card for American City Bank, and his green card. These identified him of as Raul Carcinira of Huron Junction, a neighborhood across the river in Rock Ridge.

"So is he dead?" asked the uniformed Freeway cop standing

over the ME and the dead man.

"Just a second," said the ME. He took a gloved hand and brushed away the snow that had caked the old man's forehead. "He's dead. And you need to call Homicide."

"Why?"

The ME pointed to where reddish snow still caked inside a wound in the old man's forehead. "Why do you think?"

Armand Cole caught a blow to the gut as he stepped into the alley behind The Phoenix Café. He knew this was business. He also knew not to resist. Nothing happened in or around The Phoenix unless Ralph Smithers said it happened. Cold as it was, Armand knew it was best to lay flat until pulled up or told to stand.

"Had to dump a stiff on the Inbound last night, didn't you?" said a familiar voice from behind. "We give you one simple job to prove yourself, and you go and fuck it up."

Two men, one on either side of Armand, hauled him to his feet, almost tearing both arms out of their sockets.

His stomach roiled, but he told himself not to vomit in front of Dmitri Reagan. No one showed weakness in front of Dmitri. Not unless they wanted to be his bitch.

"The snowstorm..." A blow to the back of the head interrupted him.

"Fuck the snowstorm. Ralph say you bring the old man to Pier Nine, you bring him to Pier Nine. You know what happened this morning?"

"I just got up an hour ago."

"Uh-huh. Prolly sticking it in that little ho of yours." Dmitri Reagan, five feet six inches of muscle and rage, stepped into view. There were days Armand was glad Dmitri wasn't a cop. This was one of them.

"The snowplows buried his dead ass," said Dmitri. "But some-how, he worked his way out. Some cracker truck driver damn near hit him, wrecked, and now the Inbound's clogged tighter than your baby sister's pussy."

For a moment, Armand wanted to wrap his hands around Dmitri's throat. Never mind the two goons next to him, the guy was a fucking monster. Survival instinct intervened. The last guy who went at Dmitri Reagan ended up on Pier 9 that same evening. The police didn't care. "Self-cleaning oven," they called Holland Bay.

"I'm sorry," Armand grunted, tasting bile as he spoke.

"You sorry. Meanwhile, Ralph's got homicide cops up his ass. You think sorry's gonna cut it when they take us down?" Dmitri nodded, and the two thugs holding Armand's arms let him go. "Get in there and wait. Ralph wanna talk to you. Don't know why. Told him we oughta cap your ass."

Armand looked down and moved away from Dmitri at what he considered a respectful pace. He would show no fear to Dmitri. None. Dmitri lived in fear. Armand promised himself that one day he would show him what fear drove a real man to when you threatened him one too many times.

"I caught a body," Branson repeated to herself out loud for the tenth time since Petrocelli had called her. "I actually caught a body."

A number of things had gone through her mind as she followed the Inland Parkway north, the Musgrave River's western bank below her. Above the opposite bank, I-73 glowed with stalled northbound traffic as something blocked the city's other freeway into Harbortown, Monticello's northern borough. Above the freeway on the opposite bluff sat Vodrey Heights, blissfully unaware and uninterested in the traffic jam below. Those in the Heights who bothered going into work would be very interested after they realized they'd have to cut through Midtown to cross the river and get to work. Midtown on the eastern bank was okay, if a bit grungy, as it went to seed. But no one wanted to drive through "the Hood," those Midtown neighborhoods just above the Foundry District, to get to the Inland Parkway. Bad things happened in "the Hood."

"They'd probably call in sick if there's a single flake on the ground," she muttered to herself. "But I caught a body."

Special Investigations detectives never caught bodies, or they turned them over to Homicide if they did. Something had changed over the weekend. Homicide was short of manpower. The lieutenant wanted to justify his budget and put his only former Homicide detective on a gang murder just to show they occasionally did police work.

She was being set up to fall.

This last thought stuck in her mind as she left the Parkway for Lake Road, the city's main east-west drag. As the downtown skyline came into view, its floodlights casting an eerie glow on the clouds above, a voice in her head repeated that thought over and over. *Set up to fall. Set up to fall. Set up to fall.*

Who would do that, though? A couple of commanders had reminded her that a posting to Special Investigations could be considered an invitation to pursue other opportunities. One such conversation ended with Branson getting a written reprimand for insubordination. Maybe Baker?

Alvin Baker's face loomed large in her mind as she left the parkway for the Hauptmann Memorial Bridge, an enormous stone arch bridge lined with statues of Civil War soldiers. It carried Lake Avenue across the Musgrave between the twin spans of the Commodore Perry Bridge and the enormous Vodrey Heights Suspension Bridge. It also went directly into Holland Bay and to Pier 9. As she crossed the river, she wondered if Baker was finally getting his revenge.

Baker, with his rubbery smile and his annoying lovely-to-see-you greeting, had ruined Branson's career. That wasn't true, she reminded herself. The higher-ups ruined her career. Baker just enjoyed his former post in Internal Affairs too much. She had done her job as a policewoman in shooting that boy. Baker had even said so. But like shooting an unarmed man, right or wrong, killing a politician's kid amounted to career suicide.

So had the finding that Branson was innocent. Last she'd heard, Baker had been exiled out to Edison, which did not use the MPD for its uniformed officers. It used the Musgrave County Sheriff's Department. And the Sheriff never let anyone working in the Edison Division forget it.

By the time she reached the river's eastern bank, her mood had become as dark as Lake Erie in the predawn gloom. As the road emerged from under the highway and into the cloud-filtered light of day, the sight of Pier 9 did nothing to lift her mood. Two uniformed officers, one in Port Police uniform, the other dressed for the Harbortown Division, leaned against the latter's cruiser, sipping coffee from a nearby Big Boy. A tow truck backed toward the charred remains of a car at the center of the pier. The car sat in a snowmelt crater, seemingly untouched by the blizzard around it.

The Pathfinder slid a little as Branson pulled onto the pier. She jumped out of the car, badge out. "Hey, what the hell are you doing?"

The Harbortown patrolman did not move to get off the fender of his car. "Ma'am, this is a crime scene. You'll have to leave."

"I know it's a crime scene," said Branson, waving her badge. "You see this? It's my crime scene." She looked at the tow truck and waved her badge at the driver. "Stop. I need to look at that car."

"Lady," said the driver, a tired-looking Mexican who probably had been out all night, "I got four cars stuck in a drift."

"They'll still be stuck when I get finished. Don't worry about it." She trudged through the snow toward the remains of the burned-out car. She could see that the door had been pried open and the car was empty. She looked over at the two cops watching. She finally recognized the Port cop. "Murdoch, where the hell is the body?"

"Harbortown's procedure for Pier Nine slayings," said Murdoch, sounding a little tentative, "is to process the body at the morgue."

"On a homicide?"

"On a Pier Nine homicide," said the other officer.

Branson squinted to read his nametag. "Officer...Ramos, since when do we release a body before crime scene technicians and a medical examiner have looked at it?"

Ramos and Murdoch looked at each other. Then burst out laughing.

"Branson?" said Murdoch, finally recognizing her. "Since when do we even bother with Pier Nine killings? They wrote this place off two years ago. They don't even send Homicide now. Just a squad from Harbortown."

"Not today," said Branson. "This is my crime scene. If you don't believe me, call it in. And while you're at it, get me some crime scene techs. Real ones, not those students from Custis University that the city uses to be cheap."

Murdoch, whose shift had ended a while ago, pulled his shoulder rig and called the Port Police sergeant back at his station. Ramos just stood shaking his head.

"It's a dead end," he said.

"What is?" asked Branson.

"This case."

"Why?"

"It's Pier Nine. They never get solved."

Branson ignored him and began examining the car. If she had her way, all that would change today.

The Phoenix wasn't so much stuck in time as stuck to it. Bits and pieces of the eras that had passed since the place opened during The Depression had attached themselves to it like flies to those ugly strips people hung in their kitchens in the summer. The booths, with their cracked upholstery and scarred tables, dated back to the seventies. Carvings in the tabletops showed their history. "Tupac lives," "Nuke Saddam," "Fuck Reagan," and "9/11 was an inside job."

Most of the clientele was male, black, and, in the case of the older ones, prematurely aged. They drank cheap whiskey from dirty glasses, even at this ungodly hour. Many had come to do business. The condition of the bar told Armand that the health department, never mind the police, rarely entered here—if ever. The cloud of cigarette smoke and the overflowing ashtrays on every table confirmed it.

Armand sipped ice water, about the safest thing he could have in the place. Even that gave him pause. He wasn't here to drink, though, or to hang out with the clientele. Dmitri had sent him inside to see Ralph Smithers. So until Ralph was ready, he'd sit quietly and wait. He wanted nothing to do with the rest of the people in the bar.

Not until business brought them to him.

One of the goons who had beat him earlier appeared at his table. There was no malice in his expression. "Yo, Ralph ready for you."

Armand did not take the beating personally, not from this guy. He was a soldier like Armand, doing what Dmitri told him. Armand nodded at the man and headed to a door at the back of the bar.

He had to go down a short hallway to reach Ralph Smithers's office. When he entered, it was as though he had stepped into a different world. The room, all paneled with dark wood and carpeted with something more recent than the nineties, reeked of expensive cigar smoke. Ralph Smithers, looking like Jay Z in his black tracksuit and smoking a long stogie, was leaning back in his chair, his feet up on a large mahogany desk.

In the other chair sat a well-dressed man who reminded Armand more of a young Denzel; expensive suit, expensive sunglasses, more comfortable with the brandy snifter in his hand than the stogie in his ashtray. Both men stared at Armand with cold, neutral expressions.

"Heard you had a run-in with Dmitri," said Ralph Smithers,

the one in the tracksuit. "He hurt you bad?"

"Nothing I can't handle," said Armand.

Ralph gave a thin smile. "This is Mr. King. He my money man. Started out like you."

Mr. King nodded. Armand nodded back.

"Dmitri just trying to teach you a lesson," said Ralph. "You fucked up dumping that body on the Inbound. Can't have that attention. But you did everything else right. That's why Mr. King has a job for you."

Mr. King shifted in his seat to better face Armand. "What do you know about Baggy Anderson?"

"Fatter than hell," said Armand. "Runs a corner on Eastern. Thinks he's badder than Dmitri."

"Dmitri ain't as bad as he thinks he is," said Ralph. "But Baggy ain't bad at all."

"Baggy is stealing from us," said Mr. King. "I got the numbers. I need some eyes and ears on him."

"Then cap him?" asked Armand. "I promise I take him to the pier this time."

"We'll deal with that when it's time to finish Baggy. For now, I want you to babysit him. We'll send you up with Dmitri…"

"After he and I have a chat," said Ralph.

"There's a free apartment in it for you," said Mr. King. "I want you on that corner reporting everything back to me. Who works for Baggy? Is he cutting product? Is he using? Why's he borrowing so much when his stash runs out?"

"And then?"

Ralph Smithers smiled like a pit bull. "We know what you can do, Armand. Maybe this time, the weather won't be so bad."

CHAPTER 3

"And this sonofabitch released the body!" Branson leaned onto the desk, red-faced and almost nose-to-nose with Sgt. Dan Petrocelli.

Petrocelli, tall and skinny and looking older than his thirty-three years, did not even flinch.

"That was Ramos," said Murdoch, still in his parka and standing near the door to Petrocelli's cramped office. "He had authorization from Homicide to handle the scene."

Branson turned to Murdoch. "This is not being handled by Homicide. It's being handled by Special Investigations."

"Which nobody bothered to tell us."

Petrocelli slammed his palm down on his desk. "Enough!"

Both cops jumped. The last time Petrocelli lost his temper like that, one of the Port uniforms had been shot in a drive-by.

"You're right, Murdoch," he said. "Harbortown Division dropped the ball by not telling you or Ramos of the hand-off. The fact is, Harbortown and Homicide have been writing off Pier Nine for two years now. Usually, it's some corner boy from Eastern Avenue or Prussian Meadow or a crack whore who pissed off the wrong john."

"See?" said Murdoch.

"But that ends today." Petrocelli got to his feet. "Go home, Murdoch. Tomorrow morning, you need to be back here for morning roll."

"Here?"

"The Port Police are moving all operations to the new facility at Port Jones out on Holland Island. The remaining uniform force will come under the command of the new Special Investigations captain."

"Special Investigations? What did I do?"

"Released a body before a detective could process the crime scene," said Branson.

"Jess…"

"Why hasn't Internal Affairs investigated that?" she said. "We got bodies going to the morgue with no one following up on who killed them."

"Jess…"

"Did anyone ever think that maybe Pier Nine's become a killing field because we've let it?"

"Yes, Detective. I have." The voice came from behind Branson and Murdoch.

Branson spun on her heel and…

"Oh, my God."

A short man with iron gray hair and a rubbery face smiled at her. "Lovely to see you, Detective. How's it feel to handle a homicide after so long?"

Branson's throat seized, leaving her speechless.

"Good morning, Captain Baker," said Petrocelli.

"Good morning, Sarge." Baker turned to Murdoch. "Go home, Murdoch. I need all my uniforms at morning roll seven a.m. sharp tomorrow. Go get some sleep. You've got a big day ahead of you."

Murdoch stalked out of the room, muttering under his breath.

"Well, that was certainly a screw job," said Branson. "Murdoch fucked up on this murder, but he's not a hump."

Baker laughed. "I never said he was, Detective. It's a new day in Holland Bay. This unit is no longer the Siberia of the Monticello Police Department."

"It just feels like it this morning," said Petrocelli.

"Let Midtown take all the humps. Your exile is over, Branson. We have a new mandate, and the chief himself has tasked me with carrying it out.

Branson found her voice. "Sir, I..."

Baker put a hand up. "No need to thank me, Branson. Now, I believe you have a car that's gone to Impound. I'm sure the medical examiner would appreciate a name to go with that charred body we sent him."

They could not have looked more different if one of them had been white. Two of Ralph's lieutenants drove Armand up Eastern Avenue. The driver, Monk, had been described as a gorilla by both black and white. The latter might have mumbled it or said it behind his back, but even Monk admitted he kind of looked like an ape with his huge head and sloping broad shoulders. Like Rufus, whom he drove for, he dressed for style and did not scrimp. He couldn't. As big as he was, he had to have tailor-made suits.

Monk's companion, Goose, Armand had seen often with Ralph. He dressed street, which today meant a North Face parka like Armand's and a battered Monticello State ball cap. Goose had a freakishly long neck and a beak of a nose. He also could hit harder than even Dmitri. Rumor had it that Dmitri feared Goose and watched his back around Monk. Armand didn't know if Dmitri was really afraid of these two men or just minding who had Ralph Smithers's ear.

"The place ain't bad," said Goose. "We used to put up Baggy there when he earned good. Place is empty now, but it sweet for a shithole like this neighborhood."

The neighborhood in question straddled Eastern Avenue and I-73. Near Lake Road, where Eastern began, Holland Bay had not gone too far to seed. The subway and Monorail station near Farnum Field had spawned chain fast-food restaurants and a scattering of bars that did most of their business when the minor-league Stallions played in the summer. Drive farther along Eastern and...

Armand had grown up here, and even he thought the place

looked like a war zone. When he was still in school, people had joked that Holland Bay existed solely to keep Vodrey Heights from sliding into the Musgrave River. Armand noticed that gas stations in the river valley tended to have a lot of plexiglass and wire mesh in the windows, and lighted signs with lights missing and flaking paint.

"Baggy's the problem," said Monk. "Sells weak stuff. Always has some excuse for why he needs a loan from Rufus."

"Meanwhile," said Goose, "he runnin' crack whores in warm weather outta that abandoned building behind the one where you be staying. Right now, he run 'em out of Wentworth, which got that crew in those towers righteously pissed."

"Why ain't they done him?" asked Armand.

"Not that simple," said Monk as they waited at a stoplight. Up ahead, a viaduct carried Harrison Avenue out of the Heights to the Vodrey Heights Suspension Bridge. Armand spotted a former ice cream stand now functioning as a barbecue joint with a ratty-looking smoker out front. Across Eastern from that sat a strip mall with a gun store, a payday loan place, and a nail salon.

"Baggy belongs to Dmitri," Monk continued. "The crews belong to Goose here. Doing Baggy might be interpreted as Goose moving on Dmitri." He pushed the Escalade through the intersection and under the viaduct. "Besides, Goose here and Dmitri both can't seem to catch him in the act."

"Keeps moving his stash," said Goose.

Beyond the bridge, Eastern became an enclosed slum. A view of the river beyond I-73 might have redeemed the area, but the view was blocked by the Midtown El. The ugly rail line erupted from the ground just past the bridge and blocked any view of the river.

"So what my job?" asked Armand.

"Either win Baggy over," said Monk.

"Or beat his ass if you catch him selling weak shit," said Goose. "Everybody cut, but when you cut so bad no one gettin' high, that's grounds for an ass-kicking."

***

As Branson fished in her purse for her car keys, she felt a tap on her shoulder. Jake Taggart, all six-foot-four of his creepy glory, stood behind her. "Got a minute?"

"Not now, Jake," she said. "The new captain's got me doing real police work, and I'm having trouble remembering how it's done."

"When you figure it out, maybe you can show Friedman how to do it."

Friedman, a tiny brunette with a butch haircut, sitting at a nearby desk, looked up from her John Scalzi paperback and flipped Taggart the bird. "Kiss my sweet tender ass, Jake."

"Maybe you can help me," said Branson. "I need someone to go with me to Impound."

"Can't. Gotta go out and check on that body from the Inbound," said Taggart. "Banner day here in Special Investigations. Anyway, I just got news about Ray Moran."

Branson sat down, not even asking if the news was bad. Considering the detective's condition when he arrived at University over the weekend, the news could not be anything but. "Did he wake up?"

Taggart pulled a chair from a nearby desk and sat facing her. "Sorry, Jess. They lost him about an hour ago."

Branson stared ahead at nothing at all, chewing her lower lip. "How close was he to Smithers?"

"Pretty damn close. We suspect it was that enforcer, Reagan."

Branson folded her hands together in her lap so tightly that her fingertips turned blood red. "I'll kill him."

"Reagan? You know he's a dead man walking. Narcotics won't tolerate that monster using oxygen that a more deserving sex offender could be breathing."

She finally locked eyes with him. "Not Reagan. I'm talking about Smithers."

"You want the big fish?"

"Not the big fish." She grabbed her purse and headed for the door. "He's the Great White fucking Whale. I'm going to harpoon his ass."

She had to wait before starting the Pathfinder despite the cold. Ray Moran had been in a coma since they had found him in an alley near Monticello State on Saturday night. Yet he still breathed as of last night. As long as that was true, there had been a chance he'd pull through.

Now there wasn't. What was this? Her first partner on the force murdered, and the man who had put her through a draconian Internal Affairs investigation had become her boss. She remembered that last conversation with a higher-up who suggested she leave the force. Right now, the Sheriff's Department looked good.

And the Sheriff hated the Monticello Police.

"This place all yours?"

Shandra Rogers, all five feet, two inches of her, looked around the apartment. The window looked out over Eastern Avenue, the main surface street below Vodrey Heights along the Musgrave River. Beyond that lay a stunning vista of the Upper Musgrave Elevated, ugly and black and blocking any real view of the river.

"All mine," said Armand Cole. "Long as I'm Ralph's eyes and ears on that corner out there."

Ralph and Rufus had not exactly gone all out to furnish the place, but they did at least order (or maybe stole) plenty of Ikea furniture. Too bad the rats had gnawed the legs of some of it. Armand had lived in enough slums in his short life to learn a few tricks to get rid of them. A little d-Con, a little Alka-Seltzer inside some candy, and the rats would be, if not gone, certainly less common.

"Someday," said Armand, "we gonna have a place like this on our own. Only nicer."

"And what you gotta do to keep this place?" said Shandra.

"Don't tell me you plan to work for Ralph the rest of your life."

Not this conversation again. Shandra wanted him out of the Game, and all Armand knew was the Game. "Baby, you know my only way out is through."

"You say that," she said. "You don't think you couldn't get into Custis U? They take gangbangers in all the time."

"If you smart enough. And why ain't you goin'?"

"You know I'm gonna start my own hair place when I graduate."

Right. Armand knew about all those places. Dmitri made no secret that, if Armand moved up in the organization, his next job would be laundering money through any of two dozen hair and nail salons in Holland Bay, Prussian Meadow, and, lately, down in Serievo over by the auto plants. Good money in that. He'd be expected to take a percentage off the top. As long as his numbers added up, he'd be making some real jack.

Maybe he could save up and start a business somewhere other than Monticello's seedier neighborhoods. Or even Monticello itself. Who wanted to make a future in yet another dying Midwestern steel town? Look what had become of Cleveland and Detroit.

"Baby, there ain't any way out of the Game except through. Not for guys like me. Not unless I join the military. These days, you know how long a guy like me would live fighting ISIS?"

"Longer than in Holland Bay. That's for sure."

Someone pounded on the door.

"Who is it?" he snapped, his hand automatically going for the Glock in his pants.

"Open up," said a high-pitched voice. "It's Baggy."

Shit. He had hoped to have some alone time with Shandra before the pig showed his ugly face. Armand kept his hand near the gun as he went to the door.

When Armand opened the door, there stood a boy not much older than Armand, nineteen if he was a day, and almost as wide as he was tall. Armand put him at five-feet-four, but that might have been an illusion because of the boy's girth.

"You Baggy?" he asked.

"Did I stutter?" The fat man pushed his way inside. "Nice place. Used to be mine until Dmitri kicked me out."

For once, Armand could say it without fear of reprisal. "Dmitri's an asshole."

"Must be," said Baggy. "Seems to think I need help on this corner. Where you been working?"

"I been doing mechanic work for Dmitri."

"Mechanic work?"

"Yeah. I fix things for Ralph. But before that, I worked on Crosley and Packard over in Prussian Meadow."

Baggy grunted. "We hardcore this side of the river."

"You better be."

Baggy looked Shandra up and down. "Nice ho. She suck a good dick?" When he turned, he found himself facing Armand's Glock. "Hey, man, I meant it as a..."

"Let's get one thing straight. This your corner. You do what you gotta do. Dmitri says I help you. But don't you ever call my woman a ho. Not even kidding."

Baggy stared at the barrel of the gun for a moment. Then he gently pushed it aside. "Fine. But this my corner. While you here, you do what I tell you. Or I shove that gat up your ass and make it cum lead." He flicked his eyes back over to Shandra. "Then maybe I show your girl what it like to fuck a real man."

Armand considered asking him when he'd last seen his own cock, then thought better of it. Given Mr. King's opinion of Baggy, he could have also shot the fat man and said he was ripping off Ralph and Dmitri. He thought better of that, as well. Instead, he stuffed the gun back into his pants.

"Come on," Baggy said. "Time to meet the crew."

CHAPTER 4

The crime scene tech was an Amazon who might have had a decent career with Monticello's WNBA team. They sat in a metal shed heated by a kerosene wall heater. The impound lot could have been a junkyard or a lower-end, buy-here-pay-here used-car place.

The tech thrust a slip of paper at Branson. "Is this what you needed?"

Branson took the slip, noticing, not for the first time, that the crime scene techs' logo resembled that of the television series *CSI*. She wondered if the Council thought that the resemblance made up for the budget cuts they had inflicted on the MPD's own CSI group. Half the work was done by students at the two major universities and the community college in Rockefeller Point.

The slip of paper had a charcoal impression of a VIN tag from the charred sedan they had taken from Pier 9. It was readable. *Thank God for small favors*, thought Branson.

"This is it," she said.

"Is there anything else you need, Detective?" asked the tech. Before Branson could answer, she turned on her heel and headed out the door. "Good. Because I have to get back downtown."

With all the real cops? thought Branson. Then again, if Baker were really serious...

That name simply popping up in her head sent her blood pressure skyrocketing. She brushed it off and turned to the clerk running the impound lot.

"I need to use your computer," she said.

The clerk, a graying man of about fifty, gave the hoarse laugh of a chronic smoker. "Why? It's a Pier Nine murder. Nobody cares."

She glanced at the clerk's rank insignia. Not even a corporal and this guy had to have... What? A good twenty-five years on the force? "Patrolman..."

The clerk winced at the mention of his rank.

"I have been ordered to work this as a homicide," said Branson. "I spent two years in Homicide before getting exiled out to that dump on Lake Avenue, so I know a little something on the subject. Now, can I run this VIN tag, or will you do it for me?"

The clerk logged into the system, then stepped aside for Branson to work.

"Thank you," she said, and typed in the VIN tag. Unfortunately, the State of Ohio's web application for motor vehicle searches appeared to have been sold to Columbus as being "Y2K compliant," a joke Jerry liked to make about antiquated technology. This did not surprise her. The clerk's PC was still running an older version of Windows with an outdated web browser. Branson was no techie, but she wondered how law enforcement in Ohio kept from simply grinding to a halt.

"I know a few things about homicides, too, Detective," said the clerk.

"And what's that?"

"I know the guy who died in that Buick you sent over died in the wrong place in Monticello. No one's going to care who killed him. Chances are, the guy who did it will end up dead on Pier Nine later this week."

"It's a new day in Holland Bay, Patrolman," said Branson.

At that, the clerk let out a full belly laugh.

"Yeah," said Branson, "that's what I thought when I heard that, too, but someone upstairs has other ideas."

"Probably that male model Safety Director. He wants the mayor's job, you know."

It was Branson's turn to laugh. "Right. The mayor's a Democrat. The vice mayor's a Republican. Either she gets reelected, or the vice-mayor has to go look for a Democrat to replace him when he moves up. It all depends on how the coin toss goes in November."

"You don't think Chalmers could win?"

Chalmers was the Safety Director and the bane of both the MDP and the fire department.

"That guy wears so much Aramis," said Branson, "that I sneeze every time I see him on television. His only job as Safety Director is to make the mayor look somewhat attractive on television and to stay out from under the chief's feet."

"Christ, you're a cynical broad, Detective."

"Secret of my success." The computer finally coughed up the details of the burned-out Buick. She scanned it, confirming it was, indeed, a 2001 Park Avenue last sold for sixteen hundred dollars. It also had a name. She pulled out her Android and dialed a number she hadn't used in a long time.

"Musgrave County Morgue," said a male voice on the other end. "You kill 'em, we grill 'em. Levinson speaking."

"Jesus, Joel," said Branson, "after all this time, and you still make corny jokes like that answering the phone?"

"Jessica Branson, as I live and breathe. How the hell are you?"

"Freezing. I'm in impound. Speaking of killing and grilling, a Port cop named Murdoch sent you a BBR this morning."

"You're calling me about a Pier Nine killing? Do you know how many seniors I've got who died for the gas company's sins this morning?"

"I hear you, but I got a name for your crispy critter. You could have him in and out today and off your slate. And you'd be helping me close my first homicide in four years."

"You? Working a homicide? All right, gimme a name."

"José Carcinira." When Levinson did not come back with so much as a smartass comeback, Branson said, "Joel?"

"Get up here as soon as you can."

"Why?"

"Because the name 'Carcinira' has everything to do with why the Inbound was shut down this morning."

Branson hung up.

"Nobody cares. Right?" said the clerk.

"Wrong. The ME is very interested." She patted the clerk on the cheek. "You have a nice day, Patrolman."

It was freezing out on the corner. Little traffic moved on Eastern, maybe the occasional MORT bus, a train on the el, or the monorail hissing by behind them. Armand wondered why Baggy had his crew out today. The users sure as hell weren't out.

"Weather don't keep no one from wanting a hit," said Baggy when Armand asked.

They were a ragged bunch, but then most crews were. You didn't sell product on street corners to pay for an M.B.A. from Custis or Monticello State.

Baggy pointed them out one by one. "That tall one's Linc. His uncle's a cop, so we got an ear inside Five-Oh."

Already, Armand saw trouble Ralph might not be aware of. "Does his uncle know he's your ear?"

"Fuck that. The short guy there, that's T-Dogg. The two youngins there are Rashid and Ike. Their moms is workin' three jobs, so she ain't got time to come after them. They our runners."

Armand wondered why anyone on the crew other than Rashid and Ike gave a shit about their mothers. Or mother. Baggy never said they were brothers. He looked around. Linc and T-Dogg obviously handled the money, but so far, they had no one to send the runners after. As far as Armand could see, Baggy probably sat on his fat ass on the front stoop while the other four did all the work.

"So whaddaya need from me?" he asked.

Baggy turned to face him and poked him in the chest. "You run. I need you to run. And I need you to stay out of the way."

Armand said nothing, just stared at him.

"I don't care what Dmitri thinks," said Baggy. "Dmitri ain't Ralph. Long as Ralph get his money, Dmitri can go fuck himself. This my corner. You do what I say."

"Long as we're clear we work for Ralph," said Armand.

"Shit."

Baggy might have blown off Armand's comment, but Linc and T-Dogg caught it. They both made eye contact with Armand. He tilted his head at them, acknowledging their stares. They nodded back and said nothing. Armand noticed their expressions were different when they looked at Baggy now. Linc gave Baggy a predatory look that suggested he smelled blood.

T-Dogg sidled up to Armand, said, "So you meet Ralph today? And his money man?"

"I met Ralph," said Armand.

"Who you work for? Goose?"

"Dmitri."

T-Dogg whistled. "You a brave man. Dmitri fuckin' crazy."

That he was. "Was staying with him up until last week. Had work across the river in Prussian Meadow."

T-Dogg shook his head. Armand thought he looked stupid. He had little patience for ass-kissers, but at least he wasn't as pathetic as Baggy.

"You see Ralph's woman?" asked T-Dogg.

Had he? Armand's interactions with Ralph took place either at The Phoenix Café or over by the football stadium at Ralph's titty bar. Ralph's woman, a looker named Janiece whom Armand had heard about but never seen, wouldn't be caught dead in either place. The Phoenix was a dump, no two ways about it. The Silver Stiletto? Armand knew Janiece helped with the money, helped Mr. King make the business look legitimate. Smart, beautiful woman like that? Why the hell would she come to a strip club unless she owned it?

"Ain't ever seen her," said Armand. "Heard she fine."

"Heard Ralph eats strippers for breakfast, too," said T-Dogg.

"Heard they like it."

Everyone knew Ralph helped himself to his dancers, paying them a night's dancing money to let him do whatever he wanted to them. They seldom complained. "Eating" them? That sounded about right. Armand couldn't imagine treating his woman like that. He never denied getting some behind Shandra's back, but she wasn't a piece of meat. Who knew? He might actually marry that girl.

"You have to ask Ralph what he do with those girls," said Armand. "Hos gotta make that jack, or they be taking their clothes off 'til they forty."

"Deceased is covered in full thickness burns over eighty percent of the body," intoned Joel Levinson, his face obscured by a surgical cap and mask. He hovered over the blackened remains of what Branson assumed had been José Carcinira. "Given the position of the body in a first responders' report, it would appear the burns are post-mortem." Levinson reached up to the mic hanging over the surgical table and flipped it off. "And he smells like burnt dead feet wrapped in bacon."

"Joel." The woman standing next to Levinson, also clad in cap, mask, and gown, elbowed Levinson, who rekeyed the mic. From the voice alone, Branson could tell it was Dr. Agrawal, one of the newer assistants who hadn't yet had time to acclimate to Levinson's bizarre sense of humor.

Branson watched the autopsy from inside a glass booth some ten feet from the surgical table. She could see them through three-inch panes of Plexiglas and talk to Levinson through a pair of rubber membranes implanted in two circular openings in the Plexiglas, much like bank drive-up windows used to use. It kept the autopsy theater sealed off but allowed communication between examiner and the observation booth in the event of a power failure. Branson wasn't sure why that was a consideration since a power failure would plunge the room, booth and all, into total darkness, not to mention bring an autopsy to a screeching halt.

"You know, Jess," said Levinson, "it's standard procedure to wait for an ME to show up before packing a burn victim off to the hospital, even if a two-year-old can see that he's dead."

"Well, Homicide has taught Harbortown and the Port Police some very bad habits when it comes to Pier Nine," said Branson. "The body was gone before I even got there."

"And Special Investigations doesn't normally handle homicides," said Levinson. "Tell me again what it is you guys do out on Lake Avenue?"

"On paper, we're the city's counter-terrorism unit. Never mind that the governor handed all our gear over to the National Guard years ago."

"Oh. Right. Catch any terrorists?"

"Aside from those guys selling hot CDs and stolen watches at the Monorail station, no."

"So what is it you've been doing these past four years? Besides fending off the unwanted advances of amorous Great Lakes sailors?"

"Normally, I slip in the door right after morning roll and hope Petrocelli or the lieutenant doesn't see me. Then I turn on my computer and zone out for an hour. In a given week, I'd say I get five hours of actual police work done."

Levinson looked up, the smile showing in his eyes through his John Lennon glasses. "So you're dating an IT nerd who loves *Office Space*."

She was *not* dating Jerry. Or was she? "I have a web developer friend who loves that movie."

"Great. Come over to my house sometime. We'll watch *Kung Fu* together."

"I hate *Kung Fu*."

"Heathen."

Levinson and Agrawal went through the normal ritual of making the Y-incision in the corpse's belly, no easy task since the skin either crumbled or was toughened by, for lack of a better term, cooking. They weighed the organs and commented on the condition. José Carcinira apparently liked his booze, judging from the condition of his liver. They then turned their attention to his skull.

"Deceased shows signs of trauma to the forehead," said Agrawal, "what appear to be two small-caliber bullet holes. I am going to remove the top of the skull to locate the bullets."

As Agrawal took out the saw and began working on Carcinira's head, Levinson said, "There was another Carcinira in here this morning."

"Oh?" said Branson. "Another gas-company victim?"

"Nope. This one was responsible for closing the Inbound this morning for three hours. Well, him and that hillbilly trucker who jackknifed trying not to hit him."

"What happened?"

"Appeared at first that the late Raul Carcinira was taking a stroll along I-73 at around midnight and froze to death somewhere around the Studebaker Avenue exit. The snow fell. The plows buried him. Then a subsequent plow pushed him back out into the open. A trucker from North Carolina thought it was a deer in the highway at first and thought he would risk running it over rather than stopping on a highway with black ice patches. Then he saw what it was and swerved." Levinson paused for effect and then continued.

"He swerved right onto one of those black ice patches he was trying to dodge. Anyway, as the M-E we sent out was looking over the corpse, he found a bullet hole in Mr. Carcinira's skull, similar to our overcooked friend here. At least the elder Mr. Carcinira had the decency to die with his green card and driver's license on him."

As Agrawal looked up in disgust at Levinson, she pulled the top of José Carcinira's skull off. Something metal fell onto the operating table. She grabbed it between two rubber-gloved fingers and held it up to the light. "Cause of trauma is two small-caliber bullets fired at point-blank range."

Levinson leaned in closer to the corpse's face, what remained of it, and said for the mic, "There are several pieces of glass embedded in the flesh of the face, so the first bullet was fired through his windshield or a window." Looking back up, he said, "So how did you catch a body four years after they kicked you out of Homicide?"

"We have a new captain," said Branson. "He says, 'It's a new day in Holland Bay, Branson,' and, 'This is no longer the Siberia of the MPD.'"

Levinson scoffed. "That first one I've been hearing from every Harbortown borough president since the city went to boroughs back in the nineties. As soon as the election's over, Holland Bay goes back to being 'that hell hole across the river.'"

"They wanted me to work this homicide. I'm working it. I have no idea what this means."

"Sounds like you have a friend in this new captain. What's his name?"

"Alvin Baker."

Levinson stopped what he was doing and looked Branson straight in the eye from across the room. "Jesus, Jess, who did you piss off in a former life for that kind of karma?"

"At least she doesn't have to work with you," said Agrawal, her own eyes betraying a smile now.

Before Branson could respond, her Android played the Imperial March from *Star Wars*. "Branson."

"Jess, if you're done with the coroner," said Petrocelli, "you need to get down to Settler's Commons ASAP."

"Settler's Commons? Why?"

"You've been summoned by the Deputy Ops."

CHAPTER 5

"Stop yammering." Baggy gave Armand a good, hard shove. "I ain't paying you to stand around and talk. Get to work."

"Doing what?" said Armand.

Baggy made eye contact, held it for a few moments then let it go. His breath came out like steam from an old-style train engine as he stomped away.

"Fuck him," Linc said in a hoarse whisper. "He mad because Dmitri coming down hard on his ass. He also mad you here, and he can't do nothing about it."

The urge to say Baggy needed to watch his ass came on strong, but Armand kept it to himself.

They hadn't sold any dope all day. The cars running up and down Eastern showed no sign of stopping. No one got off any of the MORT busses or the el to buy. It was hard to be a runner if there was no customer to run to. All Armand had done was freeze his ass off. Meanwhile, Shandra was up in the apartment, warm and watching *Maury Povich*. She should have been at work, but she pled snow drifts. Her boss didn't care. No one came in to have their hair or nails done the morning after a snowstorm.

A black Escalade pulled up to the corner, windows tinted well beyond what the state allowed. It wasn't the one Armand had arrived in, so it had to be either Dmitri or Goose. Baggy ran over to it as the passenger window opened.

"Dmitri," he said. "My nigga."

"I ain't your nigger," said Dmitri, scowling. "What the fuck you doing? Running corner boys on a day like this?"

"Tweakers gotta tweak," said Baggy. "We here selling to them."

Dmitri stuck his head out the window and looked around, exaggerating how he turned his head. "I don't see any buyers. Rock, you see any buyers?"

Armand couldn't see Rock inside the Slade, but he heard the big man mumble something.

"No buyers." Dmitri spotted Armand. "Don't tell me you got that boy running."

"He gotta earn his place," said Baggy. "I ain't running no charity."

"You must be, with the money you owe us." Dmitri reached out and grabbed Baggy's coat, yanking him up against the Slade's door. "Now listen, motherfucker. I put him here because he a good earner. He sell, like the rest of your boys sell. But not today. No one buying today. Got it?"

Baggy nodded, but didn't say anything, struggling to get out of Dmitri's grip.

"Only ones gonna stop today," said Dmitri, "be cops. They gonna see you, know what you up to, and have to get out their nice warm car to bust your ass. Then they gonna come back the next day when it warmer and bust more of you. Pretty soon, they gonna wreck this corner. Guess who gonna pay for that." He shoved Baggy backward. Baggy's feet caught the curb along with some ice, dropping the fat man on his ass. "Now get these boys indoors, and don't let me catch your ass outside again today." The window went up, obscuring Dmitri from view.

The Slade did a U-turn on Eastern and headed north toward the Vodrey Heights Bridge.

Whenever cops or criminals referred to Settlers Commons, they actually meant a five-story red brick building on the western end of the Commons called Samuel Kent Center, the official name of MPD headquarters. While the rest of the buildings on the Commons featured Greek columns and neoclassical architecture, the Kent Center clashed, resembling more a Romanesque Cathedral, minus the gargoyles and stained glass, than a 19th-century government building. The clash with the courthouse and main library would not have been so bad if someone hadn't slapped an ugly four-story parking garage on the back. It looked like the place Quasimodo parked his Peugeot during a hard day of bell-ringing.

Branson had never liked the building. The interior was a maze made all the more confusing by a holding facility for offenders, several specialized divisions (such as Homicide), the Harbortown Division, and the administrative offices of the police, fire department, and the Safety Director all competing for space. There was never a decent slot in the garage unless one worked overnight. Branson arrived late that morning. She'd have to park on the top level outside in the cold. Worse, she'd have to go to the first floor to check in.

Branson made her way from the roof parking deck down to the lobby level of the building and back up to the fifth floor. The Deputy Ops had an office on the second floor in the Harbortown Division's suite. Through a quirk in Monticello's police structure, the deputy chief of operations also served as commander of Harbortown. This was not a division matter, though. It was administrative.

"Thank God, they're finally going to fire me," she said aloud as she rode the elevator alone to the fifth floor. When the door opened, she saw...

"Lovely to see you again, Detective," said Alvin Baker, that big rubbery smile on his face. "Were you able to finish up with Dr. Levinson at the morgue?"

Branson froze as she stepped off the elevator. "Uh...Yes."

"Good. I was hoping you wouldn't have to drop what you were doing when that call came. I actually had Petrocelli wait ten minutes before calling you."

She fell in step with Baker as they made their way down the oak-paneled hallway. Portraits of previous police chiefs hung on either side, going all the way back to the Civil War. At the end hung a painting of a man who resembled Theodore Roosevelt in his younger days. The man was Byron Roosevelt, TR's cousin and the city's first real police commissioner. The portrait hung outside the suite marked "Derek Roberts, Deputy Chief of Operations."

Inside was more wood paneling, a thick, green carpet, and several padded leather chairs. It might have been the outer office of a law practice or an IT consulting firm. The woman behind the reception desk appeared to have walked out of a Victoria's Secret catalog and passed through a Donna Karan outlet along the way. An angry-looking man with a narrow face and dark hair sat in the reception area, glued to his smartphone.

"Captain Baker with Detective Branson to see the Deputy Chief," said Baker.

The receptionist looked up and gave them her official smile. "He's in with someone else at the moment. Please have a seat."

They each had a seat, both away from the angry-looking man. Branson thought he looked familiar, but she also noticed that he was studiously avoiding looking at Baker. To do this, he focused even harder on his phone, occasionally tapping it. So he was reading, not playing Angry Birds.

The receptionist picked up the phone, listened for a moment, then said, "Okay." She hung up and said, "The deputy chief will see you now."

The other man rose simultaneously with Baker and Branson. The three of them shared a confused look, then headed inside. Branson suddenly remembered that she had seen the Deputy Ops office in the Harbortown Division downstairs.

The deputy chief's office was large, typical for a division commander. But most commanders' offices had glass windows all around, usually covered by blinds. This office, at twice the size, made the typical office look like a closet. A large window at one end offered a view of Oldetown and Theater Row to the west, without showing the parking garage. A round meeting table sat at the other, where photos of Deputy Chief Roberts hung on the wall: Roberts shaking hands with the governor, another with George Bush, and a third of him escorting Barack Obama during a campaign stop. Donald Trump, somehow, had not made the cut.

Sitting in one of the visitors' chairs was a slim brunette in a business suit, a badge clipped to the belt of her skirt. She stood when Branson and the others entered, and Branson's eyes lit up with recognition.

"Sarah?" asked Branson.

"It's been a while," said Sarah Ryland. "Captain Baker, I'm surprised to see you here with her."

"I stand by my findings," said Baker.

Roberts, standing behind the desk, frowned. "If we could begin..." As everyone took their seats, he said, "Detective Branson, Captain Baker, you both already know Lieutenant Ryland from Homicide. This is Detective Kagan. He caught our body on the Inbound this morning. Detective, if you could bring us up to date."

Kagan reached into his jacket and pulled out a notepad. "This morning, shortly after the start of shift, Dispatch informed us that the fatality in the accident on I-73 Northbound showed signs of bullet trauma. Victim was tentatively identified as Raul Carcinira of Huron Junction in Rock Ridge. Victim had suffered a small-caliber bullet wound to the face. Detective Soroya and I arrived at the scene at about oh-seven-thirty." He gave Branson a dirty look. "Due to another homicide on Pier Nine, we had to wait for student assistants from Forensics to process the scene."

"They gave me a body," said Branson. "I wanted real techs to process it."

"It's Pier Nine, Detective," Kagan said, as if that explained everything, then went back to his notes. "As we processed the scene, Detective Taggart from Special Investigations arrived and revealed that the late Mr. Carcinira had been an informant."

"Jake?" asked Branson. "Running an informant?"

Baker laughed. "Just because they kicked him out of Narcotics doesn't mean he stopped working Narcotics."

Roberts did not look amused. Neither did Kagan, who continued. "Detective Taggart and I proceeded to the morgue to confirm the identity of the deceased." He gave another dirty look, this one targeted at Ryland. "Due to no senior officers present this morning, Detective Soroya proceeded to Huron Junction to inform Mr. Carcinira's next-of-kin."

Ryland found herself now under both Kagan's and Roberts's sharp gaze. "Several officers, including myself, were snowed in this morning."

"You, your sergeant, and Captain Carter may discuss this later today," said Roberts. "Here." Turning to Branson, he said, "It's bad enough that we've been routinely tolerating tardiness from detectives in certain units."

Baker put up his hand. "That sort of lax discipline will end tomorrow, Colonel. I have complete confidence in the detectives I've selected to remain with the unit."

"Good. Because frankly, while the chief is big on this project, I'm not so sure myself. Branson, do you know why you're here?"

"Because I didn't get to a crime scene before the body was released," said Branson, "though the responding officers on the scene..."

"Save it, Branson. I'm well aware of the clusterfuck Homicide and my own borough division have arranged. I believe, Lieutenant Ryland, that the detectives in Homicide refer to Holland Bay as a 'self-cleaning oven' and have pretty much dumped all Pier Nine slayings on Harbortown. Is that correct?"

"Captain Blazer agreed to process those slayings," said Ryland, "to assist with our workload. Captain Carter..."

"Is going to retire in a few months," said Roberts, "and not soon enough. I don't want someone old enough to have arrested Mayor Lapinsky running one of my operational divisions."

Branson bit her tongue to keep from laughing. Mayor Stan Lapinsky had been dragged out of his barricaded office in 1978.

"As of today," said Roberts, "a homicide on Pier Nine is the same as a homicide on Gotham Square or up in Vodrey Heights, or anywhere else in this city. Branson, you're here because you're the first Special Investigations detective to be a part of this. As of right now, the Carcinira murders are being given to Special Investigations."

Branson had been watching Ryland and noticed the relief in her eyes. Back when she and Ryland were partners, they had obsessed about the big white board listing every homicide under investigation. Black meant they had an arrest, pending trial. Red meant no progress. Holland Bay murders tended to stay red, as did those in Prussian Meadow and a few other depressed areas of the city. This took two red murders off her board.

"Begging your pardon, sir," said Kagan, "but Detective Soroya and I are investigating the Inbound slaying. Perhaps if SI could…"

"You're being detailed to Special Investigations, Detective," said Roberts. "Detective Soroya will be reassigned within Homicide."

Kagan looked as though he'd been slapped.

"As of today," said Roberts, "by order of the chief and the mayor, Special Investigations has a new mandate: Clean up Holland Bay."

Baker grinned, and it was a shit-eating grin. "The mayor wants a shiny new neighborhood to anchor the south end of her shiny new bridge."

"I'm going to the union about this," said Kagan. "This is a demotion."

"Not if your new partner is correct," said Baker. "You and Taggart are going to work Raul Carcinira's murder."

"Sir," said Branson, "does this mean I'm…"

"Partnered with Friedman. Bring her up to speed when you get back to the station."

Great, thought Branson. *I get that hothead for a partner.* "Does

José Carcinira's next-of-kin know about his demise?"

Kagan cleared his throat. "She's...um..."

"Sedated at Custis Memorial," said Ryland. "Detective Soroya said she was hysterical when she realized she'd lost both her husband and her son."

"I know the feeling," muttered Kagan. "I had the same thing happen to my career."

"That's enough, Kagan." Roberts got to his feet. "I want these closed immediately. Kagan, since Taggart was working the older Carcinira to get at Ralph Smithers, it might be a wise idea to get reacquainted with Lieutenant Kearny and his squad. Find out how close Narcotics is to getting the biggest fish in this city."

"With all due respect," said Branson, "as far as I'm concerned, Ralph Smithers is the Great White Whale."

Armand had his hands under Shandra's top when Baggy pounded on the door again.

"He gonna do this every time we get naked?" she asked.

"We ain't naked yet." He tossed a blanket to her and grabbed the Glock from the pile of his clothes. "Who is it?" He barked the question more than asked it.

"Baggy. Open up."

Armand went to the door, shirtless, the Glock down at his side, finger on the trigger. He threw the door open. "What? I'm busy."

"I can see that," said Baggy, pushing his bulk inside. He stopped when he realized Armand had pressed a gun into his enormous belly. "What the...?"

"I invite you in?"

"Nigga, I don't need an invitation."

Armand shoved the gun harder. "My house. My rules. Don't like it? We can take it up with Dmitri. Or Ralph."

"Where my stash?"

"Your stash?"

"I gave you a packet to run. I want it back."

Armand stared at Baggy, gun still pressed into his gut. "What's the magic word?"

"Motherfucker. The magic word is 'motherfucker.' Now give me the stash, motherfucker."

The Glock came up under Baggy's chin.

"I don't remember Spongebob saying 'motherfucker,'" said Armand. "I believe he said the magic word was 'please.'"

"Please give me my stash," said Baggy.

Armand withdrew the gun and turned to locate his jacket.

"Motherfucker," Baggy added.

Armand withdrew a plastic bag filled with packets of white crystals from his jacket and tossed it to Baggy. The fat man nearly dropped it. "There you go, Jabba."

"You might have that gat," said Baggy, "but that ain't stopped me taking care of business before."

"That so?"

"You tell Dmitri to think about all them problems I handled for him." With that, he turned and slammed the door.

Shandra emerged from the bedroom, still wrapped in a blanket. "He gone for the night?"

"He gone."

Roberts kept Branson back after the meeting. She hoped he would fire her on the spot. She could cash in some benefits and go look for the suburban job she should have taken years ago.

"Sit down, Branson," said Roberts, leaning against his over-sized oak desk.

She sat.

"I'm going to be frank with you," said the Deputy Ops. "I really wanted to send you out to Edison to file paperwork for the Sheriff's deputies out there."

"Then do it," said Branson. "But I'm not leaving unless you push me out the door."

Roberts smiled, but it was a cold smile. "Detective, you know we can't just up and fire you. It was hoped sending you to Special Investigations would send the right message. The fact is you're still in Special Investigations this morning for one reason and one reason only."

She thought about it for a moment. "Baker."

"Baker. Apparently, the captain shares your assessment that we treated you unfairly after you shot Mayor Kozinski's son. He insisted we keep you in SI after he took over. Since this is the chief's pet project…"

Nice. No pressure, Jess. Try not to fuck up under the watchful gaze of the chief's toadie. That's all.

"The fact is, though, many of us who were here before the chief was brought in still want you gone. You're an embarrassment to the force."

"With all due respect, Colonel, this conversation is out of line. I am a cop. I am a damn good cop. And let's be honest, if that piece of shit hadn't been the son of a sitting mayor…"

"You've got three days to find out who killed José Carcinira," said Roberts. "After that, Baker or no Baker, I'm burying you in the subways for the rest of your career." He rose from the desk and strolled over to the picture window that overlooked snow-covered Olde Towne and the Perry Marina. "Of course, you could save yourself and us a lot of trouble. Hand me your resignation, Branson, and I'll put in a word for you with one of the suburban forces. Willowbrook could use someone with a three-digit IQ on their force."

"Willowbrook is a trailer park without the wheels, sir."

"Dismissed, Branson. You have work to do. Time's a-wasting."

Roberts had his back to her when she flipped him her middle finger. She neither noticed nor cared if he could see her reflection in the window.

CHAPTER 6

"How the hell long are you going to make me pay for being Lon Kagan's son?"

The door to Baker's office might have been closed, but everyone heard Kagan shouting. Branson certainly heard it as she trudged in from the parking lot.

"How long's that been going on?" she asked as she met Petrocelli in the bullpen.

Petrocelli looked at his watch. "Twenty minutes now. I heard he tore out of Settlers Commons like he was on fire."

"And it still hasn't dawned on Kagan that Baker hasn't been in IA for years?"

The sergeant shrugged and headed back to his office. "Don't tell me you were happy when they transferred you here."

She found her way to her desk and... The other side was completely clean, not even a nameplate for Detective Pirelli. "Where'd Vince go?"

The desk sergeant looked up from his paperwork. "Transferred to Edison, the poor sonofabitch."

"Edison? Why?"

The desk sergeant, a beefy guy named English, grinned. "Special Investigations is no longer Siberia. Apparently, they meant it."

"I've heard that twice today. Has anyone noticed it's five degrees outside?"

"The homeless?"

That sucked. One of the things that made Holland Bay bearable for Branson was Vince Pirelli. He was every bit the stereotypical Italian greaser, even living in Little Sicily. He did little to fight that perception. He had no reason to. Special Investigations was where careers went to die. Vince had gotten a bit too rough with a drunk up in Old Rock Ridge, better known as Greektown. Since the drunk was black and Vince was white, the police naturally took a hit. Get into a brawl with a civilian of the wrong color and income bracket, and you ended up in Edison taking marching orders from the sheriff. Or under the city in the Transit Police. Or walking a beat in Holland Island, little more than a glorified security guard outside the new port or Eastern Shore.

Or here.

Vince was no longer here, one more reason to blow off morning roll call.

Branson booted her computer. The black box was a vintage Dell that probably rolled off the line around the time bin Laden took a bullet. The thing took forever to boot, which Branson took as her cue to get coffee. When she returned, she waited another minute for email to load, a blue circle of death blocking her for doing anything else.

She had an email from Baker, apparently a group email.

To all remaining detectives in Special Investigations:

Morning roll will no longer be optional. It is especially important that you be present for tomorrow's roll call, as I will be announcing our new mandate. Please be on time. Detectives and officers who fail to show up for morning roll will face disciplinary action. No exceptions.

Capt. Alvin Baker,

Commander, Special Investigations

Branson scoffed. The email was apparently meant for her and blanketed for the rest of the squad, what remained of it.

"Got a minute?"

Branson whirled in her seat to see the bear-like Jake Taggart hovering over her. "I thought I told you to quit sneaking up on me like that."

Taggart shrugged. "Seven years in Narcotics. Hard to break old habits."

"You haven't been Narcotics for a long time, Taggart."

He shrugged. "Really old habits."

Taggart drove her insane. He seldom spoke. When he did, he mainly offered an info dump that might have something to do with the subject at hand. She suspected he had more in common with that skinny guy on *The Big Bang Theory* than with most cops.

And why was he always so damned cryptic about everything? Even asking if he wanted a cup of coffee didn't guarantee a straight answer.

"I don't give a good goddamn what the Deputy Ops said." Kagan sounded as though he might have an aneurysm at any moment.

God help the MPD if Kagan ever made captain, Branson thought. He'd be a walking cliché.

She could also hear Baker's voice coming back as a low drone. Branson, like everyone else more than likely, wondered why Baker had not demanded Kagan's badge yet.

"He's not finished in there," said Taggart, "and he's my partner. Since your stiff and mine are related, maybe you'd like to come with me to talk to a couple of CIs."

It took Branson a moment to figure out what Taggart meant. "Oh. The body on the Inbound. That was José Carcinira's father. Right? Still pretending to be a Narc after all this time, eh?"

"Not pretending." He pointed at Baker's sonorous email on Branson's screen. "My impromptu operation has just become this squad's *raison d'etre.*"

"I have a crime scene report due any minute."

"Do you really think that's going to come back before tomorrow morning?"

He had a point. In Homicide, she worked the case until the CSI reports came back. Contrary to the TV shows, the crime labs took days to report back to detectives, weeks if it were DNA.

"What about my witnesses?" She was stalling. She really didn't want to spend an afternoon riding around with Taggart.

"Your only witnesses," he said, his Oklahoma drawl finally emerging, "are José Carcinira's murderers. And you know there were two. I saw the coroner's prelim on your desk."

That was another thing she didn't like about Taggart. When it came to his work, he had zero concept of boundaries.

She looked at her watch. Kagan's partner in Homicide had briefed the next-of-kin. Both Kagan and Taggart had been to the morgue ahead of Branson. Until the crime scene techs reported back, she was pretty much without witnesses or even leads.

"Screw it," she said. "Let's roll."

"Armand, this is Monk. Are you out on the corner?"

Monk had to know that they'd been kicked off the corner.

"I'm inside," said Armand, his arm wrapped around a naked, sleeping Shandra. "Keeping warm."

The smile in Monk's voice was obvious. "Don't get too warm. Mr. King wants to talk to you."

Twice in one day? "The Phoenix?"

"Don't be silly," said Monk. "Mr. King meets with Ralph once a week there. You think a player like him wants to be seen in a dump like that? Hell, Ralph only hits the Phoenix two, maybe three times a week, and only because he don't want some of his people at the Stiletto."

"Where then?"

Monk gave him directions, by Monorail, subway, and finally, bus, to an address on Holland Island. "Go through the parking garage. Find the freight elevator and come up that way. Got it?"

He got it. Monk hung up.

Nudging Shandra, Armand said, "Sorry, baby. Gotta go to work."

Shandra sat up, letting the sheet fall off her breasts. "Aw, baby. Why you gotta go? I was hoping we could go another round."

Armand smiled. "We can go as long as you want when I get back. Right now, I need to go see Mr. King."

"Another thug?"

"Not another thug," he said, getting dressed. "The money man." He pulled on his shoes and started searching for his parka. "My ticket out of the Game."

Armand wasn't naïve. He knew Baggy would have one of his crew watching the building. Going out the front door and walking to the Monorail station a few blocks north was out of the question. He slipped out through the basement to the fire door facing Halsted, the broken, narrow street that ran behind the building.

Across Halsted sat a gutted apartment building. No windows remained. Even in broad daylight, the interior looked dark. The walls had been tagged, though some of the symbols looked out of date. Armand learned from one of the runners that Baggy ran crack whores out of the place during warmer weather.

Armand had been in such a building before. He had lost his virginity to a crack whore kept by Dmitri over in Prussian Meadow. Dmitri had given him a couple of rocks to give the girl. She let him stick it wherever he wanted, and he did everything to her. In the beginning, it was about popping his own cherry. By the time he finished, it had become about using the girl because he could. That had been Dmitri's intent. To Dmitri, she was nothing more than a chew toy, something to use up and throw away. Armand later learned they'd found her frozen to death along Hudson Drive in Prussian Meadow. He went somewhere private when he heard so he could throw up.

Since that time, he had avoided the crack whores whenever possible. It might have been a power trip for Dmitri, but Armand had no illusions about him as a hero. The man was little better than an animal. His mother had thrown out better men than that.

Ralph and Rufus, on the other hand, were something to

behold. Ralph owned this city. If you dealt in Monticello, you got your product, whatever it was, from Ralph Smithers or a friend of Ralph Smithers. Otherwise, you didn't deal. And Rufus?

Rufus was the money man. Armand knew that he, too, had started out on a corner. He knew Rufus had taken a fall for Ralph, and that Ralph had sent him to Custis University. Now Rufus was the money man. All the cash guys like Baggy took in, Rufus made it look clean and turned it into cars and houses and businesses. Not just front businesses, either. There wasn't a business Rufus King touched that didn't turn a profit, or at least try to.

Now Rufus had summoned Armand. The lady who had called said that Mr. King had another job for him. She gave him a Holland Island address. Armand wasn't sure he'd ever been to Holland Island, even though he'd lived his whole life in Monticello. Rufus had an office there. He didn't live there.

Yet.

Armand wanted that eventually.

He slipped down Halsted and dashed across Eastern just as a MORT bus rolled by, coming down the slope from University Square in Vodrey Heights. Armand figured the bus would obscure his crossing the street. Another two blocks, and he would turn left to climb toward the Perkins Street Station. He couldn't get there fast enough. The cold bit at his nose and crept up his pant legs.

Once on the Monorail, headed down to Farnum Field Station, he sat back to try and warm up from his walk. Commuters, both black and white, gave him the eye. People from Holland Bay did not ride the Monorail. That was for downtowners across the river who were looking to get to the airport quickly, or people from the Heights or the Island who were trying to get out to Gates Park on the city's south side to their cushy tech jobs. The Monorail was supposed to insulate them from the Armands of the world. An older lady, probably some secretary for some big firm downtown, glared at him.

He glared back. "What? You ain't seen a black man before?"

The woman did not so much as blink. "The ones I see on this

train come from Holland Island."

"Public transportation," he said, and turned away, watching Holland Bay slide by below the Monorail.

Prussian Meadow sat opposite Canaan on the Musgrave River. Before the railroads came to Monticello, it had been one of the first areas to be annexed to Monticello beyond Rock Ridge and what was now called Harbortown. Germans had come to settle there. Unlike the Amish, Mennonite, and Brethren who flocked to the rural farmlands of Ohio, these Germans were Catholic and very urban. As such, Prussian Meadow soon found itself paved over with brick and cobblestones and hosting a dozen spired churches. By the World Wars, factories had replaced many of the churches and the Italianate buildings.

These days, the former German enclave, however, had more in common with Holland Bay than with Canaan. Gentrification had begun on the northern edge of the neighborhood near Monticello State's campus, only to be stalled by the mortgage meltdown. What remained were the ruins of former auto plants, crumbling tenements, and a maze of pot-holed streets, both asphalt and brick.

"I can't believe he stuck me with Friedman," said Branson as Taggart guided his aging Dodge Caliber through the Meadow's buckled streets. "I swear she has a crush on me."

"You're not her type," said Taggart. "You're too butch."

"Well, thanks a lot."

"All I'm saying is Friedman likes her women to be girlie. She wants what I want in a woman–tight skirts, perfect make-up, and high heels. You look like you're headed to a kickboxing class after work."

"I should take a kick-boxing class. I have rage issues. But I swear she keeps staring at me during roll call."

"Of course, she does. We all do. How many times have you been to roll in the last six months?"

"Point taken."

Taggart turned right on a narrow street called Packard Lane. The building on the corner had a peeling sign painted on one wall that said, "Luxury river views starting in the 250s." The sign had been there for five years, and the side of the building facing the river looked out on a taller brick building.

A few blocks south on Packard, they arrived at the building from which the street derived its name. The huge brick building sat inside a collapsed chain-link fence, faded and rusting signage for American Motors and Volkswagen lying against some of the outbuildings. Etched in stone over the front of the building were the words, "Packard Engine Plant No. 2."

"I think my dad's first car came from here," said Branson.

"Did he drive a Pacer?"

"A Matador."

"They built those in Wisconsin," said Taggart. "They built Pacers here in Monticello."

Branson almost called him a know-it-all asshole but held her tongue.

"Anyway," said Taggart, "this was just an engine plant. They built the actual cars in the Foundry District." He swung the car around behind the main building.

"So why are we here?"

"To see Plink."

It might have been nice, Branson thought, if he had explained who Plink was before they plowed into the snow-choked lot. They got out into the cold and braced themselves against a stiff wind off the river. The snow drifts didn't help things.

"Is he even here?" asked Branson. "If he's supplying Smithers out of here, you'd think he'd take a day like today off."

"Plink works at home," said Taggart. "So don't be surprised if he defends his home."

They trudged through a particularly deep drift, snow working its way into Branson's shoes. Taggart led her to a metal door that warned that the property was under surveillance. Branson figured the surveillance system had been stripped years ago. Taggart pushed the door in, allowing snow to tumble in ahead of him.

Inside, they stamped their feet. Once Taggart pushed the door back in place, Branson relaxed. It wasn't warm at all inside, but at least they were out of that hellish wind. The building smelled moldy, with a hint of kerosene and...

"Is that ammonia?" asked Branson.

"Yeah," said Taggart. "The day I take Plink in is going to be the saddest day in history for the tweakers of Monticello."

"You have information about a meth lab," said Branson, "and you're letting this guy stay in business?"

"Yeah. Why?"

"Jake, we're not supposed to let an operation like that slide. We could bring down Ralph Smithers by raiding the place."

"We will. Just not today. In fact, we..."

A Rottweiler charged at them out of the dark, teeth bared.

"Vader!"

The Rottweiler settled into a low growl. From the darker recesses of the inner plant, a small man in a ragged coat shambled into view. "Who is it?"

"Taggart."

Vader barked once then resumed growling.

The man came into view. Branson guessed he was white, though he could have been Hispanic or a light-skinned black. His stocking cap and tangle of beard made it hard to tell. What little skin she could see was clearly pale, red ringing the eyes.

"What do you want?" he said. "Get out of here. Dmitri was here earlier. Threatened to kill me."

"Why?" asked Branson.

Vader snarled at Branson when she spoke.

"Vader don't like cops," said the man. "You're not alone, Taggart. You know you're supposed to come alone."

Taggart stepped toward the man. "Plink, I..."

Vader snarled and lunged at him. Taggart jumped back.

"I told you he don't like cops," said Plink. To Branson, he said,

"You can leave now, lady."

Branson crossed her arms, looked down at the Rottweiler and met his eyes. The dog growled. Without breaking eye contact with the dog, she said to Plink, "Siccing a dog on a police officer is considered assault with a deadly weapon."

"Just defending my property."

"Plink," said Taggart, "why did Dmitri threaten you?"

"He knows."

"Knows what?"

"That I'm talking to you."

Branson knelt, still meeting the dog's gaze. The dog's growl subsided into keening.

"Vader..." said Plink.

"Did Dmitri tell you why he thinks we're talking?" asked Taggart.

Plink began to shake. "He said if I didn't keep my mouth shut, I'd end up like the old man."

"Carcinira?" asked Branson, speaking softly as she started patting her thigh. The dog stopped growling.

"Yeah," said Plink. "Said I'd end up on the Inbound just like him."

"We have our suspect," said Branson. "Is this the Dmitri I'm thinking of?"

"Reagan? Ralph Smithers's pit bull?"

"That's the one."

"Oh, yes. We're talking about him. But killing someone and dumping him on the freeway is not his style."

The dog stepped tentatively up to Branson and sniffed at her. He let out another keening noise. She scratched him between his ears. "Plink, how bad you want out from under Ralph?"

"Bad," said Plink.

"They check in on this operation?"

"Dmitri comes by to pick up his product, pays me."

"Does Dmitri know about Doby?" said Taggart.

"Doby?" asked Branson.

"Homeless guy. Spends most of his time in Serievo moving from abandoned house to abandoned house."

Plink looked down at the floor and shuffled. "I don't know."

"Maybe we ought to..." When Taggart saw Branson rubbing the dog's flanks and scratching his ear, he stopped.

"Vader!" said Plink.

The dog ignored him and rolled over on his back so Branson could rub his belly.

Branson looked up. "I know my dogs. This one isn't trained to be a guard dog."

Doby Clark's nose broke when his face smacked into the stripped hardwood floor. Before he could move, a foot on each side of him slammed into his rib cage.

"You been talking to that fucking cop from Holland Bay, ain't you?"

Doby could not look up at Dmitri Reagan. He didn't dare. "No." His voice came out in a croak.

Dmitri's own foot collided with Doby's head. He saw stars. "Bullshit! You been talking to him. I know you been talking to him."

"I haven't." Doby could barely wheeze out the words. "I swear."

"That ain't what Raul said before I killed him."

Doby could not contain the look of horror on his face. That was all Dmitri was looking for.

"Cap him," said Dmitri. "Then turn on the gas. Don't want nothin' left."

The first bullet destroyed his brain before he could hear anything else.

CHAPTER 7

The freight elevator reeked of oil and cleaning solvents and something oddly sweet, like someone had been drinking cheap wine in the elevator car. Armand had smelled worse. If you lived in certain neighborhoods, bad smells were a fact of life.

The lift jerked as it started to move, its motor loud. The car rumbled as it rose to Mr. King's floor. The front of the building had suggested to Armand that the main elevators were cleaner and quieter. Or at least smoother and less smelly. He had come through the building's two-level parking garage, circling around back and down below the first floor. The guard, an old guy who probably just manned the post to cover what his retirement and his Social Security did not, just grunted when Armand said, "Here for Mr. King." That was all anyone needed to say to gain entry.

When the freight elevator reached the floor for King Properties, the door rattled open onto an alcove. Large trash cans lined the back wall with wooden pallets stacked off to the side. Armand pushed open the metal door into the corridor and...

It was like a different world—plush carpeting, muted lighting, expensive wallpaper, and wood trim. The paint appeared smooth and flawless. Armand did a double take, glancing back into the alcove, which looked like a utility room in his building. He closed the door and strolled down the corridor to an office with a brass plaque next to the heavy wooden door that read, "King Properties LLC." The door whispered open as he pulled on it.

Inside, behind a large desk, sat one of the most beautiful women Armand had ever seen. Dark, with delicate features, she looked like what Armand imagined Shandra could be if she had a chance to doll herself up. When she rose, she revealed a stunning figure, that of a model, tastefully revealed and hidden by her long red dress.

"You must be Armand," she said. "I'm Janiece. Ralph and Rufus have told me a lot about you." She came around the desk and shook Armand's hand.

"So you Ralph's woman?" Armand asked, trying not to sound like a lovestruck schoolboy.

"I'm Mr. King's assistant," she said, "and yes, Ralph is my man. I'll tell Mr. King you're here."

She disappeared into the inner office through another wooden door, this one with a brass plaque that read, "Rufus King, President and CEO." Mr. King truly was the money man if he could have an office like this and pay Janiece enough to dress like she did. Then again, this was Holland Island, the promised land if you were black in Monticello.

Monk emerged from the inner office. "Well, hello, young man. Heard you had quite a morning."

For a guy that looked like he broke people in half, Monk sounded to Armand like a Baptist minister shaking hands with the faithful after church. At least the church his mother used to drag him to when he was younger. Armand instinctively put out his hand. "Been busy. Dmitri had to set Baggy straight."

"Be patient," said Monk. "Baggy'll fuck up sooner or later. If you don't get him, one of Goose's crew will. Either way's good for you."

That was all Armand needed to hear. "It's taken care of."

"I'm sure it is."

"Monk," said a voice from the inner office. "Don't waste the boy's time. Send him in. I've got work for him."

"You heard the man," said Monk. He patted Armand on the back as he guided him inside. "You need me for anything?"

Rufus King sat behind an enormous desk, the window revealing a terrific view of the downtown skyline behind him. "We cool. Why don't you check on our businesses down on Freitag Avenue."

That was in Little Sicily, which surprised Armand. Even now, with the Sicilian mob little more than an urban legend, Ralph's crews did not venture lightly into Little Sicily.

"Armand, my man," said Rufus. "Sit down. Take off your coat."

Armand shrugged out of his parka and sat in the leather-padded visitors' chair. It was one of the cheap chairs in Rufus's office, and yet it was the most comfortable chair he'd ever sat in.

"How's the new crib?" asked Rufus. "Furniture look good? Heat working?"

"It good." Armand decided not to mention the rats. They'd been scarce since he and Shandra moved in. "My girl loves the place."

"Good. Dmitri informs me Baggy's good and scared now that you're there. I want him like that."

"I do what I can."

"Good, good." Rufus's smile faded. "Did you notice that abandoned building behind your place?"

Armand nodded.

"I own that," said Rufus. "Only it's become worthless. I need you to check it out."

"I can do that."

"That's good. Because I have another job I may need you to do. Listen closely."

Greg Murdoch spotted the BMW coming out of his cul-de-sac as he pulled in, the driver's silver hair unmistakable. He'd seen it twice before, both times parked in front of his house. One time he went in to find the man out on the back patio drinking his whiskey with Jane.

"He's important to my career," Jane protested that time, her English accent becoming crisper as she did.

That had been the first time Murdoch had accused his wife of cheating on him. As with each subsequent time, it ended the same way: A huge argument, a few breakables thrown, and the mother of all make-up lays. If Jane were sleeping her way to the top of her profession, she certainly showed him how good she was at it.

This morning, he was not in the mood. He stomped into their two-story Vodrey Heights home, hung his jacket in the foyer, and headed for the kitchen. He did not need Mr. Silver Hair cuckolding him the same day the MPD opted to screw him over. He tossed his equipment belt onto the kitchen table and went fishing for a beer in the fridge.

"How many times have I told you," said Jane, her native Yorkshire showing as it always did when she was agitated, "not to leave your gun belt on the table?" As if just noticing her robe had come loose, she pulled it around herself more tightly and cinched the sash.

Murdoch ignored her, popped open an Old Muskie, and guzzled about a third of the can. "Well, you're in a cheery mood. Did the Silver Fox have trouble getting it up this morning? Figure out I was going to be late and catch him without his Cialis?"

"And where were you?" she said, the full Yorkshire coming out. "Your shift ended at seven-thirty."

"It ends when they tell me it ends. Anyway, I'm on days tomorrow. You can spread for the Silver Fox all day long if you like."

"*I am not sleeping with Taylor!*" She stamped her feet like a three-year-old refusing to go to bed. "If you'd have been home, you could have met him, found out what he's doing for me. Do you think I want to do traffic reports for the rest of my career?"

Murdoch drank the rest of his beer, belched, and crushed the can. Then he took his wedding ring off and placed it on the counter. "I can't deal with this anymore. Let me know when you want to start being my wife again."

He headed upstairs, stripped down to his boxers, and climbed onto the bed, leaving the bedspread in place. If Jane really had cheated on him this morning, he didn't want to find out by rolling into the silver fox's residue. He sent a text to Wilson, his FOP rep, and turned the ringer up loud before laying back and dozing off.

Serievo had not fallen as far from grace as Prussian Meadow, but it was rapidly getting there. Inland Boulevard, which paralleled the Inland Parkway, served as the former Slavic enclave's main drag. While most of Monticello's neighborhoods looked like the towns they had been in a former life, Serievo showed signs of decline. Whole strip malls stood empty. Payday loan places, gun shops, and liquor stores had replaced hair salons, clothing stores, and chain convenience stores that used to line Inland Boulevard. Worst of all, St. Jakob's Church rose above the block between Peterik and Elizabeth like a haunted mansion gone to seed. Even the ghosts seemed to have vacated.

"What the hell happened to this place?" asked Branson as Taggart drove through another intersection. "Where are the delis? What happened to St. Jakob's Church? Did Callahan Chevrolet close?"

"In order," said Taggart, "to the suburbs if they didn't close, not enough parishioners, and long before I came to town."

It was the first time Branson had heard Taggart even mention his past. "When did you come to town?"

"Twelve years ago," he said. "Right after I got out of the Army."

Branson did some quick math. At that point, the military had been trying to keep personnel from leaving to handle the wars in Iraq and Afghanistan. "Honorably discharged?"

Taggart glared at her, the most emotion she'd seen him show in a long time. "Do you think the MPD would hire a dishonorably discharged soldier?"

"Could have been medical."

Taggart pressed his lips thin.

"Was it?" asked Branson.

Taggart made a left onto a side street called Stanislaus that passed beneath the parkway and started up the steep slope to Rock Ridge. "It was medical." His tone suggested the subject had been closed.

The aging Dodge Caliber almost lost traction plowing its way up the winding switchbacks. Branson gripped the dashboard, wondering why they had not taken her Pathfinder.

"Don't they plow in this part of the city?" she asked as Taggart fishtailed around another curve.

"Take a look around," said Taggart. "This was Ground Zero for the mortgage meltdown. Only unlike Hiroshima, it's going to be decades before anyone lives here again."

"Jesus." Branson knew Serievo had been hard hit by the mortgage crisis, but she had not seen the effects up close. In Cleveland and Detroit, they had razed some of these neighborhoods. Parts of Detroit had gone back to wild prairie while Cleveland talked openly of all this new development space.

Monticello remained in denial. People would return as soon as the auto industry and the steel mills returned. Right, thought Branson. The only American cars built in Monticello were Fords built out in the suburbs with Volkswagen and Nissan replacing Chrysler and GM in Midtown. Only one steel mill remained, owned by some company from out of Luxembourg. Yet the city clung stubbornly to its memory of the post-World War II glory days.

Maybe that was why Branson refused to leave the MPD. She stubbornly clung to memories of her own glory days.

Taggart slid the car off the street onto the sidewalk. At least Branson thought it was a sidewalk. It was hard to tell under all that snow.

"We're here," said Taggart.

"Where's here?" asked Branson.

Taggart pointed at the small postwar cottage, its windows boarded up, some of the siding missing. Branson could see tire tracks and footprints in the snow drifts. "Doby's been making good use of foreclosures."

"Was someone here already?" she asked.

"Maybe," said Taggart. "He might have fled. If he's here, be ready to take him in."

"And if he's not?"

"We go back downtown and get two warrants for the Packard plant. One to search the place. One for Plink."

More snow slid down into her boots as they trudged across the yard. Branson could not help but feel she had better things to do with her time than chase one of Taggart's reluctant informants. Halfway from the car to the house, she stopped, sniffing the air.

"Jake," she said. "Do you...?"

The house exploded.

CHAPTER 8

Armand did not even bother hiding on his way back. He took a pair of MORT busses all the way from Holland Island and hopped off under the watchful eye of one of Baggy's crew. T-Dogg did a double take, already looking frustrated. Armand would be, too, if that fat ass Baggy had made him stand outside in this weather to watch Armand's place. T-Dogg probably didn't even know Armand had left, making things worse.

That would piss Baggy off. Good. Baggy needed a lesson in humility. It put a spring in Armand's step as he bounded up the stairs to his apartment. When he opened the door, though…

"Shandra?"

Shandra cowered in the corner, sobbing. She wore only her panties and sat rocking with her back to the door. Armand rushed over to her and wrapped her in his arms. "Baby, what's wrong?"

"He didn't rape me," she said. "Just wanted to scare me."

"Who?" Armand knew Dmitri had raped a few women in his time. It was a power trip for him. It was also a tool. Dmitri had gotten more than one woman to talk that way. If Baggy had done this to Shandra, though, nothing Ralph and Rufus could say would save him.

"Baggy came," she said between sobs. "Wanted to know where you were."

"What'd you tell him?"

"I said I didn't know," she said. "So that tall one…Linc?"

"I know him."

"He held my arms behind me while Baggy ripped off my clothes with a knife."

Armand looked around and spotted her torn top, shredded jeans, and bra in a heap near the sofa. He let go of Shandra and got to his feet. "He a dead man."

"Armand, no! He'll..."

"He'll fucking die for this." By the time Armand was out the door, he had his Glock out and the smell of blood in his nostrils.

Branson felt numb. There had been the smell of gas, then she found herself face down in the snow with her ears ringing.

The ringing began to subside, and her hearing had partially returned by the time the paramedics helped her into the ambulance. One of them kept talking to her, but she could only hear a muffled sound like listening to someone speak underwater. Even her own name did not come easily to her. Finally, the ringing and the pressure subsided. She could make out what people were saying to her.

"Are you all right, Detective?" asked the medic, a compact black woman with the bearing of someone who'd seen combat.

"Gas," Branson said, struggling to string a coherent sentence together and failing. "Smelled gas before... Before..."

"It's okay, honey," said the paramedic. "Just relax. We're going to get you all fixed up."

"Taggart," she said. "Where's Jake?"

"Is he the other detective we found?"

Beyond the paramedic, though the ambulance's open back door, Branson could see them lift someone onto a stretcher. Whoever it was had oxygen on as well. He was a bloody mess, even with bandages.

The paramedic caught the look in Branson's eye. "I know, honey. I've seen men, women, and children tore up by explosives. You never get used to it."

***

Not even a day here, and Armand had to go assert his presence. He spotted two of Baggy's crew watching him as he made his way down the street.

Baggy lived in the Wentworth housing project, two ugly cinderblock towers that loomed over I-73 a block south of Armand's place. It gave its upper floor residents a clear view into the Monorail as it glided by. Structurally, the building was more solid than the block where Armand now stayed. Armand's building, however, was cleaner. If developers ever made it this far north out of neighboring Canaan, they'd either have to blast the Wentworth or gut both towers.

It stank of stale pot and cooked cabbage inside, and half the lights didn't work. He tripped a couple of times on peeling linoleum in the halls. The doors looked faded and chipped with numbers missing on some of them. A few other doors had the apartment numbers written in with magic marker.

Baggy might live here, but the Wentworth was Ralph's biggest market for crack in Holland Bay. Someone else ran the building, dealing from a courtyard out back. White boys from up the slope in Vodrey Heights did not venture into the project.

The apartment number he had beaten out of T-Dogg was 1001, which meant Baggy rated an upper-floor apartment, but not a penthouse pad. When Armand reached the tenth floor, he took out his Glock. When he found 1001, he kicked the door in.

Two homeboys sitting at a card table jumped up, but Armand waved them off with the gun. Baggy sat in a battered recliner, an emaciated naked girl bobbing her head in his lap. She stopped working Baggy, looked up at Armand, and screamed.

"This between me and you," said Armand. "I got no beef with your homies."

In a sterling display of loyalty, the two men backed away from the tables, neither reaching for the guns in their waistbands. The girl rocked back, still kneeling.

"What you want, motherfucker?" asked Baggy.

"This is for Shandra." He fired three shots from the Glock.

With his fly open, Baggy looked like a massive brown fountain that could only pump out a weak trickle of yellow. Bullet holes in the upholstery ringed his head. The naked crack whore who had been working him sat back on her haunches, crying. Baggy stared at Armand wide-eyed.

"You a dead mother—"

Armand squeezed off another round, putting a fourth hole in the recliner near Baggy's head. "You may run that corner. I may have to work for you. But you ever bust in my place again or lay a hand on my woman, you gonna wind up like that old man on the Inbound this morning."

Baggy tried to make a show of not caring by zipping his fly. His hands shook too badly to grab the zipper. "You're dead, Cole." He looked up to see Armand's Glock in his face.

"I'm dead?" he said. "Next round goes between your eyes. If you want to stay alive, stay the fuck out of my crib, and you don't so much as jerk off thinking about my woman. Or I cut off your tiny little cock and shove it down your throat before I kill you, and *then* dump your ass on the Inbound. Understand?"

Baggy nodded.

"Good." He tapped a salute like he'd seen a couple of uniformed cops do. "You have a nice evening."

Cold snap fires were the worst, at least as far as Ron Corwin was concerned. An investigator for the Monticello Fire Department, he knew finding someone, especially a child, inside the remains of a burnt building was truly the worst thing that could happen at a fire scene. That said, the worst environment to fight a fire would either be a blizzard or single-digit temperatures. Monticello had endured both in the last twenty-four hours.

Corwin might not have come out until the next day had two police detectives not been injured in the explosion. Like homicides on Pier 9 in the old port facility, Serievo fires were usually left alone on streets where abandoned homes outnumbered inhabited ones by at least two to one. Stanislaus Avenue had been a ghost town for about three years now. Letting houses burn was cheaper than razing them. Never mind that the federal government kept promising funds to level the homes and buy the vacant lots. That money would not materialize until the right political calculus appeared in Congress.

Snow, of course, made getting to a fire a dangerous proposition. Stanislaus was one of those streets that climbed the hill out of Midtown, of which Serievo was a part, into Rock Ridge, the city's western borough. Corwin noted that the responding unit had come from Huron Junction, the Rock Ridge neighborhood overlooking where the Huron River emptied into the Musgrave. Belgrade Street was actually closer, but it sat at the bottom of Stanislaus, which seldom saw a snowplow anymore, since the mortgage crisis had emptied that part of town.

Corwin had to watch his step as he walked the edge of the ruin. They had pumped an enormous amount of water onto the fire, which had turned into ice almost immediately. Two firefighters had made their way down into the rubble, which had collapsed into the house's basement. Nothing would be taken out today. Corwin would need to get a crew out here the next day to help sift through it all. Right now, he wanted to know what he was up against.

"Hey!"

The voice was female. Corwin looked up from a shard of gas pipe he'd been examining to see Robin Broxterman, one of his investigators, holding onto a large timber and pointing to what amounted to a sinkhole in the rubble.

"There's a body down here," said Broxterman. "It's pretty badly burned, but I think it has a couple of bullet holes in the skull."

Shit, thought Corwin. *Bad enough two cops got flattened.* "All right. Let's call it in."

"How long do you think the coroner will take?"

"To hell with the coroner," said Corwin. "I'm going to get a doctor from Custis Memorial out here. That stiff will still be dead when he gets over to Vodrey Heights."

CHAPTER 9

Custis Memorial Hospital overlooked the confluence of the Huron and Musgrave Rivers, hence the name of the surrounding neighborhood, Huron Junction. Built in the 1920s, the original architect designed it to look like a castle in the mountains. The slope out of Rock Ridge into Midtown, however, was only fifty feet at that point. From that vantage point, the dark stone made it look more menacing than majestic. It didn't so much loom over the two rivers as glare down at them.

Branson was glad the ambulance spared her a view of the hospital from a distance. She always found the building incredibly ugly, made uglier by the boxy, lifeless wings that had been added onto the place since the 1950s. Maybe if they'd put it upriver, where Prussian Meadow and the Monticello State campus sat a hundred and fifty feet below Rock Ridge proper, the thing might have actually looked evil from below. From here, especially pulling into the parking lot, it looked like a suburb had sprung up around Dr. Frankenstein's castle. The proliferation of Starbucks and Jimmy Johns and the like to one side didn't help the image, nor did the check-cashing places, gun shops, and dirty bookstores on the other side of the hospital lot.

Branson saw only the entrance to the emergency room when her ride arrived at Custis Memorial. The ER was its own special kind of hell. Her concussion made her the guest of honor. She did not care at that point. All she wanted was relief from her headache and something to settle her stomach.

They rolled her in on a stretcher, passing a second team, a doctor, two nurses, and an orderly, who stood waiting for Taggart to arrive in the other ambulance. The doctor, named Cutler, asked her questions. His voice sounded tinny and distant. Branson assumed her hearing was not completely recovered yet. At least she hoped there was a "yet" to it. The penlight was the worst. Cutler held it close to each eye, causing her head to explode in fresh waves of pain. After Cutler administered what resembled a roadside sobriety test, the orderly helped her into a wheelchair and pushed her into a private examining room. After an hour alone, she started demanding to go home. After her third protest, Cutler entered the room. His voice did not sound quite so distant when he countered her argument that she felt fine now.

"Detective Branson," he said in his best paternal tone, "you've suffered a concussion. The first twenty-four hours are the most critical. If you do not calm down..."

"How the hell can I calm down when you dump me in a cold room for hours on end?" She hopped off the examining table. "And can I have something besides this thing to wear? I feel like my ass is on display."

"We'll bring you some scrubs," he said. "Just please, try to relax. Stress is the worst thing for you at this moment."

"That's why I want to go home now." Never mind that she'd need to go back to Holland Bay for her car.

The orderly returned with a set of surgical scrubs and asked if she needed anything else.

"My discharge papers," she said.

The orderly did not answer that, opting instead to leave the room while she changed.

The scrubs did feel better, but the examining room lacked any magazines or television. She did not have her phone and hoped they had stowed her personal items somewhere nearby. If not, her wallet, phone, and, worst of all, her gun, lay somewhere in an abandoned neighborhood in Serievo.

The next time a nurse appeared, she said, "Any news on Taggart?"

"Is he the other police officer in the explosion?" the nurse asked.

"Yes. He looked pretty bad when they put him in the ambulance."

The nurse swallowed. Cutler had probably told her not to stress out Branson any more than necessary. "He's in surgery. He has a lot of shrapnel in his back."

"Sounds like a goddamned war zone."

The nurse nodded slowly. "Was your friend a soldier?"

"You know, I'm not sure what he did in the military. I only know he used to work Narcotics and grew up in Oklahoma."

"Oklahoma? Why would anyone move to Monticello from there?"

Branson shrugged. "Beats me. I keep asking myself why I stay here."

Cutler returned fifteen minutes later to inform her they were keeping her overnight for observation.

"I'm fine," she said. "Can I go home?"

It had been almost three hours now. Her ears had stopped ringing, and her vision had returned to normal. Moreover, she was certain that the headache was being caused by the cold room and antiseptic smell, rather than any blow she might have taken. Did they want to make her stay overnight for observation? Fine. Could they at least get her into a room with a television and some heat?

"We're almost done here," said Dr. Cutler. "But we need to be sure there isn't more serious damage."

"I'm fine," Branson repeated.

"She sure is."

Both Branson and Cutler turned their attention to the entrance to the examining room. There stood Alvin Baker, flanked by Murdoch and Kagan, the Homicide cop. Kagan looked angrier than Branson, which she would have never thought possible.

"You'll have to leave," said Cutler. "I'm examining..." He

stopped when he saw Baker's badge. "Is this official business?"

"It is," said Baker. "You have two of my detectives here. Since one of them is in another room with his back sliced open, I want to talk to Detective Branson here."

Branson's headache worsened. "Can I please just go home?"

"Detective Branson has sustained a concussion," said Cutler. "I'm sure I don't need to explain to you the ramifications of that."

"I don't want to put her on the SWAT Team," said Baker. "Since Ms. Branson is conscious and clearly coherent, I only want to know what she can tell me about two of my cops getting blown up."

"It made me deaf and loopy," said Branson, "and it hurt like a mother."

"I would like to keep her here for observation," said Cutler. "Make sure there's no serious damage."

"A wise decision," said Baker, "but she looks fine to me. She seems to have quickly recovered most of her faculties."

As Cutler and Baker went back and forth, Branson noticed that Murdoch's and Kagan's expressions both changed to amusement. Kagan seemed to be trying to hide it. Murdoch did not seem to care. Then again, Murdoch, as far as Branson knew, had no history with Baker or anyone else in Internal Affairs. When Baker left that division, Murdoch was probably still writing parking tickets and pulling concert duty at the nightclubs in Olde Towne or down in Edison for overtime pay. She knew Kagan's story. Even if she didn't, he wore it in that perpetual scowl he had ever since setting foot in Holland Bay Station.

"I can't force her to stay," said Cutler. "But I strongly suggest it. There may be damage we're not seeing yet."

Baker took Cutler by the arm. "I understand that, doc. I really do. But I need to chat with Detective Branson. And if she doesn't want to stay overnight..."

"I want to look at her first thing in the morning."

"I will have her checked out before she sets foot in morning roll."

"I'm right here, guys," said Branson, which got a chuckle from Murdoch.

"Detective," said Cutler, "if I release you, you are not to drive and not return to work until you've been cleared by me."

"Finally," said Branson.

"So what do you want to do, Detective?" said Baker.

"Get the hell out of here."

"Doctor, as soon as she's dressed and ready for discharge, I want to spend a few minutes debriefing her. Only fair." He turned to Kagan. "You can drive her home."

"Fine," said Kagan.

"And pick her up in the morning."

"Captain, I live way the hell over in Vodrey Heights..."

"Nice part of town," said Baker. "Our Mr. Murdoch lives in another part of Vodrey Heights. Either way, I want one of you picking her up tomorrow morning. Murdoch's had a long day, so it's you."

"I don't have to..."

"It's an order." To Murdoch, he said, "How about a drink, Murdoch? What's your poison?"

Branson thought she heard him say something about Cabo Wabo.

Mexicans populated the bar, but that was par for the course in Huron Junction. None of them took notice of Baker and Murdoch when they entered. The waitress didn't even bat an eyelash when Baker ordered a Jameson and Budweiser. Murdoch, aware of what the Romans did in Rome, ordered a Modelo Negra. The waitress smirked as she left to get their drinks.

"So tell me, Murdoch," said Baker. "How long have you been on the Port Police?"

"Two years," he said. "I'd planned to transfer when they finally closed down the old port this summer." He hoped the beer wouldn't make him sleepy. He'd only had four hours of sleep before Baker summoned him to the hospital.

"Consider yourself transferred."

Murdoch said nothing, trying to hide the kick in the gut he felt.

When their drinks arrived, Baker swallowed his Jameson in one gulp without making a move for his beer. "I suppose you think this is a backhanded demotion."

Murdoch thought about how to answer as he sipped his beer, tossing the slice of lime aside. "The thought crossed my mind."

"It should," said Baker. "Special Investigations, as it's been utilized by the MPD, should never have existed. The only one doing real police work was my predecessor, and he's been transferred to the Port Police out on Holland Island. Same job, just without having to babysit the force's undesirables." Baker finally took a pull on his Bud longneck. "Those days are over, Murdoch. SI now has real work to do. And you're going to help me do it."

"How's that, sir?"

"I've got Kagan detailed from Homicide on this Carcinira thing. Branson's hurt, but she'll be back on her feet tomorrow. I guarantee it. It's Taggart I worry about. He's the key to every-thing. If he were at least awake and able to talk, I'd leave my original plan in place. I'd put Friedman with Branson and..." He saw Murdoch laughing. "What's so funny?"

"Friedman?" Murdoch signaled the waitress. "With Branson?"

"Well, I know she's a disciplinary problem," said Baker, "but I know how to deal with that."

"I meant Friedman has the hots for Branson." The waitress came. Murdoch ordered a shot of Cuervo. "I mean literally."

Baker shook his head. "I can see you guys need more to do than prowling shipping containers and handing out OVIs to drunken sailors. Which is why I'm putting you on plainclothes to work with Branson and Kagan."

Murdoch's mug stopped halfway to his mouth, threatening to spill if he didn't either drink or set it back down.

"Yeah," said Baker. "Thought that's what you'd say."

***

At the merge with I-673, the highway traversing the Big Mac Bridge and linking the airport with Monticello's inner boroughs, the Inland Parkway narrowed from six-lane freeway to four-lane boulevard. Its proper name was US 250 North, and it began outside the former village of Camelot in the city's southern borough of Edison.

Camelot itself was only a recent addition to Monticello. In 1994, when all the unincorporated space north of the city of Milan suddenly became part of the larger city, the village of Camelot declined the invitation. It made too much money off traffic fines to surrender home rule to the urban behemoth to the north. But it wasn't always like this.

The main route of US 250 bypassed Monticello into Sandusky, home of Cedar Point Amusement Park and one of the main jumping off points for the Lake Erie islands. After World War II, an enterprising gentleman named Rankin L. Harrison built a hotel, tavern, and diner at the spot where Inland Road and US 250 split. He'd catch coaster freaks and island hoppers coming and fleeing Monticellans going. From 1948 to 1958, it was a sweet setup. The diner became a Big Boy. Gas stations, bars, and chain motels sprang up, the cash machine made only sweeter with the conversion of nearby Doolittle Air Force Base to Rooney International Airport.

Then President Eisenhower decreed that his new interstate system would run along the east bank of the Musgrave River through Monticello before connecting the city to Columbus, one hundred miles to the south. Interstate 90 and the Ohio Turnpike connected I-73 to what soon became John Glenn International Airport, and business dried up in Camelot.

Harrison cashed out, retired to Florida, and left the town he founded to wither and die. So Camelot turned to that tried-and-true means of survival, the speed trap. And oh, what a speed trap it was. When the state built the Inland Parkway as a companion freeway on the Musgrave's western bank, a ridiculous amount of speeding fines kept Camelot flush with cash well into the 2000s.

At least they did until the State of Ohio passed a bill dissolving all villages with populations less than one hundred fifty residents as incorporated entities. It took less than a day for the Musgrave County Prosecutor to file a suit to dissolve Camelot as an actual town and have it absorbed into Monticello.

By the time Kagan drove Branson home to Camelot, the town was still in evidence, but it looked abandoned. Rank's Diner, what became the Big Boy in the late fifties, had stood vacant since the 1990s, Big Boy himself flaking and violated with graffiti. The one remaining gas station still sported a Pure Oil sign out front, despite selling some off-brand of gas these days. It looked like Norman Rockwell gone to seed.

"Oh, if you only knew how many tickets I got out of driving through here," said Kagan.

"Even a few years ago," said Branson, "you could get twelve points on your license just driving down Main Street." Main Street had become Norwalk Road, Inland Boulevard's name when it originally left Monticello proper. "How'd you get out of those tickets?"

"My dad saved Gino Fasano's life in Vietnam. So, I had a guardian devil."

Branson snorted. "Must have been hell growing up in your household. And you married a prosecutor?"

"Not just any assistant prosecutor. I married Ken Tierny's daughter."

Branson remembered Tierny. Among other things, he had made his name as a young assistant prosecutor on the team that pressed state charges against Mayor Stan Lipinsky. Lipinsky went to prison. Now he had his own AM talk show and a weekend gig on Fox News. From hippie to wingnut, Mayor Stan would not go away. "So, you had a guardian angel and a guardian devil."

"Not until after Maria and I married. When I was a teenager, Ken hated my guts. Thought I was going to corrupt his little girl."

"Did you?"

"In a good way."

That made Branson laugh. "All right, give. What's your beef with Alvin Baker?"

"Well," said Kagan, looking calm but gripping the steering wheel to the point of white knuckles, "when they investigated my old man, they decided I'd be guilty by association. Dad's a dirty cop, so I'm a dirty cop."

"And Baker had your case."

"Baker put me in the rack and broke out the hot pokers, same as he did to anyone he investigated. I understand he was the one who found you innocent."

"Only after my husband decided it was bad for his career to be married to a woman who shot a sitting mayor's son."

"Where is Mr. Branson?"

"Loring."

"What?"

"My married name was Loring. The day I signed the divorce papers, I went to the Social Security office and changed my name back to Branson."

Kagan smiled. "I hope you banged his best friend to get even."

She debated whether to tell him what she did do the day the papers were signed, then thought better of it. The less other cops knew about her personal life, the better. "I celebrated my freedom. Let's leave it at that."

They entered Camelot and drove past the abandoned Big Boy. It made the one on Pier 10 look like it was merely closed for remodeling. "So, how'd you end up out here?"

"The house in Vodrey Heights we could afford comfortably. Actually, *he* could afford it nicely. On a cop's salary alone, especially one that went stagnant like mine, it was a foreclosure waiting to happen." She smiled. "Sometimes, when the woman gets the house, it's a curse."

"Sell it?"

"Renting. It's still underwater, so I'm pretty much stuck with it." She frowned at the thought of having to work a second job if her tenants ever pulled up stakes and left. Maybe it was time to see if she could land in the suburbs, make a little extra cash as a sergeant or even a captain. Her record up until shooting Ray Kozinski had been stellar. "Hell, if it hadn't been for that monster, I might have made sergeant by now."

"Or lieutenant. Remember, your old partner is my boss now."

"Someone told me today that you're up for Landsman's job as sergeant."

Kagan seemed to focus harder on the road ahead. "Yeah, well..." His jaw shifted a little as he appeared to struggle with whether to say anything. "Hey, about Moran. I'm sorry to hear what happened."

It was Branson's turn to grind her teeth. "Well, with Taggart down, maybe it's a sign."

"A sign of what?"

"That maybe I'm the one who should take that motherfucker Smithers down."

Kagan laughed. "Good luck with that. We've been chasing that sonofabitch since I was in Narcotics." He made a left onto a small side street leading into a shabby apartment complex. It wasn't a ghetto, but it looked like a place where one lived until something better came along or circumstances warranted something cheaper. "We're agreed. Baker is a prick."

"I have mixed feelings about him. He cleared me."

"He put me through six weeks of hell because Ken Tierny's word wasn't good enough for him."

Branson leaned her head back and closed her eyes. "If I recall correctly, you got my slot in Homicide not long after that."

"So?"

"The only reason I'm not in Sarah Ryland's place is that I shot a sitting mayor's son. Baker was even told to find me guilty. I don't hate him for investigating me. I do hate the passion he had for the job."

Kagan pulled the car into a slot in front of Branson's building. "Six of one, half a dozen of the other. Need help?"

Branson opened the door. Her headache came back in three

quick waves. Nausea rolled in her stomach, but then subsided. "I think I can manage. Six o'clock tomorrow?"

"Yeah. Captain says he wants you at the station instead of Custis Memorial."

"But Dr. Cutler wants to check me out before I go on duty."

Kagan grinned. "I'll give Baker this. He only promised to have you checked out and cleared. He never promised Cutler that he'd be the one to do it."

If Branson felt better, she would have laughed. "Six a.m., Kagan. Don't be late."

If Armand were Baggy, he would have had someone at every entrance to his apartment building, waiting for Armand to come out. Armand was not Baggy. He told Shandra to keep the door locked and to keep a baseball bat handy, just in case. At around six that evening, he slipped out of the building on the far side from his apartment and into the alley between Eastern and Halsted. The temperature hovered around zero again, but the cold did little to stifle the smell of fresh garbage. He ignored it. By spring, it would start reeking of urine or worse.

Armand's building looked shabbier in the dark, but inside, it was solid, more solid than one usually found in Holland Bay. If Rufus were smart, Armand told himself, he would rewire the place, rip out all the pipes, hang drywall in place of the plaster, and paint it something other than the bland puke color that coated the walls inside. Who knew? Maybe he would. They were only a few blocks from Canaan, where his mama grew up. His mama couldn't afford Canaan anymore.

The other building...

Across Halsted, fronting Delaware, sat what looked like something left by a bombing sortie. The hulk might have resembled Armand's building in an earlier life, maybe when dockworkers and truck drivers still lived here. His mama sometimes talked about the old Holland Bay. It was rough back before Armand was born, but it wasn't the hell it had since become. Back in those days, Canaan had been the ghetto, whereas Holland Bay was just a rough-and-tumble blue-collar neighborhood. The faces were white with last names from Poland or Italy or Ireland. There were a few black faces there. Mama had implied that one of them might have been Armand's father, but she'd added that the blacks back then weren't like the blacks you see these days in Holland Bay or Prussian Meadow. They were the poorer relations to the Holland Island blacks. They didn't have the money, but they had the standing.

Now, only Holland Island blacks could afford Canaan, and none of them would be caught dead in Holland Bay outside the Monorail or Farnum Field, down by the lakeshore. Their poor relations had fled for the new borough of Edison or out to the suburbs like their white brethren. Holland Bay was a dumping ground, like Prussian Meadow had been for decades.

This building was emblematic of it. No windows, crumbling brick, power lines ripped out of the walls. Armand almost feared going inside. He'd gone inside just such a place once as a kid on a dare. Back before the gangs permeated every aspect of his life, he and his friends would swarm through the neighborhood, doing what kids did everywhere. One time, Isaac, a tall kid who later left Holland Bay for a suburb and was now a star on the Custis University basketball team, told the urban legend of Rot Face. Rot Face was a zombie who had been a hobo in life and now hid in this abandoned tenement on Feemster Avenue. Isaac dared the group to go inside and stare down Rot Face. Only Armand took the dare.

Rot Face never showed, but the building itself damn near killed him. The stairs on the fourth floor collapsed under him. Had he not been eight, he might have simply hung there until he either fell to the third-floor landing (and possibly through it) or the police rescued him. And his mama always told him, "Armand, you stay away from them po-LEECE! They get you. Like they got…" And here she would insert the name of whatever boyfriend she had just kicked out of the house.

At eight, most boys can swing around in high places. At eighteen, he could move with the best of them, but he was no eight-year-old swinging on monkey bars and fire escapes. Rock climbing was definitely not in his immediate future.

This building, the one on Halsted, had stairs like those on Feemster. For a brief moment, Armand imagined Rot Face lurked somewhere inside, and from the looks of things, maybe he did. Armand now carried a nine, which would take out Rot Face quite nicely, thank you very much. The stairs?

He'd have to go slow and hope the fire escapes still held.

He found nothing on the fourth floor, where the stairs were at their weakest. The only signs of any human presence in the last five years came from smashed plaster and wood that had once made up the walls. Not an inch of copper wiring remained. PVC piping, most of it filthy, lay about the doorless apartments' bathrooms and kitchens. Scrap dealers didn't want PVC. They wanted copper and stainless steel and aluminum. The third floor was much the same, but there was the smell of stale urine and old feces. Abandoned now, these rooms showed every sign that Baggy had run crack whores out of them. Armand wondered why anyone in their right mind would want a blowjob off one of those nasty girls. Never mind the girl Dmitri had once bought for him.

The girls had to have bugged out when the weather turned cold, which, in Northern Ohio, meant October. Assuming Baggy survived and held onto the corner, he'd simply get a few more teenage girls hooked on crack and put them to work in these same apartments. Armand knew it was bad in Holland Bay, but he'd heard about conditions in Haiti. This made Haiti look like the resort on Put-in-Bay. For that alone, Armand decided he would kill Baggy. The old man might have been snitching on Ralph. Baggy was just scum.

The first and second floors had clearly been used. Baggy was smart enough not to put his stash in here. Scavengers had avoided the bottom two floors, expecting someone to walk in on them, possibly the owner or the cops. The upper floors provided plenty of places to hide, but those had been picked clean. Someone, probably Baggy, had smashed the wall between two of the apartments on the second floor and pushed the debris into the corner. There was a kerosene heater, which Armand thought might be useful in Mr. King's plans. There were also a couple of mattresses, one of those camping stoves Armand had seen in a sporting goods store somewhere, and a cooler, probably empty. The mattresses were dirty, and used condoms lay scattered around one of them. Baggy had made himself a nest.

Like the second-floor apartments, the first floor had been altered with a sledgehammer. This "suite" was arranged like an office. Armand searched the desk, found a couple bags of weed, and helped himself to one. He and Shandra would get high tonight. High on pot, Shandra was freaky and would do anything Armand wanted.

Most of the basement was locked. There was a huge storage room similar to one he had seen in his own building. Armand wondered why it was locked if no one, aside from Baggy, used the building. He doubted it was the stash. He decided to go out behind the building and look at the old coal chute.

It, too, was locked with a chain and padlock. He found a metal pipe lying in a corner and began beating on the doors. The thin metal began to dent and collapse with each blow. Finally, it fell into the cellar. Armand slipped in, shining a flashlight around the room.

Bodies in various states of decomposition stared back at him.

CHAPTER 10

By five, as Armand Cole was reconnoitering Rufus's abandoned building, Branson was bored to tears. By six, she had scarfed half a cheese pizza from Papa Gino's. Bad idea. She puked it back up, which in turn left her dizzy. She put the rest in the fridge and decided to risk yogurt later, assuming it hadn't gone bad. On the other hand, she couldn't stand sitting around doing nothing.

On a normal night, she would go run in the park. She'd hang out at a bar and, if sufficiently bored enough or drunk, bring home a playmate. In light of Jerry's overly concerned phone call earlier, though, the thought of screwing some random barfly out of boredom seemed less appealing than that yogurt she'd brave later.

And that explosion bothered her. It wasn't just the concussion or the bruises or the frostbite. It wasn't Taggart in surgery having chunks of wood and concrete extracted from his shoulder and back. It bothered her because this was her first homicide in four years, and someone had tried to stop her investigating it by blowing up a house. Flipping on Fox 18, she caught blonde anchor Jenn Acosta starting the newscast off with the story. She was surprised Jenn hadn't called her, but the station probably thought she was still at the hospital.

Acosta was a high school friend of Branson's, a real party girl in her early days. Branson, already attached to Gary when they graduated college, played wingman to Acosta, who looked a little like Marilyn Monroe if Marilyn had been a hair metal groupie in her youth. Branson was almost butch, something she hadn't thought about until Taggart had explained what Friedman wanted in a woman.

By the time Branson made Homicide, Jenny Acosta was the pretty, bubbly street reporter stuck doing fluff pieces for WMON, the city's CBS affiliate. She wanted to be taken seriously, and Branson obliged her, leaking choice bits of information to her on cases. When Branson shot Mayor Kozinski's son, who thought "questioning a witness" meant "stopping by for nookie," Acosta was the only reporter she would talk to. Acosta treated her with respect, making the fall from grace and divorce from Gary bearable. The interviews got her the weekend anchor position at Fox 18, which led to her current gig at six and ten.

Jennifer Acosta only introduced the story from the desk. The street reporter, some twentyish girl with a model's looks, did mention Branson, but had not contacted her. Either the girl didn't know her job or Acosta was running interference. She'd expect a phone call sooner or later, but Branson hadn't talked to Acosta in about three years. She didn't appreciate her friend going out with Gary Loring after the divorce, even if it was only one date. She doubted Acosta even had her phone number anymore.

"Firefighters also made a gruesome discovery after both officers were taken from the scene," said the reporter. "While sifting the rubble, they discovered the body of what appears to have been a homeless person who had taken up residence in the house. Police are not saying if they have any theories, but one officer at the scene told Fox 18 that Homicide was already working with Special Investigations, formerly the city's counter-terrorism unit..."

That made Branson snort. Special Investigations had not done a minute of counter-terrorism work since about 2005, when council pulled its funding.

"...on the deaths of a father and son, both murdered last night, one of whom was found on I-73 Inbound this morning."

Oh, shit. Someone had talked out of turn. Not Murdoch, not after his come-to-Jesus moment with Baker. Kagan had been at the hospital with her, Baker, and Murdoch, then driven her home. She bet it was either Petrocelli, looking to raise his profile, or Friedman, making sure she, too, was still attached to what was her first real case in years.

That was it. Even the media were interested now. She might be sidelined, she mused, but there was no reason she couldn't do a little homework before they cleared her again.

As she booted up her laptop, an Acer that had seen better days, she dialed a number at Settlers Commons, looking for the sole exception to her iron-clad rule never to date a cop. It made her smile, then tear up a little, as she remembered that rule had been Ray Moran's suggestion.

"Systems," said a bored male voice on the other end. "Clayborne speaking."

"Hello, baby," said Branson in a voice that had melted lawyers and hard-bitten bikers since her divorce. "It's Jess. Listen, I really want to get a line on who killed my old partner, Moran. Think you can get me into his files?"

Clayborne, a nerdy fellow not unlike Jerry, but in ways that bothered Branson, chuckled. "And what's in it for me, gorgeous?"

"My gratitude?"

"Uh-huh. Which means you buy me a couple of rounds and sweet talk me for about an hour. Then I go home in frustration. Do I have this right?"

"That's exactly what I'm offering. Do we have a deal?"

"That's what I love about you, Branson. You know what men really want. Emailing you the password to Moran's account now. Does your boss know I'm doing this for you?"

"My boss will thank you when I break this case. One more thing?"

"Your wish is my command, though I can't figure out why."

"Damn right it is. My new partner, Taggart, got himself blown up, and I really need to look at his notes, too. Do you think you could get me into his folder?"

Murdoch returned home to an empty house. At first, he thought Jane had gone to bed since she had had needed to be at the studio for her morning drive shift. Yet he found the bedroom empty.

"Jane?"

He went down to the garage and flipped on the light. Empty, except for Murdoch's Ford. In the kitchen, no dishes sat in the drainer or inside the dishwasher. No plates lay in the sink. She had not been at home when he woke up, but she also did afternoon traffic for several radio stations in the afternoon. Murdoch had assumed she'd been at work when he awoke.

He checked his phone for messages. The last text had come in this afternoon, when Sgt. Petrocelli called about Branson and Taggart. Jane had left no note, not even a message on the phone's voicemail. Murdoch's beat-cop instincts kicked in. He headed to the basement and quickly searched it. Since it was all one room, he needed only to turn on the light and look around from the base of the stairs. It was empty.

Finally, he climbed back to the second floor and checked her dresser. Some of her underwear was missing, including a lacy thing from Victoria's Secret that she liked to wear when she and Murdoch got along better. From another drawer, he found most of her jeans gone. Several pull-over tops had disappeared from a third. He didn't bother with the closet. He knew he'd find her shoes and a couple of dresses or skirts missing.

Murdoch did the only thing he could do in a situation like this. He took off his shirt and pants and tossed them casually on the bed. Clad only in boxers and a T, he trudged down to the kitchen and dug out an Ol' Muskie from the fridge. Some of the foam from the can spilled onto the floor, but he didn't care.

How could he clean up when the Huskies, Monticello's hockey team, were playing Columbus on ESPN? He tuned into the *Sportscenter* to wait for the game to start and did something that would have set Jane frothing in that Yorkshire accent of hers.

He put his bare feet up on her prized antique coffee table and sat the beer next to him on the couch. "Daddy's house now," he said out loud.

Armand found himself back on Holland Island for a second time that day, once again in Rufus King's office. At close to seven-thirty now, the man himself was still there. Mr. King offered him a drink, which turned out to be cognac.

"So, tell me what you found," said Mr. King.

Armand outlined how the upper floors had been stripped by scavengers. Someone had been running crack whores out of the second floor in warmer weather, and Baggy had converted the first floor into an office, using kerosene heaters to make the place habitable during the day.

Mr. King nodded. "What about the rest of the building?"

"Someone been stashing bodies in the basement," said Armand.

That made Mr. King sit up. "Bodies?"

"At least ten of them. Some been there for a while. One was a skeleton."

At first, Mr. King looked horrified. Then something changed in his eyes, the first hint of a smile. "Did it smell?"

"No," said Armand. "Place was locked up. Like someone knew somebody'd come looking."

"Surprised no one smelled it already. Was it the big storage room in the basement?"

"Yeah. There's one just like it in the building you set me up in."

Now the smile came out. Mr. King rummaged around in his desk and came up with a set of car keys. He tossed them to Armand. "Corolla in lot D-Twenty-Five, over at Port Center." He reached into his jacket and pulled out a C note and a couple of fifties. "Give a fifty to the attendant. It's been there a while. Drive out to Norwalk to that Walmart where you've been dumping cars for us. Pick up four of those five-gallon gas cans."

"Why?"

"Because you're going to need a lot of gas."

Both Moran and Taggart had taken copious notes about the drug operation that dominated Monticello. Moran had names of corner boys, of distributors, runners, even enforcers. He knew where they worked, their last known addresses, and their specialties. Doby Clark, Taggart's informant, for instance, had been a go-to guy for smack until he started using too much of his own product. At the time of his death, he was little more than an errand boy for a guy named Dmitri Reagan.

Branson cross-referenced this with NCIC, VICAP, and existing police reports. Reagan, she learned, was the only suspect in Moran's death. His notes on Reagan dated back to when Moran had been in the van running the wire on Jeff Kagan's partner a few years ago. That particular incident resulted in Detective Gordo Pearson, working undercover at the time, taking a bullet in the gut.

"The plot thickens," Branson muttered to herself, cringing at the cliché as soon as it escaped her lips. Pearson's shooting resulted in an overzealous lieutenant in Internal Affairs reaching the inescapable conclusion that Kagan, son of the MPD's dirtiest cop, had arranged his partner's murder. Unfortunately for that lieutenant, Pearson lived, causing the Deputy Ops to intervene and give the case to Alvin Baker. Like Branson, Kagan found himself getting cavity searched by Baker. However, Baker ended up exonerating them both. Subsequently, exonerated him. Unlike Branson, Kagan's clean bill of health landed him a plum transfer.

Moving back to Moran's notes, Branson looked up "Plink." Most of the thugs in his vast casebook had street names tied to their real names. Guys like Calvin "Goose" Mallory or Albert "Monk" Diggs all had arrest records. Plink she had to look for in Taggart's notes. Even then, it took her the better part of ten minutes to figure out that his legal name was Victor Wallend.

Wallend had no arrest record to date. She Googled the name and learned only that he'd served two tours in Iraq before being honorably discharged. His last known address came up on Google Maps as a vacant lot not far from Branson's apartment. The land had been cleared by a developer who had hoped to build on the cheap in the wake of the mortgage crisis. That entire block had become foreclosures, the result of a shaky homebuilding scheme that collapsed along with the rest of the economy. Nevertheless, the developer had managed to knock over the houses before he himself went belly up. Branson guessed that Plink had developed his habit when he left the Marines and simply drifted away from the house, unaware that it no longer belonged to him, or even existed.

A knock came at the door. "Who is it?"

"I come bearing gifts."

"Jerry," she muttered under her breath. Hoisting herself off the couch, she made her way to the door and opened it without removing the chain. "I'm really tired. What do you want?"

Jerry looked like a big kid, grinning and holding up two sacks from Shanghai House, around the corner from Branson. "Since when are you too tired for broccoli chicken and egg rolls?"

She wanted to slam the door and tell him to go away, but Jerry had driven all the way over from the eastern part of Edison, bringing dinner. And, she had to be honest, it'd been a while since a man had given a damn about her, beyond trying to get in her pants.

Of course, Jerry had done just that. Maybe that's why he was such a puppy dog around her. She undid the chain and let him in.

"You know I have to take it easy tonight," she said. "I was just getting ready for bed."

Jerry parked himself on her sofa and started unpacking the food. "That why you have a bunch of police records and notes up on your laptop?"

Branson tightened the sash on her robe and came over to the

couch. "Some people do Facebook. I do criminal records."

"I thought you weren't supposed to be working."

"I thought I said I wanted to be alone."

He looked up at her, obviously a little hurt. "I was worried about you."

She sat down next to him and took an egg roll. Smelling it made her hungry, a good sign. "You're sweet." The first bite steamed in her mouth. "And you deserve better."

"Maybe," he said. "But you're the first woman who hasn't judged me for being a nerd."

She grabbed his arm. "Look, about last night..."

"I know. You were drunk. I get that. I'm sorry. When we made that bet, I didn't think you'd actually..."

"Save it." She let go. "You can sleep here tonight if it makes you feel better."

Jerry looked like he'd been told Cedar Point would open on his birthday for him and him alone.

"But you sleep on the couch. Okay?"

"Okay."

Branson wanted to tell him they needed to find him a real girlfriend. But she said nothing. Most of the women she could introduce him to would stomp all over him and make him beg for more. Then she'd have to kill them.

It left her wondering who was taking care of whom.

The Silver Stiletto catered to the businessman, the mover, the shaker in Monticello. For fifty dollars a song, a professional exotic dancer would grind in a patron's lap in little more than a thong or even less. For five hundred dollars, the patron and the dancer could adjourn to the privacy of one of the Stiletto's VIP rooms for an hour. There, certain dancers would do more than dance if she and the patron could come to a reasonable arrangement. After all, what two consenting adults did in private was nobody's business.

Armand had visited the Stiletto before but never as a patron, except when Ralph Smithers once told him to help himself to a girl on the house. The girl had been a short white girl with huge breasts and a mouth that wouldn't quit. Unlike Dmitri's crack whores, this woman would probably survive her time working for Ralph with money in her pocket and her parents none the wiser.

Tonight, however, Armand came to the Stiletto after Ralph texted him. He slipped in the side door, trading fist bumps with one of the guys who had given him a beat-down that morning and headed straight to the back office. If Ralph wasn't there, Dmitri would be. If neither was there, he would head across the river to the Phoenix Café before his trip to the suburbs.

He found both Ralph and Dmitri. Dmitri looked like Armand must have when his mother yelled at him as a child.

"You used to be the shit," said Ralph. "Now Moran dead— because of you—and two cops got blown up. One of them, Taggart."

Armand had heard of this Taggart before. Strange guy, Dmitri had said. If anyone knew strange, it was Dmitri Reagan. Taggart had a string of informers all through Ralph's organization, yet never did anything about it. According to Dmitri, the undercover cop had been pulled from Narcotics after pissing off someone upstairs. Taggart had found himself exiled to a useless squad called "Special Investigations" but never stopped working his case against Ralph.

Dmitri sniffed as though he had a cold. "I swear to you, Ralph, I had no idea Taggart and that bitch would be there." His voice cracked in places. "Please, you gotta let me make this right."

Armand watched from the corridor as Ralph stood over Dmitri, who looked like some white schoolboy caught smoking pot in the john by his prep school's headmaster.

"You goddamned will make this right," said Ralph. "By midday tomorrow, I want Plink under my thumb again. I want Baggy scared of more than just you. I want him to wet himself like a baby every time he hear the name 'Ralph Smithers.' Take that boy Rufus sent you and go bust some heads, assuming Rufus ain't got him on another job."

Dmitri bobbed his head rapidly as though he couldn't say yes fast enough. "I'll do it, Ralph. You'll see."

Ralph leaned into Dmitri's face. "And then, motherfucker, you climb on a bus for Columbus or Cleveland or I don't give a fuck where. I don't wanna see your ugly face in Monticello ever again. If I do…" Ralph made a gun with his thumb and forefinger, the finger in Dmitri's face. The thumb came down as Ralph mouthed the word "boom" at Dmitri. "Now get out of here. You make me sick."

Dmitri scrambled out of the room. When he saw Armand, he bumped him into the wall and stormed down the corridor toward the showroom. Ralph spotted him. Immediately, his expression changed.

"My man," said Ralph. "Come on in. Sorry you gotta see that, but it probably good news for you. You see Mr. King?"

"Yes, sir," said Armand, taking the same seat where Dmitri had sat moments before.

"Knock off the 'yes, sir' shit. I ain't yo' daddy, and we ain't in the Marines. So, Mr. King give you more work?"

"Yes, si… Yeah."

"Good. Mr. King got big plans for Holland Bay. Big plans. Play your cards right, maybe you be part of that. No more corners. How you like that?"

Armand liked that very much, especially in this weather.

"I only got a few minutes," said Ralph. "I'm about to have dinner. So you know if Baggy cuttin' yet?"

Armand spread his hands. "Fat fucker took my stash away after Dmitri chased us off the corner today."

Ralph spread his hands. "Least Dmitri got one thing right today. Tomorrow, Baggy might have to stay off the corner as well. Don't want our crews gettin' picked up because he think he can sell to tweakers in ten-degree weather. That happen, you tell Baggy that Dmitri wants you to see the operation. Got it?"

Armand said he got it.

"Good. From now on, you Dmitri as far as the Holland Bay crews concerned. That includes your corner, the Wentworth project, and all up and down Eastern." Ralph turned his head as someone knocked on the doorframe to the office. "Dinner's here."

In the doorway stood the most beautiful red-headed white girl Armand had ever seen. She wore only a silver teddy, and that dangled from her hand. Her other hand rested on her beautiful naked hip. "Hi, I'm Fyre. You wanted to see me, Mr. Smithers?"

"Call me Ralph." He gestured to Armand and introduced him. "He work for me."

"I thought you were having dinner," said Armand.

"I am," said Ralph. "Fyre gonna let me eat her up."

Fyre swept into the room, draped her teddy around Armand's neck, and perched in Ralph's lap. "Will Armand be joining us?"

"Naw," said Ralph. "This your employee evaluation. But if you want, maybe you can help Armand celebrate his promotion in a few days."

Armand took that as his cue to leave.

Fyre squealed and pulled Ralph's face into her ample breasts. "Well, daddy, let's get started while I'm feeling yummy."

Armand left before things became even stranger. He wondered about that woman who worked for Rufus, Janiece. He knew she was Ralph's woman. Ralph talked about her quite a bit. Yet here he was getting freaky with this white girl. Armand might have indulged in some strange once in a while, but he doubted he could forget being with a girl like Janiece. He couldn't forget Shandra.

It took Branson about two hours to piece together what both Taggart and Moran had been doing. Taggart's notes caused the most trouble, being rambling, scattered, and seemingly uncon-nected.

The operative word was "seemingly," which would drive Branson's grammar-nit ex-husband up a tree. Moran's case made sense at first glance. Taggart had made Ralph Smithers his pet project since getting kicked off Narcotics, but with no clear objectives. She decided to work backward from his most recent notes.

Plink, whom she had met earlier that day, had only started talking to Taggart recently. That partly explained why Taggart hadn't busted the lab over the last two years. He needed a legal way inside, and Plink had only given him one six months earlier. Normally, any cop would call in a raid as soon as she or he knew a meth lab existed somewhere. Not Taggart. Taggart was patient to the point of madness. Branson suspected that he was really a more socially adept version of that tall skinny nerd on *The Big Bang Theory*.

Working back, she learned that the late Doby Clark had a long grudge against one Dmitri Reagan. Once upon a time, Doby had not only been Ralph Smithers's main distributor on the city's west side, namely Rock Ridge and the west bank of the Musgrave, but he had once owned Serievo. He owned the Foundry District. He even owned white-bread, picket-fenced Shawnee Heights. But Serievo was dying. The banks couldn't level foreclosures fast enough, not without some federal help. With the Rock Ridge Division aggressively booting dealers out of their nice, clean middle-class borough, Doby's turned to his own product for comfort. His territory went to Reagan, and Doby's rage went into getting even.

Doby Clark had been introduced to Taggart by Raul Carcinira, whose corpse had shut down I-73 Inbound that morning. Carcinira had come to Monticello in the eighties from Tijuana, which confused Branson. She got why people left Mexico. But why come here when there were warmer places like Arizona, New Mexico, and California? He took a job with Ford in 1985, got his green card, had a son, José, in 1992, and took the buyout from Ford when they closed the Midtown plant.

Raul Carcinira had approached Taggart four years earlier. He had concerns about young José running with those Estradas.

Once upon a time, the Estradas owned Monticello, forcing the black gangs into submission and driving the old Sicilian crime family out of business. But then someone shot old Pablo Estrada at a Chuck E Cheese in Rock Ridge at his nephew's birthday party. Suddenly, Ralph Smithers ruled the city, at least its darker corners. He also became Taggart's biggest target.

Only Taggart had not worked at all with José. Ray Moran had. And Branson already knew first-hand how Moran had a boner for putting Dmitri Reagan away. Before Homicide abandoned Pier 9 to Harbortown and the Port Police, Moran had been called in to work on a handful of bodies found there, some of them mutilated horribly.

It didn't take long for Moran to home in on Dmitri Reagan. Word on the street said Dmitri was crazy. Dmitri loved killing. Dmitri loved it more than sex. One corner boy Moran questioned said the enforcer openly talked about wanting to strangle a woman to death during sex. Moran, well away from suspects and their attorneys, quietly talked about finding a way to kill Reagan and make it look righteous.

Moran's notes had become more sporadic in the past two weeks. He had managed to get assigned to an undercover detail that eventually would bring him into Reagan's orbit. The operation did not target Reagan. It targeted Ralph Smithers himself.

Moran's last note mentioned a visit to the Silver Stiletto, a high-end strip club near the football stadium. It ended with "SMITHERS?" in bold type. They found him beaten and bloodied on Saturday in Prussian Meadow off a jogging trail near Monticello State. Within two days, both Carciniras and Doby Clark would die.

Something rumbled next to Branson on the couch. She looked up and realized Jerry had fallen asleep during a rerun of *Chopped*. Standing up, she took the blanket she'd wrapped around herself and tossed it onto him. He snorted and looked up, eyes half shut.

"Wha'?"

"My hero," she said, shutting her laptop down. "Go back to sleep. I have to be to work early."

He was snoring again by the time she reached her bedroom door.

Armand first stopped at the Walmart in Norwalk, a small city eleven miles south of downtown Monticello. Dressed in his parka and a Browns cap instead of a hoodie, he looked like just another shift worker from the Ford plant in Milan, stopping in for a late-night purchase. Mr. King had planned it that way. Armand needed to look like anything but a gang banger.

The cans cost him sixteen dollars apiece. He wondered when plastic gas cans had gotten so expensive. He expected to pay only eight dollars or so for the nice ones. Nonetheless, no one seemed to be surprised to see his purchases.

"Snowblower?" asked the clerk, a slightly overweight redhead in her forties.

Armand smiled and said, "Yeah. Easy money in this weather."

The clerk shook her head. "Couldn't get me to go out in that weather for more than a few minutes."

"You snooze, you lose," said Armand, trying to sound folksy, and off he went to the Toyota Mr. King had given him.

The gas station proved a bit more difficult. Armand decided to get gas off I-73 in Edison. He picked a Speedway on Amherst Pike, thinking that getting gas far from where he bought the cans would make him harder to identify. And of course, buying both far from Holland Bay would make it harder to find suspicious buys when the building went up.

Unfortunately, the manager of the Speedway proved to be a paranoid type. "Hey, what are you doing?"

Armand had just started his second can of gas when the manager came rushing out, seemingly oblivious to the cold.

"I'm pumping gas," said Armand. "What does it look like?"

"Why so many cans?"

Funny. The woman in Norwalk immediately thought snow blower. This chump thought he was getting robbed.

"I'm gonna blow snow tomorrow. Need the gas."

"What?"

"Snow."

"Cocaine?"

Armand started on his third can. "No, stupid. See all this white shit laying around? People want it off their sidewalks."

The manager stared at him. "You're not from this area. Are you?"

As he topped off the third can, he said, "Naw. Holland Bay."

"Holland Bay? Why are you all the way down here? Why not get gas up there?"

Armand grinned, remembering what he and every other kid at school said about Holland Bay. That is, when he bothered to go to school. "Are you kidding? With all those niggers down there? I might get robbed."

The manager slunk away after that, looking very confused by Armand's joke. Since he'd already paid for his gas, he put the cans in the trunk and drove away. The trip from Holland Island out the Inland Parkway to Norwalk and back into the city took about an hour altogether.

At around midnight, in the abandoned apartment building on Halstead and Delaware, a fire broke out in an upper room. By twelve-thirty, the entire building was engulfed in flames. The fire department had it out by one-thirty. By two a.m., they had found the bodies Armand had discovered earlier in the day.

Armand Cole knew nothing about this. He did see the flames as he came up the Inbound. The gas, however, still sat in his trunk.

CHAPTER 11

Branson's head still hurt when she woke up, but at least she woke up alone. She probably would not have minded Jerry coming to bed with her, especially if her concussion got worse. The trouble was, Jerry was too clingy for her to handle sober.

She padded into the bathroom and splashed cold water on her face. Her reflection looked pale, dark circles under her eyes. At least she looked like she felt. Giving her head a quick shake, she did not feel nauseous from the sudden movement. The doctor would probably clear her.

In the kitchen, she started the coffee maker then went over to nudge Jerry, who lay snoring on the couch. "Hey. You need to get out of here. My partner's picking me up in half an hour."

Jerry's eyes fluttered open. "Wha'? Oh. I'll take you to the hospital."

"I'm not going to the hospital. My partner's taking me into the station."

Jerry sat up. "No, he's not. You need to be seen by a doctor before you can go back to work."

Branson put up her hand. "Save it. A police doc will look at me. Even if he doesn't clear me, I need to pick up my car, which is still at the station."

"Half an hour. Aren't you getting a shower?"

"I'll put my hair up in a clip." Though she had to admit to herself that a hot shower would have felt wonderful. "But you need to get going. I've got Special K and toast. Sorry, I'm not much of a breakfast person."

"Did you even have breakfast yesterday?"

"I was lucky to get out the door yesterday." In the cabinet, stale Pop Tarts awaited, blueberry, her favorite when she was a kid. "You remember that, don't you?" She waggled her eyebrows at him.

Jerry pressed his lips thin and looked away.

"Oh, Jerry, don't be like that." As the coffee maker started gurgling, she went over to the sofa to sit with him. Handing him a Pop Tart, she said, "Hey, we were having fun. Did you have fun?"

"I thought it was more than that," he mumbled.

She kissed him on the cheek. "You're sweet. I don't know why we're friends. You deserve someone who's not going to do that to you."

"I wanted to do that with you."

"Yes, but you're smitten. I was drunk and bored, and you deserve better than that." She draped an arm across his shoulders. "But you came here last night worried about me. You know how many guys I've been out with who would do that for me?"

He blushed. God love him, Branson thought, but he was actually blushing.

"Hey," she said, "I know what you want."

"But you don't want that."

"No. But I think you've earned the right to change my mind." She put a finger under his chin and gently turned him to face her. "You ought to try. Stubborn girl like me, you could consider it a challenge."

Finally, he smiled. "Next time, I make you breakfast." He held up the Pop Tart. "And not this crap, either."

"I'm fond of protein bars, too."

Murdoch awoke with a stiff back, a crick in his neck, and no one beside him in the bed. He checked his phone to find no texts, no missed calls, not even a Facebook message. He also felt like his bladder was about to explode.

He stood, stretched, and pulled a pair of suitcases from the closet and left them open on the bed. Then he began his morning routine: morning piss, long hot shower to the point of using up all the hot water, and a shave. He'd left his clothes from the night before strewn all over the bedroom and didn't bother to clean them up as he got dressed.

For breakfast, he had two jelly donuts instead of the usual one and left the plate on the table, along with a coffee mug with a half inch of coffee left in the bottom. He looked at Jane's favorite coffee cup, rinsed and left in the drainer next to the sink. It slipped, or so he told himself, from his fingers, shattering as it hit the floor.

"Oops." Grabbing his phone, he dialed a locksmith after finding it in Google. "Mr. Tully, Greg Murdoch from the MPD." He gave the address and his phone number. "I need you to redo the locks on my place. I'll swing by this afternoon, pick up the keys, and pay up then. Will that work?"

It would work, and Murdoch hung up.

When Greg Murdoch left for Holland Bay Station, two suitcases full of Jane's clothes sat on the front step.

Branson still did not feel one hundred percent, even though her headache had largely subsided with the little bit of food she had. She looked forward to having Kagan drive her into work, even if she did have to make roll call for the first time in months. That is, she looked forward to it until Kagan arrived at her door just after Jerry left.

"Hey," he croaked, "late night." His bad breath hit her full on as he spoke.

"You kiss your wife with that mouth?" She let him in.

"I had to go to my spot last night," he said. From the looks of him, he hadn't showered or shaved. "You know. And I got home after Maria was asleep."

"I see." She grabbed her coat, her sidearm, and her badge,

which she clipped to her belt. "Gimme your keys."

"Huh?"

"Your keys, Kagan. I'm not riding with you in that condition."

"You're not supposed to drive."

"Not on duty." When Kagan did not move, she added, "If you want to explain to Baker why I'm late and had to take a cab—on department expense, no less—be my guest. Or you can just gimme the damn keys."

Kagan tossed her the keys. "Blue Ford with the Tigers bumper sticker."

Branson rolled her eyes. "Tigers? Come on, Kagan, even on the west side, this is still an Indians town."

Armand Cole lay back on a mattress in the spare room of a house, cell phone to his ear. "Baby, soon as I can, I'll pick you up. Right now, I gotta lay low."

"Why didn't you take me with you?" Shandra asked. "We get this new crib, and you take off again."

Armand did not answer.

"A lot of police around. They started knockin' on doors."

Armand sat up. "You tell them about me?"

"I say my boyfriend live here, but he out of town. That good?"

"And are they gone?"

"They knockin' on other doors. Most people won't talk to them."

Of course not. It was Holland Bay. No one talked to the cops except to say, "Fuck you!" Ralph had taught him better, though. Ralph told Armand to always talk to the cops, to tell the truth when he could get away with it, wrap his lies in the truth when he couldn't. Be respectful. Smile. Most cops, even black cops, didn't trust black youth, not unless they had that Holland Island aura about them. Most Holland Island kids looked like they stepped out of Abercrombie & Fitch or Hollister. Guys like Armand reeked thug. If a thug smiled and answered questions, he didn't look like a thug in the cops' eyes. He looked like a wannabe.

"Where you at?" Shandra asked.

"You'll see." He hung up and looked around the place. It was barely furnished, with an old tube television but no Internet. Whoever owned the place or rented it from Mr. King had a king-size bed in the upstairs bedroom. As long as he stayed here, that room might make a nice playpen for him and Shandra.

His phone rang. The name read "Rufus King." Armand did not dare let it go to voicemail. He snatched up the phone and answered. "I didn't do it."

Branson slid Kagan's car in next to her now-iced-up Pathfinder. Kagan had fallen asleep before she'd even reached the Big Mac Bridge. He spent the entire ride in snoring and drooling, his head lolled to one side. She felt sorry for his wife.

It looked like every Port Police cruiser in Holland Bay was there. She'd forgotten exactly how many uniforms the Port Division had assigned to the old piers. Baker had already told her and Kagan that would all end today. Hell, Murdoch was in plainclothes as of last night.

Unless that was a murky dream from her concussion yesterday afternoon. They pushed their way in, Kagan clearly moving on autopilot. Even the squad room, where the detectives spent their days not doing real police work, was crowded.

Ana Friedman, five-foot-four and built like an attractive fire plug sidled up to Branson. "Maybe they're kicking us off the force finally."

Branson laughed. "Right. They won't spend the money to defend against the lawsuits, or we'd have been gone years ago." She looked at her watch. "Wow. Six-fifty-two. This is the first time I've made it to morning roll in..."

"Four months, sixteen days," said Friedman. "We've had a betting pool going since the last time."

"Who won?"

"I did. By the way, why's Murdoch wearing a shirt and tie?"

A hush swept through the room as a group of uniformed cops from the MPD's Protective Services swept into the room. Behind three of them, another officer in an elaborate uniform strode into view, gold birds on his collar and lots of braids on his epaulets and sleeves,

"Holy shit," said Branson. "Is that...?"

"Steve Hudepohl," said Friedman. "We're getting a visit from His Holiness himself."

Mr. King had listened patiently when Armand explained what had happened the previous night.

"I didn't even make it back to Eastern Avenue when I saw the building go up," he said. "And I didn't want Five-Oh finding me with a trunk full of gas."

"Smart man," said Mr. King. "How your clothes smell?"

"Might have some gas on 'em."

"Which safe house did you go to?"

Armand gave the address. It was a Shawnee Heights address, a place where Ralph's operation had little presence. As Armand began working for Dmitri more and more, he learned that Mr. King had purchased several homes around the city for flipping. He made his buys in neighborhoods not too wealthy, but not too poor. The neighbors were mostly white, but enough blacks would live in the area that a strange black person spending a few nights in one of the rehabbed homes would not seem out of the ordinary. To any onlookers, Armand was watching the property for a night before contractors returned to resume work.

Ralph had strict rules. No dealing, no pimping, no anything took place in these homes. They had to look like any other place under renovation. Dmitri kept Armand supplied with two or three addresses around the city if he ever got into trouble and needed to lay low.

"You did good, Armand," said Mr. King. "Do you know where

the subway station in Shawnee Heights is?"

"Yes," said Armand. He had made a point of finding it before going to the safe house.

"Good. Take the train to the Stiletto. I'll send a change of clothes on ahead. Ralph is going to want to see you, so you tell him exactly what you told me."

"What if he doesn't believe me?"

"Armand, if I say my boy didn't set that fire, Ralph knows he didn't set that fire. Now get down to the Stiletto, tell your story to Ralph, and wait for instructions. You got a big day ahead of you."

"It's an open secret," said Chief Steve Hudepohl, standing up in front of the remaining detectives of Special Investigations and the assembled patrol officers, "that this unit is basically the trashcan of the Monticello Police Department. Those of you who are not in uniform have been told this. As chief, I am here to tell you those days are over. If you're still here after Captain Baker cleaned house yesterday, I want to personally welcome you back from exile."

That earned some scattered applause from the various officers in civilian garb.

"Now, those of you in uniform probably think you're being punished for some unknown violation of department politics, like giving the mayor's daughter a traffic ticket or something."

Several pairs of eyes went to Friedman, who counted such an offense among her many sins.

"In reality, we need you here," he continued. "The new Port Division headquarters at Port Jones will send officers to patrol the remaining open docks. As of this morning, all of you report to my friend, Captain Alvin Baker.

"Now, some of you have complained that the Harbortown Division ignores this neighborhood, despite it being in the same borough." He looked pointedly at Jessica Branson. "I will deal with Harbortown and Homicide's oversights shortly. Since, however, your brother officers over at Settlers Commons believe somehow that Holland Bay is just a means to get to Canaan, I am taking away both of that borough's neighborhoods on this side of the river. Today, they are your responsibility. Starting today, we are cleaning up this godforsaken place. Give the mayor a safe, clean, respectable neighborhood, and you can all count yourselves heroes in the eyes of this department."

Left unspoken was "Fail, and we'll find you a new place of exile, like subway duty."

"Holland Bay," said Hudepohl, "has been ignored for too long. It's time it rejoined the rest of Monticello. It's time we take out the parasites turning it into a war zone."

Baker started clapping, which triggered a wave of applause.

Standing unsteadily next to Branson, Jeff Kagan cringed as the noise crescendoed around him.

As the chief went on, sounding more like a politician starting his campaign than a police chief rallying his officers, Baker sidled up to Branson.

"I need you, Kagan, and Murdoch in one of the interrogation rooms after this," he said. "The chief wants to talk to us."

Branson nodded then glanced nervously at Kagan. The Homicide detective looked like he would lose his breakfast at any moment.

CHAPTER 12

Armand remembered the redhead from the night before. She called herself Fyre. This morning, she could barely walk. She smiled at Armand, however, and stopped him as he walked past her.

"Ralph says if you come by tomorrow night, you and I get a private room all to ourselves," she said. "Just ask for me when you come in." She kissed him, her breath smelling of cigarettes and...

Armand didn't want to know what else.

The house lights were up, the room fully lit, but the stage was dark when Armand entered. A pair of bar backs cleaned while a Mexican woman ran a vacuum cleaner. He made his way down the corridor to the back office where he found a somewhat blissful Ralph leaning back in his chair, his pants up but still unzipped. In his hand, a blunt gave off a stream of smoke.

"Armand," he said, "I got stress this morning, but I at least got me a redhead to help me with that."

"She look like you had her all night long."

Ralph grinned. "I did. I good and sore this morning. So's she." He held up the blunt. "And this better than coffee." His face became serious. "So Rufus sent you on an errand, and someone did the job for you. Tell me, you think it Baggy?"

Did he? He could lie about it and send Baggy to Pier 9. If it wasn't Baggy, however, then whoever did the building might decide to cap Armand to cover his tracks. "It was someone who knew I was supposed to torch that place."

"Only people who know be me, Rufus, maybe my woman Janiece, and..." A dark expression clouded Ralph's face for a moment. "You seen Dmitri since yesterday?"

"Last time I saw him," said Armand, "was here yesterday. Before that, when he chased us off the corner. Told Baggy he'd cap him if he caught us out there again."

"Well," said Ralph, "Baggy a fucktard. Still got your burner from yesterday?"

Armand held up the cell phone, the latest in a long line of disposable phones he'd used since going to work for Ralph.

"Good. Hold onto it one more day. Lay low. Listen to Dmitri. If he call you, you ask him straight up. Did he do that building?"

"Got it."

"Now, go back to that house. Do not go back to Eastern until I tell you. Cops hassle you, you know what to do. Change of clothes for you in the dressing rooms. You talk to Fyre?"

Armand just grinned.

"Yeah, she tasty," said Ralph. "You show up tomorrow night, she all yours for however long you want her. Now get dressed. You smell like a BP truck sprung a leak."

As Armand started to leave, an older guy with an ugly nose and a long neck came into the office. He recognized the newcomer as Goose, part of Ralph's original crew.

"Yo, Dmitri out in the parking lot," said Goose.

"Let's welcome him home," said Ralph.

Armand went to the dressing room to change. Rufus had sent him all new clothes, nothing expensive. They would, however, keep him from looking suspicious to the eyes of Shawnee Heights residents.

Once he finished changing, he started out toward the stage area. He could hear the sound of a struggle, like someone getting a beat down. Armand decided to leave by the rear exit instead. As he turned around, he heard Ralph growl, "Dmitri, you motherfucker. What did you do?"

***

The interrogation room made a horrible conference room. Seven people crammed into a space that usually held three. And then there was that smell, a stench hundreds of crime novels from the most placid cozy to the most horrific noir described as the "smell of fear and desperation." It actually smelled of years of BO, urine, institutional cleaning fluids, embedded tobacco smoke, and ancient flatulence. None of the scents by itself was overwhelming or noticeable. Together, they made an odor that was hard to miss.

Branson thought the interrogation rooms at Holland Bay Station did not smell as bad as those at Settlers Commons or the various borough divisions. Then again, only the Port Police had brought anyone in here for questioning up until this morning. On the rare occasion Branson or her fellow detectives had a case worth mentioning, they often took the suspect to Settlers Commons and used Harbortown's interrogation rooms. It put them across the river where they could lock up a suspect.

With all the people in the room, one of them not in the best condition, Branson found the room oppressive. To make matters worse, she found herself uncomfortably close to Kagan, whose breath carried the scent of hangover and bad sleep, not to mention stale booze.

"Since you three are the first to get a real case under the new mandate," said Chief Hudepohl, who, besides Baker, was the only one seated, "I'm going to tell you first. Officially, you will all still report to Harbortown Division. All that means is Captain Baker sends his paperwork to the Deputy Ops and leaves his assistant out of the loop."

"So we're our own division, basically," said Petrocelli.

"For all intents and purposes."

"What about patrols in Canaan? The port cops you gave us can handle Holland Bay, but if the crime rate doesn't drop..."

"*When* the crime rate drops, Sergeant. 'If' is not acceptable.

The mayor won't allow it."

Does that mean the mayor has been allowing this place to be-come a war zone since she took office? thought Branson. *Or did the new bridge bring that problem up on her radar?*

"I am personally reassigning a contingent of Harbortown uniforms here. For now, they'll come out of Settler's Commons, but they report here for assignments and paperwork." Hudepohl looked around the room, more at the walls and ceiling than at the assembled cops with him. "I've managed to convince the Safety Director to budget money to open up the building's second floor to make room."

"Wow," said Branson, "a budget?"

Hudepohl ignored her. "We have ten new cruisers, all Dodge Chargers, coming in this month. I'll have them decaled for Har-bortown Division, but I'm putting new lettering reading 'Holland Bay Squad' on the front fenders. Those will replace the Port Division cars your uniforms will have to drive until then. Now, the reason I called you three in particular in here."

Hudepohl studied the three of them—Branson, Kagan, and Murdoch. He reserved a scowl for Kagan. At least, Branson told herself, he wasn't actually standing next to Kagan. "You three have the Carcinira murders. I haven't told homicide this, but I'm giving you the house explosion in Serievo as well. Speaking of which, Branson, have you been cleared yet?"

"I'm having the free clinic doc check her out when we finish here," said Baker.

"Good. I'm convinced that explosion has everything to do with the bodies on the Inbound and Pier Nine. You and Taggart were headed to that house when it blew. That can't be coincidence."

"And if the body they found turns out to be a random home-less guy?" asked Branson.

Hudepohl's smile did not reach his eyes. "You used to be Hom-icide, Detective. Time you got back into practice. Speaking of which…" He focused on Kagan. The temperature of the room seemed to drop suddenly. "Kagan, you and I need to talk. Alone.

After we finish." He relaxed a little. "The rest of you I want to coordinate with Homicide on the Delaware bodies. That building is right above the corner on Eastern, and that's been a thorn in Narcotics' side for years now. Let's shut it down. If something ties in with your new cases, jump right in. If Homicide resists, Captain Baker will call me directly. Dismissed."

The filed out of the room, leaving Kagan looking like a man condemned.

Murdoch started to follow Baker into his office to find out where he would sit. Friedman intercepted him.

"So," she said, "you're bumping me for the Carciniras."

He looked down to see Ana Friedman staring back up at him as though she towered over him. Absently, his hand went to his crotch, the other hand ready to block if Friedman took a swing. "Captain's idea."

Friedman stared for another moment before laughing. "Jesus, Murdoch, you should see your face. I'm just busting your balls." Her eyes went to the hand over his fly. "Okay, not literally. Anyway, I got a call on hold you'll want to take. Some guy out in Edison says he might know who torched that building last night on Eastern." When Murdoch didn't move, she said, "Well, go talk to the guy. Maybe your first case in plainclothes will be to crack twelve murders."

Murdoch went. He picked up the phone, took the call off hold, and said, "Special Investigations. Officer Murdoch."

"This is Alex Remmick," said a tired male voice on the other end. "I manage the Speedway out on Amherst Pike in old Eastfield Village."

Great, thought Murdoch, part of Edison. If a deputy sheriff showed up, he'd make it a point to remind Murdoch that the borough used the county instead of the city for police protection. Never mind that the MPD still had jurisdiction in all of the city, regardless of borough. "How can I help you, Mr. Remmick?"

"A guy came by here about eleven yesterday and bought about twenty gallons of gas. He said it was for his snow blower."

Murdoch wondered if Remmick had noticed the foot of snow now blanketing the city or all the snowplows that appeared almost the second the Super Bowl ended the other night. "Lots of people buying gas for that, Mr. Remmick, even at night."

"He was black."

Murdoch looked at the back of his own hand. "Many people are, sir. Forty-nine percent of Monticello, according to the last census."

"That's not what I mean," said Remmick. "He was the wrong kind of black. Wrong for Eastfield Center."

And now the other racial shoe dropped. If you had dark skin, you were fine if you looked like you came from the Island or from Upper Musgrave or maybe one of the suburbs. If you looked even remotely like a rapper... "And what's the wrong kind of black for Eastfield Center, Mr. Remmick?"

"He came out and said he was from Holland Bay."

"Really?" That was the wrong kind of black for Eastfield Center. "Give me your address. I want to talk to you."

As soon as he hit the street, Armand called Shandra. Her phone went to voicemail.

"Hey, it's me," he said. "Call me. I got a place to lay low for a day or two."

If Shandra had gone into work, she would text him as soon as she got a second.

He trudged his way across Lucas Avenue and into the parking lot for Bernie Kosar Stadium. The billboard flashed "Get Commodores season tickets now!" He shook his head. Nobody he knew followed Monticello's soccer team. But college football ended in December, and the city needed a tenant for Kosar Stadium to pay the exorbitant mortgage in the off-season. Right now, the stadium served as commuter parking.

Beyond the stadium lay Kosar Station, which serviced not only MORT but Amtrak as well. The Lakeshore Limited stopped here, but Armand knew of no one who took passenger trains anywhere but in the city. Armand wanted the train back to Rock Ridge. He might have taken the bus, but he hated buses. They were crowded, smelly, and depressing. He bought a token and a transfer that would get him back to Shawnee Heights. As the train rolled up to the platform, he looked down at his phone.

No Shandra. He called again. "Hey, it's me. Take the subway over to Greektown. I pick you up at the station. Call me when you get this."

"Well, you look a little more sober," said Branson as she guided her Pathfinder onto the Hauptmann Bridge. A cold-induced fog drifted up from the Musgrave, giving Lake Road a dreamy quality and blurring the skyline behind a veil.

"Getting ripped a new asshole has that effect," mumbled Kagan, leaning his head against the passenger side window.

Branson had been checked out by a doctor from the neighborhood free clinic. He gave all the usual warnings doctors give to the recently concussed: Avoid any more blows to the head, go immediately to the hospital if she felt any dizziness or confusion, no strenuous activity for the next five days. Ironically, she was still healthier than Kagan this morning. "I've always found Mondays to be really bad nights for heavy drinking. Unless I had Tuesday off."

"How would you notice in Special Investigations?"

She thought about responding to that, but he had a point.

"So where are we going?" he asked as Lake Road entered the northern edge of downtown.

"A strip club. Don't you feel lucky?"

"Actually, that kind of makes things worse."

"I'll bet."

The high-rises of downtown slid by to the right, the Bixby

Building, the Emerald Spire, and the American City Bank Building, forming a three-tower crown to the business district. Up ahead, Lake became Lucas Avenue after passing under the Shoreway, with Bernie Kosar Stadium to the left. To the right, a string of bars, print shops, and assorted businesses common to the fringe of a city's downtown lined the right side of the road. Branson parked in a loading zone in front of an office building under renovation. The Silver Stiletto occupied the first floor.

"We're here," said Branson.

"I'll bite. Why."

Branson hung a police placard on her rearview, letting the parking Nazis know not to ticket a sister officer. It seldom worked, and the city generally ignored complaints from Special Investigations. Branson had a feeling that was about to change. "Baker sent two uniforms over to park outside the Phoenix Café, and Smithers hasn't shown all morning. If he's not there, he's either at home or here banging a stripper."

"Can I stay here?" asked Kagan.

Branson jumped out of the Pathfinder. "Oh, sleep it off, you big baby. I'll be back as soon as I put the fear of Jess into that prick." She slammed the door and tried not to laugh when Kagan visibly winced.

She had her first good look at Ralph Smithers when he emerged from the club. Short, solidly built, he looked more like someone pulling a morning shift at Nissan or Volkswagen than Moran's Great White Whale.

"May I help you, Officer...?" He offered his hand, trying his damnedest to sound like a bond trader instead of a thug. The sound of it made Branson struggle not to laugh since he sounded a little like Ron Burgundy.

"Branson," she said. "Detective Jessica Branson. You're Ralph Smithers?"

"I am. Branson. Why do I know that name?" He made a show of searching his memory, but even this thug probably remembered who shot the previous mayor's kid. Maybe it made her a hero in his mind. "Ah, yes. You capped the mayor's degenerate brat."

His smile told her he knew the consequences of her righteous kill.

"Ex-mayor's. And that's right, Mr. Smithers. I killed a would-be rapist." It was her turn to smile, and hers felt predatory as it stretched her lips. "Do you know a Raymond Moran?"

Again, Smithers made a pretense of searching his memory. "Saw it on the news this morning. That would be the detective who died yesterday from a severe beating. Have you caught his killer?"

Smithers's struggle to speak like a citizen amused Branson. His smile made her want to put a nine-millimeter slug between his eyes. "No, Mr. Smithers, we have not. We're looking for a man named Dmitri Reagan. We have reason to believe he frequents this club."

Smithers gave what had to be the phoniest laugh Branson had ever heard. "Ms. Branson, many people frequent this establishment. Business executives and garbage men. City officials and auto workers. And, to let you in on a little secret, maybe a few students from Monticello State. If a common street thug wants to pay us to watch naked chicks..." He had almost said "bitches." Branson saw the word form on his lips before he caught himself. "...his money spends as good as the Safety Director's."

"I see." She fished a faded and yellowed card out of her purse. She'd had little reason to leave a card these past four years. "Well, if you see Mr. Reagan on these premises, give him this."

Smithers took the card and studied it. "And why should I do that?"

"Because," said Branson, "Ray Moran was my first partner when I became a police officer. And I'm the motherfucker who's going to shove his killer's balls down his throat."

She could not be sure, but she thought Smithers lost a little color. She straightened her coat and her purse. "You have a nice day, Mr. Smithers. I hope your girls give some really good blowjobs in those private booths of yours. Make you lots of dirty money." She spun on her sneakered heel and walked out.

Armand waited in a loading zone across the street from the subway station in Greek Town. The area, also known as Old Rock Ridge, hadn't been very Greek for about a decade, which was longer than Armand could remember anything about it anyway. All he knew was that a lot of Greeks lived here before he was born and that the exodus started when he was a kid. The place now looked like one of those white suburbs going to seed.

Parked as he was in front of a Jimmy John's and a FedEx Office, he sat with the engine running to keep the car warm. Across the street, the station disgorged commuters every few minutes. At around nine twenty-five, a smaller knot of people than he'd seen over the last half-hour made its way up from underground. No Shandra.

Someone behind him honked their horn. He looked up to make sure it wasn't a cop, then proceeded to flip the impatient taxi driver the bird. If Armand wasn't supposed to be sitting in the loading zone, a cabbie wasn't either. The cab pulled around him, passenger window down. Armand lowered his own window and caught a stream of some damn language or another. It wasn't Spanish, which Armand could at least recognize.

"Learn English," he shouted back, "you raghead motherfuck-er."

The cabbie made a gesture, which Armand assumed suggested he molest himself and disappeared into traffic.

By the time the crowd dispersed, five minutes had passed. He looked at his watch and his MORT rail schedule. Another train would arrive in ten minutes or so, with one more arriving around nine. If he did not see Shandra by then, he'd go back to the safe house and call Mr. King. In the meantime, he dialed Shandra again. Again, her phone went to voicemail.

***

Packard Lane followed an old, crooked railroad spur that cut a swath through ancient red brick buildings. Most of these had, at one time or another, housed suppliers for the auto plant where Plink now lived. Half of them stood abandoned. Branson spotted a garage that she doubted was certified, probably doing business for cash off the books.

The Packard plant itself sat low and dark in the middle of a parking lot that hadn't been plowed since Sunday night. Then again, why would anyone bother? Branson pulled into the same space Taggart had used the day before.

"Come on, whipping boy," she said. "Time to do some police work."

"Can I wait in the car?"

"No." She jumped out and slammed the door behind her, making Kagan jump. She trudged through the path already made through the drifting snow. She noticed there were a lot more tracks, both car and human, in the snow surrounding the side of the building where they had entered the day before. She stopped and sniffed the air, catching a faint whiff of ammonia. Branson had never dealt directly with meth labs before, but she knew ammonia was involved in the making of crystal meth. She'd even caught the scent of it the day before, only fainter and well inside the building. Kagan, if he ever dragged his hungover ass out of the car, would have to tell her if this was normal.

The door had been forced. Branson turned, seeing Kagan's first tentative steps out of the Pathfinder into the snow. "Kagan, bring me a flashlight. I have a feeling the power's out in here."

"There's power?"

"There was yesterday."

She waited, her hand on her weapon as she watched Kagan battle the snow and his own faltering metabolism for balance. When he reached her, she said, "You shine. I'll take point." She removed her Glock from the hip holster and motioned for Kagan to move inside. The weapon hung at ready by her side.

The first thing she noticed was the increased smell of ammonia, much stronger than the previous day. No one could miss it. They made their way into Plink's outer sanctum, where she and Taggart had met him yesterday. This time, no large, black hellbeast came bounding out of the shadows.

"Did it smell like this yesterday?" asked Kagan, looking green even in the building's dim light.

"You mean the ammonia?" said Branson. "Not like this. There's supposed to be a Rottweiler threatening us."

"Rottweiler?"

"Yeah. Hates cops. It's named Vader. Tried to eat Taggart yesterday."

"Um… Why does it bother you that the Rottweiler's gone?"

"No Vader, no Plink." She smiled at Kagan, who looked even greener now in the ambient light from the flashlight. "Besides, the dog loves me."

The day before, Plink had emerged from a metal door. That door now sat open, and the ammonia smell was overwhelming. No Plink plus two forced doors constituted probable cause, according to every academy instructor she'd had as a cadet.

"We're going inside," said Branson. "Can you sweep that room with the light without throwing up?"

"Very funny."

"Hold the light to the side. I'm going in low. Should make us both hard to hit."

Kagan held the light straight out at his side about shoulder level, pointing it at the door. Branson crouched and pushed the door open farther.

The ammonia nearly suffocated the two of them. What they managed to see was not a working meth lab, but one that had been smashed up and partially burned in a fire only hours earlier. Branson fell back and crab-walked as fast as she could from the opening, kicking the door shut.

Coughing, she said, "Call the fire department. We need a Haz Mat team. Then call your buddy Kearny."

CHAPTER 13

"I can't believe you changed the locks on the house," Jane shouted over the phone. "Leaving my things on the front steps?"

"Least I could do after five years of marriage," said Murdoch. He really did not want to have this conversation. Baker had tossed him the keys to an unmarked Ford Fusion before he headed off to the gas station on Amherst Pike. It was bad enough he was driving out to a part of the city that wasn't really the city. He didn't want to spend the drive on the Outbound listening to Jane shrieking.

"Least you could do?" she said. "You could have left."

"Hey, you're the one who didn't come home last night," said Murdoch, casually whipping the Charger around a slow-moving container truck lumbering south from the port. "Why the hell should I leave?"

"I'm calling my lawyer."

"I thought that was the point. Do you need my lawyer's number?"

"Fuck you!"

Murdoch cut the call short and tossed the Android in the passenger seat. Outside, the smoked brick and dirty corrugated steel of Midtown slowly gave way to billboards, post-war single-family homes, and big-box grocery stores all packed together and huddling in the dirty snow from the other night. The Big Mac Bridge loomed to the right as he blew through the Airport Interchange, and Midtown's decay gave way to Edison, Monticello's southernmost borough.

Even twenty-plus years after the city line moved all the way south to Milan, this area still felt like unclaimed territory. Edison blended seamlessly with the endless parade of suburban sprawl beyond the city limits. Drive far enough south, and the illusion of a city dissolved into Ohio's Amish country for about twenty miles.

Murdoch's turn-off came just beyond the Turnpike. A 757 roared overhead toward Glenn-Armstrong International Airport. He headed in the opposite direction, to the former village of Eastfield Center. Edison's inclusion as part of Monticello was so invisible that Eastfield had left up its corporation limit sign, faded and rusted though it was.

Edison made Murdoch nervous. Under the borough system, sections of Monticello could opt out of city services and contract for their own. Rock Ridge, for instance, had privatized its EMS system, and Vodrey Heights used some company out of Cincinnati for its waste pickup, rather than the city trash service. Edison opted to use the Musgrave County Sheriff for police protection. MPD still had jurisdiction, and the department's Edison Division still supplied plainclothes officers, but the uniforms and radio cars all answered to the Sheriff.

And they never failed to remind the MPD officers of this.

Nonetheless, Murdoch felt better as he approached the gas station. The fire on Delaware had yielded ten bodies. If this manager had a lead that could crack the case, the resulting promotion might ease things with Jane.

For now.

As he pulled into the lot of a busy Speedway, he glanced at the phone in the passenger seat. "Fuck Jane," he said.

Inside, he badged the cashier and asked to see Remmick. The man who emerged from the back office did a double take when he saw Murdoch. It made Murdoch wonder how rare black people were in this part of the city.

"You that cop I talked to?" he asked.

"I'm Officer Murdoch. Are you Remmick?"

"You're not a deputy?"

Murdoch did not feel like explaining Edison's stupid arrangement with the county. "It's a city case."

"Of course." Remmick motioned him back into his cramped office. The store itself was clean and well-lighted. That hygiene did not extend to the office, where the desk was strewn with paper, used food containers, and soda bottles still containing puddles of whatever someone had been drinking at the time. Even though the computer, with its small archaic monitor, came in the standard black of business computers, it looked as filthy as some of the beige machines Murdoch remembered from elementary school. "It's really strange, a young black man out here buying gas."

"Oh?" said Murdoch, removing his gloves and revealing his dark brown hands.

Remmick blanched. "I don't mean that. I mean he didn't look like the typical customer we get around here, black or white."

"And what kind of customer might that be?" he asked.

"You know. Some are high school kids and farm boys, but most of them are middle class. Soft."

Like you? thought Murdoch.

"Boys that age around here are driving their daddies' cars or something their daddy bought for them," said Remmick. "This guy had a certain swagger, like he wasn't posing."

Now we're getting somewhere.

"Most of the kids that age come in here and look like they're half asleep. Or they're hopped up on energy drinks and soda."

Murdoch gestured at the computer. "Let's see the footage."

Remmick worked the screen and took the recording to where the security camera's digital clock read "11:05 p.m." from the day before. It showed a Toyota Corolla, roughly five years old and due for a paint job (visible even in this grainy video), rolling up to one of the gas pumps. A kid, definitely black and packed in a heavy parka, got out and opened the trunk where he retrieved five large gas cans.

Moments later, Remmick could be seen running out to talk to the kid. They had a conversation, more heated on Remmick's end than the kid's, then parted company.

"What did he say to you?" asked Murdoch.

"He told me he was snow blowing at twenty bucks a pop down in Holland Bay," said Remmick.

"Did he say why he was all the way down here in East Bum-fuck, Egypt?"

Remmick gave him a dirty look. "It ain't like in the city, Officer."

Murdoch motioned for him to continue.

"Well, he said...um...I don't know how to put this."

"Just say it."

"He said, and I'm quoting here, 'Gas in Holland Bay? With all those niggers up there? I'd get robbed.'"

Murdoch laughed, which seemed to make Remmick more uncomfortable. It had been years since he'd heard that joke, but he grew up saying it whenever he was in another part of the city. His middle school basketball coach made the team do extra laps once when he caught them saying it to some players over at John XXIII Middle School. "Yep, he's from Holland Bay all right. Did you make me a copy?"

Remmick seemed relieved as he killed Windows Media and popped the CD tray open. "Thought you'd never ask."

The wind swept upriver from Lake Erie, funneled through the streets of Prussian Meadow, and cut through Packard Lane. Uniformed police, winter-clad firefighters, and a hazmat crew milled about the lot, moving in and out of the former engine plant. Branson had been inside until a few minutes earlier, helping catalog evidence. A short, thin figure emerged from the building, looking pale and gray wherever his winter clothes did not cover him. The man had a high-pitched voice and a loud laugh.

Branson did not recognize him, but Kagan clearly did.

"Lieutenant Kearny," Kagan called out, trudging through the snow over to the man.

The gray man broke off from a knot of uniforms and a couple of detectives. "Jeff Kagan, as I live and breathe." Kearny's voice was so Irish that one would swear he'd just gotten off the boat from Galway. Never mind that Kearny had lived in Monticello for the past thirty-five years. "How the hell are you?"

"Cold," said Kagan. "Quite a prize our lady Branson's found, wouldn't you say?"

Kearny laughed. "Oh, I think it's been found a long time. If I know that fooker Taggart, he's been sitting on this a long time, waiting."

"Waiting? For what? Why wasn't this busted months ago?"

"Try years. Taggart fancies himself Eliot Ness. He's been building a case to take down Ralph Smithers ever since he had Pablo Estrada whacked."

Whacked. Branson had not heard that term since the Mafia was still a going concern in Monticello. "I'd say we have it, then."

"Maybe," said Kearny. "Branson, you seem to think..."

They heard the growl first. Moments later, a very large Rottweiler with teeth to match came tearing around a corner, charging at the three of them.

"Vader!"

The dog was about to lunge at Kagan, who had drawn his weapon. Upon hearing Branson shout his name, he skidded to a stop, turned and charged toward Branson. Kagan and two uniforms trained their weapons on the dog, but Branson held up an arm.

"Don't shoot!" She crouched down, and the dog skidded to a stop once again and began barking. This time, the dog did not sound menacing. He sounded desperate, whining between bursts.

"What's that, Lassie?" Kagan said to Kearny. "Timmy fell down a well again? And you think we should leave the stupid little shit there this time? Me, too."

Branson glared at Kagan for a moment. "Vader, where's Plink?"

The dog made a questioning noise and cocked his head.

"Plink."

The dog turned and charged off across the lot. He stopped, turned, and gave Branson a couple of yelps before moving again.

"Let's go," she said, pushing through the snow in the trail Vader had made.

Kagan and Kearny fell in behind her, along with the two uniforms who had drawn on the dog. Vader led them all the way to the back of the lot to a storage shed, then started barking, whining again as he did so.

Branson ripped open the door, not locked but drawn tightly.

Inside, a haggard-looking man, who would not have been out of place downtown, begging for change, sat shivering in the dark.

"Hello, Plink," said Branson.

Armand sat in the recliner of the safe house, not really paying attention to the yammering from the judge show on television. He had called Shandra every ten minutes since leaving the subway station in Greektown. She never answered.

Finally, he spoke to voicemail. "Baby, it's me. You never showed. Where are you?" He swallowed as that voice in the back of his head started whispering about Baggy and what he might have done to her. "Baby, please hurry. I promise you if you show up, I get a job. I'll quit the life. Just please get here. Please."

He cried when the voicemail cut him off. He stopped crying when he called again five minutes later with still no answer.

"Fuck this," said Armand, leaving the TV running as he grabbed the keys to the Toyota. He didn't even notice the smell of the gas in the trunk as he made his way back to Holland Bay.

"He's going to lawyer up the second we get him to the station," said Kagan.

Two paramedics hovered around Plink at the back end of an ambulance. Plink sat shivering under two heavy blankets.

"He's tweaked," said Kearny. "That's for sure. Anything we get out of him will be useless. Even if he tells the truth."

"Taggart's been getting information out of him for six months," said Branson.

"What makes you think what Taggart's been doing is any good?" said Kagan. "Crazy bastard got himself blown up. Got you blown up, too."

Branson put up her hand, her face pained as though a migraine had suddenly exploded behind her eyes. "You know, I'm really sick of everyone assuming we're useless down in Special Investigations. We're not useless; we're ignored. Now, let me go do some real goddamn police work, Detective. One of us ought to do it today." Before either Kagan or Kearny could respond, she spun on her heel and marched over to the ambulance.

Plink looked up at her, eyes ringed with red. "I'm screwed. Aren't I?"

"Maybe," said Branson, "but Taggart made you promises I might be able to keep."

"Jake is dead," he said.

"Not yet. I was in that explosion, too." Vader nudged her leg, and Branson idly scratched his head. "Look, you've been running the biggest meth lab in the city. Taggart, by all rights, should have had you in Mansfield by now. You know something he's working on. Would you be willing to share that with me?"

Plink closed his eyes. "I have a couple of conditions."

"Okay."

"First, I don't want Lew Steinberg as my lawyer. I don't care if it's a public defender. I want someone else."

Lew Steinberg. Branson knew the name. "I can arrange that. I'll have Lieutenant Kearny phone for a public defender. What's the second condition?"

"The dog stays with me, at least while I'm questioned."

Branson watched as Plink's shaking waxed and waned before her. His eyes, with their dilated pupils, looked terrified. She would have to acclimate the dog to Kagan just to get him into the room. And most likely, the county prosecutor would send someone in to interview Plink. Never mind the public defender. "I'll take care of it."

She marched over to Kearny, cutting Kagan off in mid-conversation. "Plink's going to talk about this place. He'll give up the owner. He'll give up his contacts. That's what Taggart's been working on since you booted him from Narcotics."

Kearny's face split into a big grin. "I didn't boot him, girlie. That self-important prick running the Midtown Division had him buried. Whatever you gotta do, Branson. Kagan'll bring this in for a landing."

"*I* will bring this in for a landing." She motioned over to a uniform. "As soon as he's cleared, bring him down to Holland Bay Station."

"Wouldn't Midtown or Settlers Commons...?"

"Harbortown doesn't have a goddamned clue what's going on here." Never mind that the uniforms' cars all had "Harbortown Division" emblazoned on their fenders. "And Midtown's been fucking this up for years. Take him to Holland Bay. It's our case. Got a problem with it? Go see that man." She pointed at Kearny, who watched with an amused expression. She looked at Kagan. "Let's go. I want this guy processed and talking by dinner time."

"Yes, ma'am," said Kagan, looking surprised.

She whistled. "Vader."

The dog, sitting a short distance from the ambulance where Plink sat, turned at the sound of its name and made a questioning noise.

"Go for ride?" If Vader jumped at that, it would explain why he was such a lousy guard dog.

The dog barked once at Plink and ran toward Branson. She triggered the rear door on the Pathfinder, letting Vader jump inside as though he'd always ridden in the car.

"What are you doing?" asked Kagan as they moved to get into the car.

"Plink wants his dog with him. He's in withdrawal, and I want anything that gives us an edge."

Vader started growling as Kagan got into the car.

"Was this such a good idea?" he asked.

"Beats how this has been handled up until today."

The fastest way back to Holland Bay was the Vodrey Heights Bridge, the enormous suspension bridge that connected Rock Ridge to the borough on the opposite bluff. Unlike most of the bridges across the Musgrave, which ran from one bank to the other, the Vodrey Heights Bridge ran between the two bluffs over that loomed over Midtown, Canaan, and Holland Bay. It afforded drivers some spectacular views of downtown from its one-hundred-foot-high span. Unfortunately, it also afforded views of Prussian Meadow.

As Armand started across the bridge, he happened to look to his right and down onto Prussian Meadow. Several lights flashed around an old factory. He could make out people in hazmat suits moving into the building, as well as several police cruisers. The building looked familiar, but...

He pulled the Toyota over and got out to look. The street ran along the abandoned rail line, which meant it was Packard Avenue. Armand pulled his burner and dialed Dmitri.

Ralph Smithers answered. "Who this?"

Oh, shit. Armand knew he'd just disobeyed Ralph and had to tell him. He decided to plunge ahead. If it got him in trouble, well, Shandra wanted him out of the life anyway. "This is Armand. I was headed back to pick up Shandra."

"Didn't I tell you to stay put?"

"Five-Oh taking out Packard Lane. They all over the place."

"Where are you?"

"Vodrey Heights Bridge."

Ralph didn't say anything for a long time. Armand thought he might have hung up.

"Go get that shorty," Ralph finally said. "Get her back to the safe house. Call me when you get back." He hung up.

Armand hopped back over the railing between the road deck and the pedestrian walkway. He wondered what Ralph would say next. Maybe, he thought, he really should leave the city.

"I grabbed a couple of hits on my way out the door," said Plink, handcuffed and rocking in his seat. He, Branson, and Kagan sat in the interrogation room. Vader lay behind Plink, snoring. "I should be good for a while."

His left eye twitched as he spoke. If this was Plink high, or at least calmed down, Branson did not want to see withdrawal.

"You're okay with this?" she asked. "I know Taggart wasn't ready to bring you in yet."

He stopped rocking and looked first at Kagan, then Branson. "I'm ready to get off of this. I'm ready to get out from under their thumbs."

"Whose thumbs?"

"Dmitri Reagan, for one."

"Really?" said Kagan.

"I'll roll on Dmitri," he said, "if you protect me."

Branson looked at Kagan. "Can your wife get him into Fair Oaks down in Norwalk?"

"She can," said Kagan. "Whether the Sheriff will put a guard on him is another question."

She turned back to Plink. "You know Dmitri's a glorified corner boy, right? We need someone higher up the food chain."

Plink started shaking, yet there was a faint little smile on his face. "Oh, I can give you the biggest fish of all."

"Ralph Smithers?" asked Branson.

"The same."

Branson felt like running through the station and shouting

"Hallelujah" at the top of her lungs. "Plink, if you give me that sonofabitch's head on a platter, I will kiss you harder than any woman's ever kissed you before."

"Jesus," said Kagan. "You must really want Smithers."

"I want him dead, but this will do."

Armand stowed the Toyota behind a front he knew Ralph owned, letting the manager know the car belonged to Mr. King. That was all they needed to hear. He walked the remaining six blocks south on Eastern, barely noticing the cold. If Shandra was okay, even if she was upset with him, he'd never do another job for Ralph Smithers or Rufus King.

A couple of people coming out of the building looked sadly at Armand before rushing away. He didn't like that. They had looked at him with either fear or apathy before. One lady, her baby always on her hip, smiled at him whenever she saw him. He couldn't help but smile back. It made him want to put a baby in Shandra. If she were okay, he would. He knew she wanted one.

The door opened readily for him, its lock busted. Already Armand felt sick.

"Shandra?"

She didn't answer.

Armand took out the Glock and hung it at his side, finger inside the trigger guard. Carefully, he nudged the bedroom door open.

Shandra lay naked on the bed, her neck snapped.

"Motherfucker's going to die," he shouted.

Randy Dugan needed a break. He had spent the morning stringing lights on the Voinovich Bridge's cables, a job made harder by a combination of temperatures in the teens and gusts of wind cutting across Holland Island into the sound. Dugan nearly fell a couple of times and thanked a God he no longer believed in for his safety harness. Lunch break, sitting in the orange construction pickup, came as a welcome relief.

Dugan wished the old piers had not been closing so fast. Of the five remaining active piers, only one was close enough to observe anyone there with any degree of accuracy. Oh, people visited the other piers: homeless, drug dealers, the odd trucker or cop pulling over for a few moments of privacy.

Today, he noticed a white, unmarked van pulling onto Pier 9. That was strange. He watched it closely. What else did he have to do besides munch on his stale turkey sandwich and listen to Rush Limbaugh on WMNT?

The van pushed through the deep snow and into where the burned-out car had been found the day before. The back door opened, and a body rolled out. Dugan couldn't see at this distance who it was, but it was clearly a dead body.

CHAPTER 14

Murdoch was grateful the surveillance footage was digital. Too often, he had seen security camera footage recorded on videotape, usually VHS on the slowest speed, making everything grainy. This footage would never win any Oscars, but Murdoch could make out details.

He watched over the shoulder of Alan Tera, one of the MPD's resident nerds from Settlers Commons. Tera was able to load the footage into a specialized video editing package on his laptop that let him focus in on various details. At the moment, he was trying to bring the license plate of an aging Toyota sedan into focus.

"There we go," said Tera, a thirtyish guy with wire-rimmed glasses and a mild case of acne. Murdoch doubted that Tera ever went outside if he could avoid it. "It's starting to pixilate, but the lettering is there."

Murdoch spun around in his seat to face a desktop computer he had booted up. He called up the BMV website, logged in as a police officer, and asked Tera to read off the plate number. Moments later, he had a name.

"Doby Clark," said Murdoch, disgusted. "The guy who got blown up yesterday with Taggart and Branson."

Tera already had a public records web site up and Clark's last reported address cut and pasted into the site. "17175 Sandusky Boulevard, Apartment 412. That's a Rock Ridge address."

And probably fake. Murdoch pulled up his own Google session and punched in the address to Google Maps. Switching to Satellite and zooming into street level, he said, "It's a storage company. That address is probably a locker."

Tera spun in his chair. "Wanna look the perp in the eye?"

"We don't know he's a perp yet."

"We have a guy claiming to blow snow in Holland Bay way the hell out by the Lorain County line, pumping ten gallons of gas and driving a car registered to a dead, homeless guy at a fake address. If he's not the perp, what is he?"

"Stupid?"

Tera unplugged his laptop from the wall power supply. "Bring up mug shots. I'll get this guy's face. Let's see if we can find him." Tera manipulated the footage to focus on the Toyota's driver. He had to expand that slice of the video on a frame where the driver was getting out of his car. It was grainier than Murdoch liked, but he could tell the driver was probably in his late teens—early twenties at the most.

Tera had expanded the face of the driver to where Murdoch could see the face, despite pixilation. Tera leaned over to look at the mug shots. They had managed to filter it by race and facial features. It took Murdoch awhile to find a face that matched. If the kid hadn't put the hood up on his parka, he might have found it faster.

Tera pulled up the mug shots on his laptop and looked at them side by side. The hairline in the mug shot was covered by the kid's parka in the video, but he had not worn sunglasses. For that, Murdoch was grateful. Even if they recovered the car, the video would have been otherwise useless. The kid could very well have bought gas to run his snowblower, and the car could be stolen.

Murdoch knew in his bones that that scenario was complete bullshit. A defense lawyer could sell it to a jury, who did not have to deal with such details on a daily basis and wanted to get home in time to watch *Dancing with the Stars* anyway. The face, however, had a record attached to it.

"Armand Cole," Murdoch read off his own screen. "Aged eighteen, last known address 815 Cumberland Street."

"Holland Bay," said Tera. "Color me surprised."

"Record indicates he was a guest of the juvenile system," said Murdoch. "Assault, petty theft, possession. The usual hobbies in that neighborhood."

"Take it to the leads on this case?"

Murdoch chuckled. "Nerds. Always afraid to get their hands dirty. No, I'll get APB's out on the car and Cole. Then I'll pay 815 Cumberland a visit. It's only a few blocks from here anyway. Want to tag along?"

"You mean in the field?" said Tera. "No."

Murdoch shook his head. "Nerds."

"Where you at now?" It was the second time today that Ralph had asked Armand that in an angry tone.

"The corner," he said, the phone screwed in his ear. When Ralph responded with little more than breathing, Armand added, "Baggy killed my girl."

"Oh, he did, did he? You call Five-Oh?"

"I was going to call Mr. King." Armand did not like the pause that came when he said that. "Was I wrong?"

"No, man," said Ralph. "You did good. Rufus say you didn't torch the place."

"I didn't. What about Shandra? I call Five-Oh, they bust me for killing her."

"We take care of Shandra for you. I need you to help me clean a little house. Heard what else happen?"

Now what? He knew about Packard Lane. What else could have happened? "I haven't heard anything."

"Dmitri got got," said Ralph, "You Dmitri now."

Did he want to be? "Meaning?"

"Meaning you my muscle now. And as a present, I'm giving

Baggy's fat ass to you. You wanna cap his ass, it yours to cap."

"What about Shandra?" He knew he could only press Ralph so far on what to do about her body, but he had to know.

"We take care of that. I send Rock up to move her someplace Five-Oh can't tie to you."

Beyond that, Armand did not want to know. He did, however, want to square it with her mama. She had been good to him. "Got a last message for Baggy?"

"No. Just grab one of the crew, any of them, and tell them Ralph wants you to see Baggy. Then he can join Dmitri on Pier Nine."

"I make no guarantees," said Maria Kagan. "I'm here because Jeff called and because Pulaski can't be bothered to come to a police station for anything that doesn't promise to get him on YouTube and the six o'clock news."

Pulaski, as in David Pulaski, was Mrs. Kagan's boss, the Musgrave County Prosecutor. Or, as Kagan had frequently mentioned in his two days with Branson, the one his wife called "Lord Voldemort." For a fire in a warehouse in a heavily poor black neighborhood on the fringes of Harbortown, Pulaski sent his minions. Since Jeff Kagan had called it in, he sent Maria Kagan.

"I doubt," she said, "he'll want to spend the money on protective custody."

"We could house him out in Greenwich," said Kagan. "They have a drunk tank."

"He needs to be in a hospital," said Branson. "The only reason he's not freaking out on us now is that he's seen me with Taggart."

"And the dog's with him," said Kagan. "I don't think that Rottweiler's a guard dog."

"Wanted to chew your nuts off," said Branson.

That earned Kagan a strange look from Maria.

"Right..." said Kagan.

"Look," said Branson, "Taggart's been sitting on the biggest meth lab in the city's history. Now that it's been wrecked and exposed, it's time to find out what Plink knows. Why did Taggart look the other way for so long?"

"He's going to have to give me something," said Maria. "The fire department pretty much handed over the meth lab. I've got no 'who' or 'why,' just an abandoned building with fire damage."

A smile spread over Branson's face. "What if I told you he promised us Ralph Smithers?"

Maria threw her arms around Kagan's neck and kissed him hard. "Did I ever tell you what a wonderful husband you are?"

Armand found the tall, skinny one named Linc loitering in the lobby of Wentworth's northern tower. He had his gun at his side, index finger along the barrel like he'd seen a few cops do. "I need Baggy. Now."

"Fuck you," said Linc. "Baggy's going to cap you if you don't start..."

The Glock swung up into Linc's face. "This come from Ralph."

Linc put up his hands. "A'ight, a'ight. Let's go."

He turned and led Armand to the basement of the tower. At the bottom, they trudged through a poorly lit hallway that opened to a laundry room and a bank of storage lockers. At the far end of the hall sat an apartment. Linc kicked the door open.

Inside, baggies of meth and crack sat in neat piles, ready for sale. The crack, Armand knew, came from the crew that ran the towers. If Baggy cut that, he would have been dead by now. The meth on the other hand...

Baggy and his crew had emptied all the bags of meth from the lab on Packard Lane and dumped them into a bowl. On the table at that end sat a rolling pin and a gallon jug of kitty litter crystals. He could see where the litter had been crushed.

"Oh, Ralph gonna be pissed," said Armand.

"You think?"

Armand turned and found himself facing another Glock in the

fist of T-Dogg.

"I don't give a fuck about Baggy," said T-Dogg, "but you gotta die for what you did to me yesterday."

Something very hard slammed into the back of Armand's knee. He saw that it was a baseball bat just before it knocked him out.

Patrolman Anthony Spinosa caught the first corpse of the new era on Pier 9. It sure as hell didn't feel like a new era. Half the former port cops were still patrolling the old Port of Monticello. Worse, despite all the new chief's rosy platitudes, they were doing it as part of the MPD's dead-end squad, Special Investigations. When Spinosa went to his union rep to look into transferring to one of the borough commands or operations divisions, the rep told him his choices: Transit duty, a beat on Holland Island at the former landfill, or "assisting" the uniformed deputies patrolling for the Edison Division. In short, he could be buried, trashed, or exiled.

So finding the body of yet another gangbanger, this one with a nine-millimeter third eye in his forehead, only served to send Spinosa's day deeper into the crapper.

Until two honest-to-God Homicide cops showed up, crime scene technicians in tow.

"I'll be damned," said the first Homicide cop, a large black man named Pearson whom Spinosa remembered playing linebacker for Monticello State a decade earlier. "Lexy, guess who this is?"

The other Homicide cop, a slight redhead who looked like she'd just stepped out of Macy's after maxing out three credit cards, approached the corpse, flanking Spinosa with Pearson. "Should I know him?"

Pearson grinned. "I sure as hell do. Spinosa, this is your lucky day."

It sure as hell didn't feel like it, other than Homicide not writing off a Pier 9 stiff for once. "Really, Detective? Why's that?"

"You just handed us Dmitri Reagan."

"Who?"

"Ralph Smithers's top enforcer," said the one named Lexy. "Looks like the boss was unhappy with him."

"It's better than what Dmitri did to Moran," said Pearson.

Moran. That was a name Spinosa knew. He had gone to the Academy with Moran, even rode with him for six months when they started in the Rock Ridge Division. Despite the presence of the crime scene techs, Spinosa couldn't resist.

He spit on the body.

"Patrolman!" Lexy snapped at him.

Spinosa covered it up with a cough. "Sorry. Bronchitis."

Not that the apology mattered to Dmitri. The dead man now had snot running down his frozen cheek.

A young redhead named Amanda McPhee came to represent Plink. She wore a dark blue suit and pencil skirt with a dour expression that suggested her idealism had died roughly the same day she took the job. Branson guessed her to be less than two years out of law school and thought if she held herself any tighter, she would snap in two. One look at Vader sleeping behind Plink in the interrogation room seemed to confirm McPhee's resignation, that she had signed on to defend a series of thugs, idiots, and eccentrics, few of whom might actually be innocent.

Branson sat directly across from Plink, McPhee sat next to him. Maria Kagan took a seat next to Branson. Jeff Kagan would have been there, but word of Dmitri Reagan's body on Pier 9 had reached Baker. The captain came in, practically bouncing with glee, and ordered either Kagan or Branson over to the pier to take over the crime scene. Vader had already chosen Branson to do the interrogation.

"You agree to plead guilty to possession with intent," said Maria, "and possession of drug paraphernalia. In return for your confession and testimony, the State agrees to recommend concurrent sentences of no more than five years with parole eligibility in two. Furthermore, the State will recommend you be placed in the medium security facility at Lebanon, then transferred to the Grafton Honor Farm after nine months."

That had been Branson's idea. Ralph Smithers's people, when the MPD managed to get them convicted, were almost always sent to Mansfield, the maximum-security prison fifty miles south of Monticello. Lebanon was north of Cincinnati, on the other end of the state. Plink's incarceration there would be public knowledge. A transfer, however, would not be noticed. Medium security, Branson reasoned, would be rough on Plink, but maximum security would kill him. And if Plink could hold out in Lebanon for nine months, he could finish his sentence at the honor farm, even if the parole deal fell through.

"Do you understand these conditions as I have explained them to you?" said Maria.

"Yes." Plink sounded listless now. He was coming down from his last hit of meth. They'd lose him soon to sleep. The hell of withdrawal would start when he awoke.

"We will take you to the holding facility at Norwalk," said Maria, "which has a better infirmary than the lockup downtown. It'll also get you out of the city. I can't imagine Ralph Smithers is going to be happy when he finds out you're alive and talking to us."

"I talk to her. Right?" He pointed at Branson.

"As long as I'm in the room to hear it." Before McPhee could object, Branson quickly added, "And your attorney is here to protect your interests."

McPhee relaxed a little, though Branson was hard pressed to call it "relaxed." The young public defender had been wringing her hands the whole time.

Vader, for his part, snored. Plink was there. Branson was there. The other two women were not cops, though the dog had watched McPhee with a wary eye. Her stiff posture and abrupt manner probably told him "cop."

"Can I have a cigarette?" asked Plink.

McPhee said, "I don't think…"

Branson took a pack she'd borrowed from Friedman and shook out a Virginia Slim. Plink took it and accepted a light from Branson.

"Thank you," he said.

"Let's get started," said Branson. "Today is February sixth. The time is two forty-four p.m. This is Detective Jessica Branson of…" What was the squad called now? The name "Holland Bay Task Force" was being used in the hallways, but no one had made the name official yet. Until so ordered, the name would remain… "Special Investigations, questioning Victor Wallend, alias 'Plink,' aged thirty-one, last known address 1717 Garland Avenue, Monticello, Ohio, in connection with the methamphetamine lab discovered at 2825 Packard Lane, also in Monticello. Present are Amanda McPhee, acting as counsel for Mr. Wallend, and Maria Kagan of the Musgrave County Prosecutor's Office. Mr. Wallend, for the record, please state your name and your acceptance of the plea terms as agreed to by your attorney and counsel for the State. You agree to plead guilty to possession of an illegal substance with intent to sell and possession of drug paraphernalia. In exchange for your confession and information regarding the operation of that lab, the State agrees to favorable sentencing and incarceration terms, as well as treatment for your dependency on methamphetamine."

Plink gave his name and his verbal agreement to the plea deal.

"Then let's begin. Do you work for Ralph Smithers?"

"Yes."

"And did Mr. Smithers ever come to the Packard Lane location to discuss production of methamphetamine with you?"

"No. He would send someone else to talk to me."

"And do you know these people's names?"

"There was an older guy, about my age…"

Branson bit her tongue. At thirty-four, she did not think Plink or someone his age was "an older guy." She didn't think she herself was "older."

"...Had a street name of Goose."

Branson met McPhee's eyes with a questioning glance. When McPhee nodded, she continued. "Do you know Goose's real name?"

"No," said Plink. "But I could pick him out of a lineup."

That was what she wanted to hear. She knew Maria wanted to hear that, too. Branson scribbled a note to get with Kagan first, then Kearny from Narcotics, about a street thug named Goose. She would also pass on Moran's notes.

"Anyone else?"

"A young boy named Armand Cole," said Plink. "But only in the last couple of months. He works for Dmitri."

"Dmitri?"

"Dmitri Reagan."

Dmitri Reagan, the corpse Jeff Kagan now stood over while crime scene techs photographed and collected evidence.

"And did Mr. Reagan ever come to Packard Lane?"

"All the time," Plink began to shake uncontrollably.

"That's enough," said McPhee. "He's having a panic attack."

As if in agreement, Vader raised his head and barked once.

Before anyone could respond, Branson said, "You told us Dmitri tried to burn you out last night. Plink, did Dmitri Reagan try to kill you?"

"Yes."

"Did he say why he was trying to kill you?"

"He said Ralph wanted me dead and the evidence gone." Plink began rocking. "If Taggart hadn't been blown up, I'd have gone to him for help."

"You're referring to Detective Jake Taggart?"

The shaking did not subside, and Plink began rocking in his seat. "Yes. The only reason I'm talking to you is because my dog likes you."

"Detective, he's..."

"Plink, when you made up a batch of the product," said Branson, "what did you do with it?"

"I called a number and told someone to 'Send the van.'"

"Explain?"

"They would send a white panel truck, usually driven by Goose, Dmitri, or Armand."

"Did they leave the van at Packard Lane?"

"No. I rode in the van once. When I had to go meet with Ralph."

"Where was that?"

Plink smiled, revealing some missing teeth. "A strip club near Kosar Stadium called The Silver Stiletto."

Branson decided she was going to take Maria's husband to a strip club once more. It's what cops did for their partners all the time.

Cumberland Street was only a few blocks from Holland Bay Station, but a world away. The station sat tucked under the Cleveland Shoreway, a small brick building in a sea of crumbling asphalt. Beyond that lay the piers and what little remained of the supporting businesses that serviced the original Port of Monticello. Cumberland had been a thriving blue-collar neighborhood in the 1940s and '50s, but since had gone to seed. Many of the houses had been clumsily converted to four-family units in the 1970s, and quite a few had not seen a fresh coat of paint since Kurt Cobain still walked the Earth. Different streetscape, same atmosphere of desperation and apathy. Murdoch had grown up in this area. Since his stepfather had a good job at Volkswagen, they were able to escape to one of the neighborhoods of Rock Ridge.

Murdoch parked across the street from the tenement, Eastern Avenue some four blocks in his rearview. Three boys sat on the stoop of 815 Cumberland, all of them eye-fucking him. He eye-fucked them in return.

"Even in this weather," said Murdoch, "you boys loitering outside?"

"We ain't doing nothin'," said one of the boys.

"Of course not," said Murdoch. "It's got to be only fifteen out here."

The boys did not move.

"If you'd like to sit in my nice warm car, all you gotta do is keep sitting in my way. Be happy to take you in on vagrancy charges."

The tallest boy stood up and came nose-to-nose with him. When Murdoch did not say anything, the boy said, "Shit. Let's go."

The boys abandoned the stoop, the last one making sure to bump Murdoch. He grabbed him by the arm. "That's assault, son. Try it again. Find out what a bad day I'm having."

The boy shrugged himself free and walked off.

Murdoch went inside. The floorboards creaked underfoot, and the carpet had very little color left, even where it still had pile. He started up a set of uneven stairs, grasping a loose banister. "Surprised it's not condemned."

He had lived in worse after his father died. It didn't add to the building's appeal, only put it into perspective. Apartment 4 sat at the top left-hand side of the stairs. Out of Apartment 3, hip-hop blared, some rapper with a fake-gang background and one hit. He probably called himself the new Elvis or Michael Jackson or something equally stupid. Murdoch shook his head. He missed the nineties.

No one answered when he knocked on Apartment 4's door, but a door opened behind him. He turned with his badge out and glared at a man with a joint dangling from his mouth. The man dropped it, crushed it out with his bare foot, and ducked back inside. Murdoch knocked again.

The door finally opened. A small woman who looked like she was in her late forties poked her face out the door. Murdoch knew she was younger. He recognized her for the hard thirty or thirty-five she was.

"Yes?" she said in a small voice.

Murdoch held up his badge once again. "Officer Murdoch,

ma'am. Special Investigations. I'm looking for an Armand Cole. We understand he lives here."

"What's my boy done?" she asked. "Tell me. I haven't seen him in weeks."

"Would you mind if I looked around?"

"I mind very much," she said, her expression hardening.

"Please, ma'am," said Murdoch. "A quick look to verify he's not here, and I'll leave you alone."

"I don't trust no plainclothes."

He studied the woman's face. "Don't I know you?"

The woman's face became darker. "Can't get in my door, so you gonna hit on me?"

Murdoch took out a card and handed it to her. "No, I mean you went to Darius Reed Middle School, didn't you? Had Mrs. Kaminsky's homeroom?"

Something changed in her eyes. She took the card and studied it. "You was the boy whose father died in that bus crash."

"Yes, ma'am. Greg Murdoch. We moved to Shawnee Heights after my mom remarried."

A smile fought its way onto her face. "I remember you."

"Althea Cole," said Murdoch. "I used to have the biggest crush on you."

"Well..." She looked away, blushing. When she looked back, the hard expression had returned. "What's my boy done?"

Murdoch frowned. "A building several blocks up Eastern Avenue burned down last night. We think Armand knows something about it."

Althea pressed her lips thin. "I knew that boy would get into trouble with that Dmitri."

"Dmitri. Reagan?"

"You know him?"

"Yes, ma'am. They found his body on Pier Nine this afternoon."

"Armand did not do it."

"I certainly hope not." Murdoch put his hands on her shoulders. "Althea, if Armand is in trouble, I can help make things easier on him. But we need to talk to him."

Althea swallowed. "He told me he was living in Serievo."

Great. Another trip to the Third World. "Did he say where?"

"He say he was living in an apartment off Inland on Wotyla. Brandon Lane Apartments."

"Give me your phone number. I'll call you when I find him."

When Armand opened his eyes, the first thing he saw was Baggy standing over him. "You a dead man," the fat man said.

Then Baggy's cell rang. He looked at the display, annoyed, then his eyes went wide. "Yo." He waited while someone could be heard yelling at him. "I got him. What you want me to do...?" The yelling continued. "But I...He...Come on, Ralph, I..." He hung up. "Dammit!" He nodded at someone behind Armand.

Armand felt a pair of hands turn him over on his stomach. A blade cut his wrists as it sliced through the duct tape binding him.

"You in luck," said Baggy. "Ralph say you live. But I ain't taking you to him. Find your own way, motherfucker. Come on. Let's dump this loser at Farnum Field."

CHAPTER 15

Murdoch called Baker after talking to Armand Cole's mother. Baker, in turn, called Narcotics and the Midtown Division commander. Lt. Kearny in Narcotics jumped at the chance to grab Dmitri Reagan, if only posthumously. The Midtown commander?

Not so much. So Baker called his friend, Chief Hudepohl, who in turn called the Midtown commander. The Midtown commander came to Jesus rather quickly and sent two uniforms to meet two of Kearny's detectives at the Brandon Lane Apartments in Serievo.

The uniforms arrived to find the detectives already in the apartment, looking for evidence. It appeared the apartment manager had taken the opportunity to serve the late Dmitri Reagan with an eviction notice. Since Dmitri now lay on a slab in Vodrey Heights, the detectives needed neither the notice nor a search warrant to enter the premises.

They also did not need much technical skill to get into Dmitri Reagan's computer. Reagan was a busy man, too busy for petty stuff like Windows passwords on his aging desktop machine. Luck?

Possibly, since no self-respecting gangbanger these days even used a laptop—if they owned a computer at all. No, sir, the stylin' banger these days had an iPad. Never mind that their phones would embarrass teenagers from 2005, let alone the present day. Then again, the police could put a wire on a cell phone, which forced the gangs to use cheap, disposable phones.

Dmitri Reagan, tech-savvy guy that he was, kept a list of such phones on his computer. He also used an email client, which stored several emails indicating that business at the Silver Stiletto strip club involved more than just professional naked women committing the occasional misdemeanor.

By the time Murdoch returned to the station, the Monticello Police Department had something they had never been able to get on Ralph Smithers since the last time he left prison.

Hard evidence.

The first thing Armand wondered was why they hadn't just let him go. If Ralph had saved Armand's fat from the fryer, why hadn't Baggy turned him loose?

Then he wondered where Baggy found someone with a car to do his work. Baggy, like most guys in the Game, didn't drive. Armand had come to Dmitri's attention because he owned a driver's license. Even though a stint in juvie had cost him that license, he knew how to drive. And he could always use the poor man's excuse for driving without a license: "I'm sorry, officer, but if I don't drive, I can't work. Please don't tell my parole officer."

Never mind that Monticello had more public transportation than Cleveland, which had always had a rail system, or any other major city in rail-phobic Ohio.

But none of Baggy's crew owned a car. They had no access to cars, and no ability to drive one if they had. Armand not only drove, he stole cars, originally. He'd never been caught, but he'd learned some skills.

Nevertheless, Baggy's crew stuffed Armand into the trunk of a dying Chevy Malibu with Swiss cheese for a tailpipe. He spent the entire trip sucking fumes.

At the end, they yanked him out onto his feet and shoved him into an alley. He fell face down into some frozen garbage as the Malibu rumbled away. Getting to his feet, he did not need a mirror to know what he looked like. But he'd need to call Ralph, which required a phone. He'd need money for the subway or the Monorail, assuming they would allow him aboard.

As he staggered out into the street, he saw Farnum Field, "Home of Triple-A Stallions Baseball," its flashing sign proclaimed. So they'd dumped him off at the Monorail's end, still in Holland Bay. He knew how he'd raise money. After fifteen minutes of drooling and talking with an improvised speech impediment, Armand managed to shame or horrify enough commuters into giving him about twenty dollars. A transit cop started to run him off. Armand asked if there were any payphones nearby. Mercifully, they still existed below street level near the subway platform, probably the last ones in the entire state.

He dialed a number he'd memorized when Ralph first noticed him.

"Stiletto," said a rough voice.

"Armand for Ralph." Blunt was the only way to get through. They put him on hold. Seconds later, Ralph Smithers came on the line.

"Where you at?"

"Farnum Field Station," said Armand. "Baggy tried to kill me. Dumped me here when you called him."

"Is that so?" said Ralph. "Look for Goose. We need to talk."

"Branson."

Branson wondered if she would ever get used to Alvin Baker as her commander. "Sir?"

The short, pudgy man strolled up to her with his rubbery smile in place. "I can't believe Taggart was sitting on that lab for as long as he was."

"Six months, sir," said Branson. She caught a weak smile forming on her lips. "I...er...had a friend hack his notes. Moran's, too."

Baker's expression fell. "Oh. Right. He was your first partner. Sorry to hear about that." His face lit up again. "Tell you what. How'd you like another shot at Ralph Smithers?"

"Dmitri Reagan recovered," said Branson, "and I get to finish him?"

"Branson…"

"Sorry, sir."

He gestured down the hall where Murdoch was chatting with another Port cop named Velasco. Velasco was in uniform. Murdoch looked uncomfortable in the shirt and tie Baker had made him wear today.

"Murdoch got a lead," said Baker, "on some kid who pulled into a gas station in Edison last night with five brand new gas cans. He brought back the security video and worked with some whiz kid from Settler's Commons to identify him."

"You can identify someone off a gas station security camera?"

Baker shrugged. "The kid's good. Care to guess what our firebug's name is?"

"Armand Cole?"

"Give the lady a cigar." Baker turned around. "Murdoch. Get over here."

Murdoch broke off his conversation with a uniform and made his way back to them.

"Update Branson here on your busy day," said Baker. "Give her the whole story about Armand Cole."

"You mean how he was staying with Dmitri Reagan?" said Murdoch.

Branson wasn't sure he heard that right. "What did you say?"

Murdoch recounted his visit to Cole's mother, who told him her son had been staying with a thug named Dmitri. She had the address and only gave it to Murdoch because she remembered him from Middle School as "that boy whose father died in the bus accident." Branson wondered if that had anything to do with Murdoch's perpetually sour expression.

"Since Reagan's body was found while we were headed across town," said Murdoch, "we didn't need a search warrant for the apartment. The manager was already going to evict him."

"And our boy Dmitri was not the most technically brilliant

computer user," said Baker.

"Narcotics found a solid connection to Reagan and that strip club over by Kosar Stadium," said Murdoch. "I was getting ready to head over there and have a chat with Mr. Smithers."

Baker's smile slid back into place. "Why don't you take Branson with you? Seems she already paid our man Smithers a visit this morning. Maybe we can put the fear of Jess into him once more."

Branson wasn't sure if Baker was making a joke or just being condescending.

Armand looked like hell when he walked into the office at the Stiletto. Goose brought him in the side door so that the club's clientele wouldn't see a battered, frost-bitten gangbanger wandering in the crowd. The Stiletto might have been a titty bar with a little pussy sold on the side, but it was also a respectable joint.

Armand watched as Ralph looked him over. He was shivering now, the cold reaching his bones. Goose had made him ride in the back of the van, too. Baggy, or rather Baggy's crew, had done a number on him, all right. His ribs, bruised but not broken, throbbed with pain. One of his eyes had swollen halfway shut. He knew the other one was black—he could feel it swelling.

Ralph smiled. "Got a little too close to Baggy's secret, did you?"

"I'm going to kill the fucker," said Armand. "But first, I'm going to cut off his dick and make him suck it."

That made Ralph laugh. "Dmitri used to talk like that. Even done it. He'd make some dude suck his own cock after it got cut off, then kill him with it hanging out his mouth. Got so bad with Dmitri, he'd make them blow him before he kill them."

That made Armand a little sick. "Ain't that kind of stupid?"

"You know it. All kinds of DNA in that jizz, if anyone care to look." Ralph leaned in toward him. "You want Baggy that bad?"

Armand's fists balled at his side. "I wanna kick his head all the way down Eastern to the lakeshore and punt it to Holland Island."

"I'll give you that chance," said Ralph, "if you answer one question for me."

"He cuttin'. Big time."

"That's what I wanted to know.

Branson rode with Murdoch on this trip to the Stiletto. Unlike the earlier trip, Murdoch opted to take the Shoreway across the river. Never mind that rush hour had begun. He gripped the steering wheel like he was going to bend it in half.

"Christ, Murdoch," said Branson, "what's your problem today? You just made plainclothes, and on a day the chief declared us his chosen people."

Murdoch didn't say anything, simply continued weaving in and out of traffic, narrowly missing a semi.

"Okay," said Branson. "That's it. Pull over."

Murdoch stared straight ahead.

"I said pull the fuck over. *Now.*"

When he saw the look on her face, he took his foot off the gas. "Sorry."

"Sorry won't cut it if you wreck us. I've already had one concussion in the last twenty-four hours. I don't need a second one."

He worked his way over to the far-right lane, taking the exit for Lucas Avenue and Bernie Kosar Stadium. "It's not you or even the job. Trouble at home."

"Well, pull it together. And if you get trigger happy, try to aim for Smithers's balls."

That made Murdoch laugh. "You know, I believe I may do that."

"I get first shot." As they took the exit, Branson relaxed. "So what's going on that you have to drive like Mad Max on an icy bridge?"

"Jane and I had a fight this morning," he said. "A really bad one."

Mrs. Murdoch, better known as Jane Hyde, the Traffic Wench on WMNT, WONK, and a few other stations, was famous for her bawdy sense of humor and an English accent that kept men in Monticello slobbering during their commutes. Branson had met her a couple of times. "Well, she is kind of a bitch."

Murdoch tried not to laugh as he pulled into the parking lot between the Silver Stiletto and the print shop next door.

Ralph's people gave Armand an ice pack and two shots of Jack to ease his pain. Goose pushed on his ribs. It hurt like a mother, but they determined Baggy's crew had not broken them. Ralph gave him another shot of Jack for his trouble.

"Not too much," he said. "I need you sharp. Feel me?"

Armand nodded and pressed the ice pack back to his swollen eye.

"Baggy has disrespected me for the last time. No more." Ralph stood up and started pacing the office. "He cuts my product. He shorts Rufus on money. He makes the whole operation look bad. I don't need some fat ass idiot selling weak-ass shit in my name." He looked over at Goose and nodded, then back to Armand. "As of today, you have two new jobs."

"Lay it on me," said Armand, trying not to sound apathetic. What he really wanted was half a bottle of aspirin and some really good weed. Ralph might respect that, but they had business to attend to first.

"Dmitri disappointed me," said Ralph. "By now you know he dead."

Armand knew better than to ask for details. As he rode in the trunk of that old Ford, he had overheard one of Baggy's crew talking about how Dmitri ended up on Pier 9 already, and that Ralph probably did Dmitri himself.

"You showed balls," said Ralph, "barging in on Baggy like that. Twice. And he already yours to kill for what he did to your girl. You were stupid the second time, but we all get our asses kicked when we stupid. Learn anything?"

Armand nodded. "Yeah. Don't be stupid. Especially around that nigger."

"Good. So from now on, *you* are my boy. You enforce the rules. When I got righteous anger, you deliver my wrath. Feel me?"

Through all the pain, Armand managed a smile. His mouth was still bloody, but his teeth were intact. "I feel ya."

Ralph motioned over for Goose to approach. The big man handed Armand something wrapped in oilcloth.

"Baggy is now yours to do whatever you want with."

Armand took the oilcloth package but did not open it yet. "What's that?"

"You gonna go to Baggy and effect a management change on Delaware and Eastern. In fact, all of Holland Bay is yours. I put the word out to the boys in Wentworth that you coming to make the change. Goose will tell them you speak for him now. Do Baggy, and they respect your authority." He gestured for Armand to open his package.

Inside lay a polished Smith & Wesson .45 magnum and three magazines.

"I wanna see that motherfucker's dead ass on Pier Nine by sunrise tomorrow with a hole in him big enough to drive a Hummer through. You feel me?"

Armand sat up and showed an energy that had been absent since he'd arrived at the Stiletto. Fyre poked her head in the door. "Hey, boss. Some cop's here looking for Ralph Smithers."

Ralph laughed. "Don't know no one here by that name. You, Goose? How about you, Armand?"

Reynaldo Estrada marched into Ali's Corner Grocery like he owned the place. Unofficially, Renaldo did, because Ali, the Palestinian owner of the shop, was into one of Estrada's loan sharks for about twenty-five grand and way behind on his payments. But Reynaldo was a merciful creditor. He did not threaten to break Ali's legs like the Italians might have done back in the day. He didn't shoot his deadbeats—at least not until every other option had been exhausted—like Ralph Smithers's crazy black motherfuckers.

No, he just turned Ali's Corner Grocery into his personal piggy bank. He made Ali his personal bitch. True, Ali had video surveillance on the place and could easily go to the police with tapes of Rey Estrada helping himself to whatever was on the shelf, in the register, or even in the lottery displays. Occasionally, he helped himself to Ali's wife, and truth be told, Ali's wife kind of liked it. After all, Rey Estrada was a powerful man who took what he wanted. Ali was merely Rey's bitch.

So the same afternoon Ralph Smithers sentenced Baggy to death, Rey Estrada waltzed into Ali's and grabbed his complimentary case of Yuengling (because he was sick to death of the piss water Mexico was shipping to Ohio), helped himself to a sandwich, and grabbed a copy of the *Wall Street Journal* and the Spanish-language edition of the local *Herald-Star*. It was the last time Estrada would walk out of Ali's.

A bullet destroyed the back of his head as he stepped out onto Barnett Avenue.

The shooter, moving back around the corner, pulled out a newly purchased cell phone, activated that morning, and speed-dialed a pre-programmed number. "Yo. It's Jules. Yeah, he down."

The phone would end up in a trash can in Vodrey Heights by sundown.

CHAPTER 16

Murdoch had to pay the ten-dollar cover to get into the Silver Stiletto. Branson just smiled and mumbled a comment about whether it was amateur night. The guy at the door told her he'd like to see her fine ass up on the pole. Branson pretended that was a compliment, and in she went.

They had already agreed to separate and use their phones to keep in contact. It wouldn't be hard for Murdoch to cover Branson's texts as coming from his wife. Jane had started texting him every fifteen minutes, which only served to keep the scowl fixed upon Murdoch's face. Branson decided she would pretend she was flirting with someone whenever Murdoch texted her.

She started a circle of the room, trying to spot Smithers or one of the better-known members of his crew. Instead, she spotted at least three misdemeanors and a probable felony. An assistant coach from Monticello State's basketball team tried to snort a line of cocaine without looking like he was snorting a line of cocaine. She opted to ignore it. They weren't here to ruin some idiot celebrity's life, not that the assistant was a celebrity.

As she made her way over to the private rooms, she saw Murdoch show his badge to the bartender. He did it smoothly. To anyone not in the know, it looked like he slipped the bartender something extra, maybe for drugs or to get a particular girl to dance for him.

She moved over to the stage area, smiled at some of the men

who seemed amused to see a woman in the Stiletto. In the middle of the room, she spotted a familiar face admiring the breasts of a rather curvy black dancer. The girl let him motorboat her as a fifty appeared in her garter. Branson took this opportunity to check her phone.

And discreetly snap a photo of Deputy Chief Roberts, who apparently did not see her.

Then she saw *her*, a statuesque redhead in a silver teddy, striding across the room like she owned it. The woman headed straight for Murdoch, who was either texting Branson or his wife. Her phone buzzed.

"Contact," her screen read, Murdoch's number at the top. She watched. The redhead certainly had Murdoch's attention. He followed her back toward the dressing rooms and, Branson assumed, the office. She circled back to the bar and waited.

"Can I help you?" said the bartender, a forty-something guy with a comb-over, trying desperately to look younger than thirty-five.

Branson slapped a five on the bar. "Ginger ale. And keep it pure."

"You a cop like that black guy?"

"My daddy can shut this place down."

"And who would that be?"

"Remember Mayor Kozinski?"

When the color drained from the bartender's face, it gave her great pleasure to use the man who destroyed her career to help rebuild it. "Yeah. Bad enough his daughter's a lesbian."

That made the bartender smile, and he poured her a ginger ale. "Really? So... See anything you like?"

"Naw," she said, "I like my women butch."

Detective Eddie Soroya pulled his collar up around his neck as a stiff breeze blew in from downriver and the lake. Rock Ridge uniforms had cordoned off the sidewalk around the entrance to

Ali's Grocery, effectively closing the corner store. The owner did not look too upset. One look at the deceased told Soroya and his partner, Bosic, why.

Rey Estrada's sightless eyes stared back at them when the responding officer pulled the sheet down from his face.

"Well, this hasn't happened in a while," said Bosic. "They put you on spic detail again, Eddie?"

Soroya shrugged. Most people assumed his name was "Eduardo" or "Edward," and he never corrected them. Since 9/11, he had made a concerted effort to conceal the fact that "Eddie" really stood for "Ahmed." During his patrol days in Rock Ridge, he found that his looks, along with a decent ability to speak Spanish with a passable Mexican accent, and his last name got him a lot more cooperation than his Anglo and black counterparts on the MPD. Even some of the Hispanic cops had a rougher time of it than Soroya, most likely because Eddie's baggage did not come from living in Huron Junction. His baggage came directly from Iran with a dose of the Monticello suburbs thrown in for that authentic middle school experience. "First time I've seen an Estrada in the line of fire. Anyone talk to the owner?"

"Ali Rasaad," said Bosic. "Moved here from Palestine in the nineties. Has owned this store since he arrived. Says Estrada was boorish and threatening and helped himself to the inventory whenever he wanted, but he didn't kill him."

"Of course not," said Soroya. "Otherwise, we'd be policing the area for buckshot from a thirty-aught-six." He studied Estrada's ruined head. "No exit wounds. Large entry point. A .22 at close range, you think?"

"No self-respecting gang banger carries anything else these days. Not even a Glock Nine."

Soroya laughed. "God, I miss the nineties. Pearl Jam and Heavy D."

"You have some fucked-up taste in music, Eddie."

"I prefer the politically correct term 'eclectic.'" He stood. "You know, if one of Ralph Smithers's boys hit this guy, the shit's going to hit the fan."

"Yeah. In hours instead of days, too."

"Better call this into Kearny over in Narcotics. Tell him he's got a war on his hands."

"Great. I could use the overtime."

"Bet on the Steelers over the weekend?"

"Goddamned hillbilly patsies."

Murdoch had been gone fifteen minutes without any contact. Branson had texted him twice before abandoning the bar. She made her way toward the dressing rooms. A large man with bad breath tried to block her way. She palmed her badge and held it in his face.

"Ever been to Mansfield?" she asked.

The way he moved aside told her he had, and it probably hadn't gone very well. She pushed past him and headed down the corridor. The door to an office stood ajar.

"Murdoch?"

She heard a grunt and pushed the door open.

"Shit," said Murdoch as the redhead, now sans teddy, stood and wiped her mouth.

She kissed Murdoch on the cheek. "You sure go down smooth, daddy." She turned and walked past Branson.

Branson had often heard the expression "caught with his dick in his hand." She never expected to see it so literally.

Murdoch struggled to tuck his penis back inside his pants. "I...um..."

"Save it," said Branson. "Let's go. If I'm in a good mood, you might get to stay on the force."

She was halfway back down the corridor before she heard Murdoch's footsteps behind her.

***

They stood in the office across the lobby from the Stiletto, Ralph on his cell phone, Armand with an ice pack still on his eye, Goose watching the street. With the lights out in the empty storefront, the shadows kept them from being seen. Armand watched with his good eye as the black cop walked past the building, keeping pace with an angry-looking white woman.

"Must be his wife," said Goose in a low voice.

It was the first time Armand had laughed in a while. Ralph did not seem to pay attention. "Okay, hoss. I'll send him your way." He clicked off his phone and pocketed it. "Soon as we clear, you need to go see Rufus."

Armand's stomach rolled over. He hadn't talked to Mr. King since this morning.

"Keep that burner for a little while longer," said Ralph. "You got a busy evening ahead of you. Rufus got some chores for you after you cap Baggy. Do all this, and we have a sit-down with the Wentworth crew tomorrow. Hell, they probably think you God tomorrow if you get rid of' Baggy for them."

The rear door to the storefront opened. Fyre, adjusting her teddy, stood silhouetted in the light. "They're gone. And I took care of that black cop for you."

"You suck his dick good?" asked Ralph.

"He was happy until that lady cop came looking for him. She's pissed."

"Told you it was his wife," said Goose.

This time, even Ralph laughed. To Armand, he said, "Got your gat?"

Armand patted the pocket of his parka.

"Good," said Ralph. "Go see the money man. Then go wipe Baggy off the face of the earth."

CHAPTER 17

They reported back to Baker, informing him that, yes, the Stiletto was a den of drugs and prostitution. The force could shut it down simply by having three Vice cops walk in undercover without even going into the booths. Branson showed Baker the photo she had snapped.

Baker laughed. "That's funny. Don't think of putting that up on Instagram, though. Roberts will invent a way to fire you if he thinks his job is on the line."

"I plan to save it for a rainy day," said Branson.

Baker turned to Murdoch. "So Smithers gave you the slip?"

Murdoch's face changed color.

"They sent someone out to distract Murdoch," said Branson. "We tried to be discreet, but that bartender probably tipped them off to us."

"Well," said Baker, "given the delicate nature of the Stiletto's clientele, we can't afford to raid them without something big." He looked at Murdoch. "Or knowing some of our own people are compromised."

Branson knew the captain had figured out Murdoch's secret, even if Roberts was the real reason they could not just burst in, guns blazing.

"Stick around, Murdoch," said Baker. "I want you to get with Kagan when he gets back from the Morgue. Let's see if we can find this Armand Cole." He turned back to Branson. "And you."

"Sir?"

"Go home."

Well, that felt like a slap in the face. Before she could respond, Baker added, "You're on restricted duty, Branson. If something happens to you, it's not just your ass on the line." He put a hand on her shoulder. "You did good. You got us the lab. You came within sniffing distance of Smithers. Don't worry. The chief will know what all you did today."

"Sir," she said, "I feel fine."

Actually, she felt cranky. And hungry. She and Kagan had skipped lunch. Beyond a stale cruller in the break room and a candy bar from the vending machine, she had not eaten anything since that Pop Tart for breakfast.

"Bullshit," said Baker. "You look exhausted. Go get some food. Go home. Get some rest. If you want to do something police related, go see Taggart on your way home. If he's awake, tell him his ass is in a sling. He can get it out by telling us everything he knows."

Well, it was something, or so Branson told herself. She headed toward the back of the building and the rear parking lot where her Pathfinder still sat. One of the uniforms, Velasco, stopped her. "Hey, Branson, what are we going to do about that dog in Interrogation Room Two?"

Oh, shit. Vader had been left alone inside a police station all afternoon. Had it not occurred to anyone to call Animal Control? Of course not. None of these idiots, and Branson included herself among them, had done real police work in so long they had forgotten protocol.

Branson did not want to deal with Animal Control. If she wasn't going back out with Murdoch or Kagan, she sure as hell didn't want to spend another hour doing paperwork.

Vader still slept in the interrogation room. When he looked up to see Branson, his untrimmed tail began thumping on the floor.

"Vader," she said, "go for ride?"

As the now-former drug dog scampered toward the rear entrance, not even bothering to bark at the uniformed cops milling about, Branson realized that this definitely had been somebody's pet, maybe even Plink's.

The freight elevator in Mr. King's building had an odd reddish stain on the back wall that hadn't been there the last time Armand had ridden in it. Someone had tried to scrub it away, but the best they could do was blend it in with all the grease and grime embedded in the rest of the car. Armand wondered if this place had been the last thing Dmitri Reagan had seen before his death.

And who did him?

No one sat behind the receptionist's desk this time. Last time, it had been Janiece, Ralph's woman. She was fine, but she seemed too...

She seemed too Holland Island for Ralph. Ralph, for all his wealth and power, was still street. This woman belonged in an office, but not behind a receptionist's desk. The way she talked to Mr. King and even to Armand, she had to be doing more than getting coffee and taking phone calls. Being Ralph's woman, she probably watched his money closely.

She probably wanted to make it her money.

Monk emerged from the office. "Hello, young man. Come on in. Mr. King's waiting for you."

They went into Mr. King's office. King paced behind his desk, cell phone in his ear.

"I give you my word, Miguel," he said. "I knew nothing about this." King waited as someone shouted back at him through the phone. "Well, have you considered it might be mutiny?" More shouting.

Armand could almost make out what the other person was saying. He caught the line, "What if I decided to go after Ralph?"

"If that's what you think," said Mr. King, "then you do what you gotta do." He hung up and looked at Monk. "He's pissed."

"If it was your brother, wouldn't you be?" said Monk. "Besides, them Estradas are crazy."

They both looked at Armand.

"You don't know nothing about this," said Monk.

"Do you still have all that gas you bought?" said Mr. King.

Armand nodded and said nothing.

"Good. I understand Ralph gave you Baggy to cap. Go take care of that first. After that, I need you to finish the job Dmitri started last night."

"That building already gone, man," said Armand.

Mr. King smiled. "I know. I need both those lots cleared. Understand?"

Armand understood. Before he could say anything, Janiece swept into the room, wearing a tight black dress that showed off all her curves and quite a bit of skin.

"Are we ready to go yet?" she said, looking at Mr. King like he was a piece of candy.

"Almost, baby," said Mr. King. "Armand, I'm going to ask you a very important question. Would you kill for me?"

That was a stupid question. He was about to go kill Baggy. "Of course."

"Even if it was someone high up in the organization?"

Armand did not like where this was going. Still, he thought, Mr. King would not ask unless he had a good reason. "Depends on who ask."

"What if I asked you?"

"I would."

Mr. King came over and put his arm across Armand's shoulders. "You go take care of Baggy. That's for you, even if it's because we want him gone. Go do that building where we set you up. That's for me. Don't worry about the police. We'll cover you."

Armand nodded, wondering what Mr. King would say next.

"Janiece and I will be laying low tonight," said Mr. King. "So when you finish your business in Holland Bay, you call Monk. He'll have one last job for you tonight."

"And then?"

"And then you own Eastern Avenue."

Armand could not help but smile.

"That's right," said Mr. King. "You're my boy now. I want you to be my man in Holland Bay. I've got big plans for that neighborhood."

Armand noticed that Mr. King had said "my man in Holland Bay," not "Ralph's man" or "our man."

Big things were about to happen. So why did Shandra's voice come back to him, warning him to leave the Game?

Picture someone who walked too close to a roadside bomb but missed getting blown to pieces by it. That was Jake Taggart when Branson arrived in his room. A white bandage wrapped his head. One tube stuck out of his arm while another snaked out from under his sheets. Branson recognized this last as a Foley catheter and did not envy Taggart if he got out of bed.

Assuming he could.

"I think we got too close to someone," said Taggart as Branson entered the room. "But I don't think they were expecting us."

"Well," she said, "it started a shit storm in Holland Bay, in case you were wondering. Guess who else got killed today."

"Plink?"

"Dmitri Reagan. Plink is on his way to the infirmary at the Norwalk lockup, if our idiot prosecutor did his job."

"You didn't shut down Packard Lane, did you? I was going to arrange for Narcotics to raid the place in another..."

"Save it," she said. "I raided your notes last night. Yours and Moran's. Anyway, we think torching Packard Lane got Dmitri killed. He tried to burn out that lab you've been sitting on."

"You got into my notes?"

Branson rolled her eyes. "Really, Taggart. You could have at least kept Lieutenant Kearny in on your operation. It's not like he was saving Ralph Smithers for a special occasion."

Taggart folded his arms and sulked. It made her want to slap him.

"Plink's in custody," she said. "He's rolling on Smithers. Reagan is dead. They dumped him on Pier Nine. If you and I hadn't gotten blown up when we did, Baker would be feeding you to Internal Affairs." She waited a beat for Taggart to respond. Of course, he didn't. Social skills were never his forte.

"And," she added, "I know what Baker's like if he suspects a cop is dirty."

"So..."

She pulled up a chair. "Jake, you've got to come clean on everything. Now. No more holding back. You were running Plink, Doby Clark, and Raul Carcinira as informants. Give it all to me, and Baker will make sure you get proper credit. Hell, you got blown up for the team."

Taggart frowned. "I worked two goddamned years on this. I really thought..."

"Oh, for Christ's sake! Those two fuckers killed the first partner I ever had. You owe me, Taggart. You owe me Ralph Smithers's head."

Branson's outburst made Taggart flinch in his bed, then groan. "Did you put that stupid dog of Plink's down?"

She began laughing.

"What?" said Taggart.

"Don't bad mouth my dog. I still haven't let him out of the car yet."

"Aye yi yi."

"This isn't just disrespect," said Miguel Estrada, pacing the office of the Mexican restaurant that doubled as his headquarters. "That fucker Smithers killed my brother. His money man all but said it."

Marco Trujillo sat listening to his employer. Most of the time, Marco tended bar at the restaurant. Most of the time. Estrada had a different job in mind for him now.

"No one will come out and say it," Estrada continued, waving his hands as he talked, "but you know he had Uncle Pablo done right there at Chuck E Cheese. In front of my goddamned nephew."

Marco knew his boss to be a devout Catholic under normal circumstances, more so than his brother Rey. Rey never hid what he was, a wealthy man of dubious means who indulged every carnal pleasure he could. The only time Rey Estrada ever saw the inside of a church was at weddings, christenings, and funerals. Rey's own funeral would be in a couple of days. Because of this, Miguel's devotion to the One True Faith had gone out the window.

"You have equipment?" asked Estrada.

"I have my usual sources," said Marco. "One phone call, and I get what I want. The usual terms." Which meant the restaurant would be billed for electrical repairs that never happened. Marco's weapons supplier used his cousin's heating and cooling company as a front.

"Good," said Estrada. "Here's the job. I want you to hunt down Ralph Smithers, get him alone, and put a very large bullet in his head." He reached into his desk and tossed him a set of car keys. "Take the Hyundai. Ditch it when you're done. Leave the bastard on Pier Nine."

Armand found Shandra's body gone and the bed stripped when he returned to the apartment. He had retrieved the Toyota from its hiding place and parked it along Halsted. This late, he did not expect fire or police to be working the building, so he doubted anyone would even notice the car, unless they tried to boost it. To keep that from happening, he popped the hood and undid one of the battery wires.

Inside, he took one last look around the apartment. It would have been mighty nice to rule his new kingdom from here instead of Wentworth. Mr. King was right. This building could have been something.

Searching the dresser, he found a locket Shandra liked to

wear. It was a cheap thing he bought off some guy selling stolen DVD's downtown, but Shandra loved it just the same. She had put a picture of herself and Armand in it. Armand opened it. The photo of her smiling next to him hit him like a hammer blow to the chest. He closed it, pocketed it, and checked the .45 under his parka.

"Time to die," he said to the fat man down the street. Baggy might not have heard him then, but he would soon.

The last time Armand had marched into Wentworth, he got resistance. This time, the word had come down. Armand was Ralph Smithers's boy. He was also tight with the money man. He was the new Dmitri. Maybe he wasn't the psycho Dmitri had been, but he still demanded respect. Baggy's homeboys cleared a path for him, watching impassively, waiting to see if the fat man came out of the apartment alive.

It had taken four guys to take Armand down last time. None of them was Baggy. Baggy had waited until the others beat Armand into submission before making a move. Then he had whined when Ralph called.

Now Armand had returned with a huge gat and murder in his eye. He kicked the door into Baggy's apartment only to find it freezing. He held the big .45 out in front of him like he'd seen the cops do. Never, Dmitri once told him, should he use the homeboy grip. It looked stupid and almost always ruined one's aim.

And Armand aimed to empty his clip into this fat sonofabitch. A rattling noise came from the bedroom. Inside, he spotted a smashed window and heard the fire escape shake.

"Oh, no, you don't," he said out loud and went through the shattered window out onto the Wentworth's fragile fire escape. Below him, he could see Baggy scampering to the ground in nothing but a T-shirt and boxers. Armand could not tell from where he was, but it looked like Baggy was also barefoot. This would be an easy kill. Dump the gun in the Musgrave, and Baggy would be just another Holland Bay stiff.

Armand started down the escape, shaking it even more than

Baggy. But Baggy was trying not to get frostbite on his feet. Armand took two steps at a time, even jumping between levels, ignoring the pain in his ribs and his knee. It actually drove him harder. So while Baggy rode the final flight down as it lowered on springs to the alley below, Armand reached the bottom and simply leaped the final story. It hurt like hell when he landed, but he was up and running in seconds.

The fat man yelled as he ran down Eastern in the frigid air. Armand followed for three blocks, nearly catching the fat ass.

When the police cruiser rolled up on Baggy, Armand had to duck into an alley. He peeked around the corner.

That motherfucker jumped into the back of the police car, not even waiting to be cuffed. Armand kicked a trashcan in frustration, spooking a rat and a couple of stray cats.

CHAPTER 18

It was along Inland Parkway that Branson realized Vader definitely was not a real drug dealer's dog. He took to her rather quickly and stopped barking at Kagan when she snapped at him. Plink hadn't found a guard dog. He probably picked up someone's stray that was wandering Big River Park. She wondered what the dog's real name was, since it was collarless.

After stopping at the Giant Eagle in Little Sicily for dog food and a couple of bowls, she came back to find the dog whining. The poor thing had been in the back of the Pathfinder or in Plink's interrogation room since that afternoon.

"What's the matter, fella?" she said as she pulled out of the Giant Eagle lot. "Gotta go?"

Vader barked three times, a high-pitched yelp that sounded nothing like the growl he had greeted her and Taggart with the day before.

"All right. I don't have a leash, but we'll find you a nice park."

She found one right outside the former borders of Camelot. In warmer weather, the place swarmed with joggers and picnickers. A mile-long running trail circled it. Its biggest feature was its veterans' memorial, a mounted Vietnam-era Huey and a Korean War-era howitzer, tucked off to one corner. Two days after the Superbowl and the worst snowstorm in recent memory, the place would be deserted. Branson let Vader loose there.

The Rottweiler leaped out of the back of the Pathfinder and

into the snow. For a short-hair dog, he certainly loved the six-inch layer of virgin snow that covered the park. After playing for a couple of minutes, nature finally asserted herself, and Vader left a token of his appreciation in the park.

"Hey! You gonna clean that up?"

Branson, leaning against the Pathfinder as she watched Vader, turned to see a deputy sheriff in his cruiser. She badged him. "That dog just brought down the biggest meth lab in Monticello. If he wants to shit in the park, he'll shit in the park."

The deputy peered out at her with contempt from under his broad-brimmed hat. "City cops," he muttered. "I'll let it pass, but I want to see a leash on that dog next time. And you bring a scooper. I don't know how they do it in the city, but out here in Edison..."

"Edison *is* the city, Deputy." She turned and whistled for Vader to come back. To her surprise, the dog made a beeline for her through a fresh patch of snow, his tongue hanging out the whole way. "I know. I live here."

"Get a leash," the deputy said, "and bring a scooper next time. Professional courtesy extends only so far."

After the deputy drove off, Branson muttered, "Ticket your mother lately?" She opened the passenger door and let Vader jump into the seat. He then greeted Branson by shaking himself off all over her.

"Vader!" If she kept this dog, he would have to attend obedience school.

Five minutes later, they were home. She opened the door to her apartment, struggling with her purse, the dog food, and bowls. Vader charged inside and started barking furiously.

"What the hell?" The dog, teeth bared and voice in a growl, had Jerry cornered in the kitchen.

"Jess, what the hell is this?"

"Vader," she said in a threatening tone, and the dog whimpered twice, growled once at Jerry, then turned around to explore Branson's apartment. "I got a dog."

"A dog? When?"

"When I put his owner in jail. He was guarding a meth lab."

Vader, as if to emphasize the point, turned and growled again at Jerry.

"So," she said, "spending the night again?"

Armand waited in the shadows of a building along Eastern, watching Baggy run into the arms of the police. He would call Ralph later to let them know Baggy had not only escaped, but he was now a snitch. He wasn't sure what was going on higher up or what job he was doing for Rufus later, but he did know Baggy was a dead man once they got him to the County tank downtown. Too bad. Armand had wanted desperately to pull that trigger himself.

When the cruiser was gone, he made his way up the street to the apartment block. There, he found the Toyota where he'd left it and replaced the battery cable. Then he popped the trunk and grabbed a couple of the gas cans. Inside the building, he found the maintenance room.

The furnace, the hot water heaters, and a workbench took a soaking before he ran back out to the car. He used the next two cans to coat the floor of the furnace room, where everyone supposedly had lockers. In reality, no one in their right mind would use them. Someone was always breaking into them. Armand suspected Baggy had used it for part of his stash. Could not be helped. This was his corner now, along with Wentworth. He'd have to get the new connect to resupply him. At least this time, there would be no bodies to draw the wrong kind of attention, just a bunch of lawn equipment, stored gasoline and kerosene, and some tools. Finally, Armand came back for the laundry room. A woman with a basket came in and saw him with the gas already spilling onto the floor.

Armand stood and stared at her, unable to grab his gun. It was that woman with the baby. He knew her husband was no gang banger and no deadbeat. He was a Marine, like Armand probably should have been. They were too poor to live anywhere else while the husband was overseas. Armand could only stare at her, watch her eyes widen and mouth open as he stood there with two cans of gas spilling down around his feet.

"Get out of here," he hissed. "Pull the alarm, grab your baby, and get out of here. This place is gone."

She cried out once, dropped the basket, and ran. Armand grabbed a blouse from her basket, dipped it in gasoline from the floor, and lit it. The alarm was blaring as he dropped the burning rag on his way out.

In the Toyota, he cranked the engine twice before it fired. The front wheels spun, then bit into the icy pavement. He did not even stop to make a left on Delaware. Something inside the building exploded. Red light or no, he gunned the motor and started to make a right onto Eastern.

A car clipped him coming around to turn left onto Delaware.

When Branson emerged from the shower, she found Jerry sitting on the couch, watching some concert on MTV Live, turning a half-empty beer bottle in his hand. Apparently, he and Vader had made peace. The dog lay snoring on the floor at one end of the sofa while Jerry sulked on the other.

"Hey," she said.

Jerry did not look up, concentrating instead on ignoring the band on TV. It sounded like The Who in one of their last concerts. His taste in music bewildered her sometimes.

"You okay?" she asked.

"I'm fine," he said as a gravel-voice Roger Daltrey tried to make "Teenage Wasteland" sound cool coming from a man in his seventies.

She sat down on the couch next to him, curling her legs underneath her. "Jerry? Are you really in love with me?"

Finally, he turned to her. "I'd like to be. If you'd stop selling yourself short."

She could not help but smile. "Well, when you get tossed aside like used Kleenex like I did..."

"That was years ago, Jess. Where's your ex now? Columbus?"

"Chicago. Office in the Loop, trophy wife in the burbs. Last I heard, she was bleeding him dry."

He snaked an arm across her shoulders. "You really think of yourself as a slut?"

"I like sex. What's wrong with that?"

"Nothing. I'm more worried about how you see yourself."

"You want to be my knight in shining armor, don't you?"

"I guess you could think of it that way."

"Do you want to spend the night again?"

"Yes."

"Then be a dear and get us some Chinese."

Jerry laughed and got up, startling Vader.

"Jerry?" said Branson.

"Yes?"

"Let's go slow, okay? I'm damaged goods, so I need to feel my way back to normal." She stood up and put her hands on his shoulders. "I'm not the most trusting person. That doesn't mean you can't earn my trust." She kissed his ear. "I want you to try."

Heather Leary, aka "Fyre," finished her turn on stage, scooping up the rain of singles, fivers, and even twenties that flooded the stage while she had worked the pole. With no one wanting a lap dance immediately after, she grabbed up her teddy and walked naked back to the dressing rooms, drinking in the appreciative hoots along the way. In the back, she stowed her cash, minus the house take, dressed again, and went back to the office to give the manager the Stiletto's cut.

She found Ralph alone. He looked angry, staring at his phone. "Everything okay, boss?" She hoped he didn't want to fuck her again. Ralph was fun to screw, but he was insatiable. She needed recovery time before she let him pound her again.

Ralph still stared at his phone. "Cops took over my bar." He looked up at her. "You believe that? Fucking cops took over The Phoenix. Just barged in and said it was their watering hole. Some old fuck named Baker. Says he's going to clean up Holland Bay."

That wasn't all that bothered Ralph. She could tell. "Tell me more, baby. What's bothering you."

"Had to cap my homeboy today," he said. "He fucked me. Burned out my main business."

Fyre had no idea what he was talking about, but it didn't matter. Making Ralph Smithers feel better had proven to be lucrative. She knelt in front of him and took his hand. "Let me make it better, baby." She began sucking his fingers slowly.

"And then my main man," said Ralph, "the man holding my money. He took my woman. He taking my money. It's turning to shit."

She reached between his legs for his fly. "Let me be your woman." She looked up before opening his fly. "I'll do anything you want, baby. You know I will." She watched his scowl soften as she reached inside his pants and began playing with him. "You like that, Ralphie? Do you want to eat me up again?"

Ralph closed his eyes in ecstasy. Then he opened them again. And smiled. That smile looked like the mouth of a shark coming at Fyre. He stood up and grabbed her arm with one hand while zipping his fly with the other.

"You know what?" he said. "You are my woman now. And right now, I want you to feel how angry I am."

This wasn't the way it was supposed to go. It was nothing like last night. "Ralph, you're hurting me."

"It's okay," he said. "You gonna take all my rage tonight. After that, I make you a queen. But I'm angry, and I need to fuck my anger away."

Fyre moaned but didn't dare resist as Ralph dragged her out into the corridor between the Stiletto and the empty storefront. As he pulled her up the stairs to one of the unfinished offices, she wondered if she would ever leave this place alive.

She screamed when he took a knife and sliced off her teddy. It only seemed to arouse Ralph even more.

They were dozing on the couch, watching *There's Something About Mary*, when Branson's phone rang, playing "The Imperial March." Jerry saw the number and grabbed the phone. Branson reached for it.

"No," said Jerry. "You're off duty. They can't make you come in."

She jabbed him hard in the ribs, winding him, then snatched the phone. "Branson."

"Hey, head case, thought you might want an update," said Petrocelli. "Looks like things are heating up around Ralph Smithers, and it's tied to your caseload."

"'Headcase'?"

"You hurt my rib," said Jerry.

She snapped her fingers at him, giving him a look that brooked no more interruption.

"That building on Eastern and Delaware," said Petrocelli, "just went up in flames."

She got up, spooking Vader and looking for her shoes. "Next to the one that burned last night?"

"The same."

"Who's there?"

"We sent Kagan. And Murdoch is questioning a suspect, a Reginald 'Baggy' Anderson. You'll love this. Norris and Mendez picked him up running down Eastern in his underwear."

"I'll be there in half an hour."

"Negative," said Petrocelli. "We're just keeping you in the loop. You might want to swing by there tomorrow morning. Let Kagan handle it. He'll be your new sergeant tomorrow anyway."

"New sergeant?"

"I know. He's pissed. At least I'm getting that freeway slot I always wanted."

"Thanks for the call, Dan. And congrats. I'll be in tomorrow." She hung up. "My ass."

Jerry was on his feet. "That hurt. Jess, I'm just trying to…"

She put up her hand. "First, do not ever do that again. That's my phone, and it's my job. Those are two things you don't want to get in the way of. Second, I am a cop. I work weird hours, even when I'm not supposed to. If you can't handle that, get the hell out of my apartment."

Jerry stared at her for a moment, then the dog. Finally, he went to the door and pulled his coat on. "Don't worry, Jess. I'll leave you alone. That's what you want anyway." He slammed the door on his way out.

Branson dodged Vader as she pulled on her sneakers. "Sorry, boy. Mommy's gotta go to work."

Vader whined, snorted, and dropped down in front of the sofa. She looked at the clock on the cable box.

"All right," said Branson, "you can stay home by yourself. But I expect you to do the dishes." She went over to scratch him between the ears before heading out the door. As she reached the stairwell, she heard Vader whine more loudly.

"Gonna have to call the landlord tomorrow," she muttered under her breath.

Ten minutes later, she was doing eighty up the Inbound, the bubble light on her car.

It had been drilled into Armand's head since he'd worked for Ralph Smithers's organization: When in trouble, go to The Phoenix. There, he could leave the car, call Ralph or some higher-up from the landline behind the bar—find someone to get him back on track. That had always been the plan.

Tonight, however, he drove out Lake Road only to find two Port Police cruisers parked alongside the bar. Slowing down, he could see a pair of uniformed cops sitting in the booth nearest the front window, sipping coffee and chatting. He stopped and squinted to see farther into the bar. It was nearly empty. One of the cops looked out and seemed to notice Armand sitting in the bashed Toyota, idling. He nudged his partner and pointed. The other cop looked out. Armand could see them laughing.

The Phoenix had been ripped away from Ralph's empire. What else would be lost tonight? He drove on down Lake past the old port and into a decaying section of Vodrey Heights called Vodrey Beach. In the dark gloom, aging wood-frame houses crowded the north side of the street, the Shoreway blocking Armand's view of anything toward the slope up to the Heights proper. He found a gas station to turn around.

He thought Pier 9 would be the best place to dispose of the car and his phone. He'd used the burner way too many times for comfort. After they pulled all those bodies out of the basement of the abandoned building this morning, Five-Oh had to be tapping phones by now.

Unfortunately, a cop car sat at the entrance to Pier 9, motor running, interior lit as the cop inside sat doing paperwork. Dmitri must have been the last straw for Five-Oh with Pier 9. He drove on, hoping the cop didn't notice the damage to the car. It wasn't a stretch that the driver of the other car would describe a Toyota Corolla driven by a black man with front fender damage. He decided to call Ralph.

Ralph did not answer, probably boning another stripper. No wonder that Janiece had taken up with Mr. King. He tried Monk next.

"He got grabbed by Five-Oh," he said when Monk answered, not introducing himself or explaining who "he" was. "Fire's going, but I got clipped, pulling out of there. This car's hot."

"Leave the car at The Phoenix," said Monk.

"Can't. Cops are there. At least two cars. Saw them in the window drinking coffee."

Monk grumbled something under his breath. "Eastern Shore. Where they're building the new Walmart. Twenty minutes." He hung up.

***

When Ralph pushed off of her, Fyre could not stop crying. He had forced himself on her in every way possible. As she lay face down on the cold concrete, she could feel something warm between her legs. Blood. Her blood.

"Oh, God," she said. "I think you tore something." A sharp pain exploded in her lower abdomen. She couldn't tell which end it came from. "Ralph, I'm dying. Take me to the hospital. I promise I'll keep quiet."

Rolling over to catch her breath, she saw Ralph standing up and zipping his fly, not even cleaning himself off. He found his coat and pulled out a wad of bills. Peeling off several hundreds, he threw them at her.

"Here. Thanks for the fuck, baby."

Fyre now cried in earnest. She had been used roughly before, but she had allowed it. Before she could always say no. Not this time. This was what rape felt like. She could not let it pass. "I can't do this anymore."

Ralph was pulling on his coat and stopped. "What you mean? You my bitch. You do what I tell you when I tell you. I give you a few days to rest up."

She couldn't speak. Everywhere Ralph had penetrated her burned. It would hurt to stand. She could only sob.

"Listen," he said, crouching, "my woman left me. Dumped me for my homeboy. They gonna end up dead by morning. But you? I like you. Long as you let me fuck that fine ass of yours, we cool. I give you everything you ever wanted long as you my bitch."

Fyre caught her breath and said, "I can't. I quit. You'll never see me again. I can't. Oh, God, it hurts. It hurts. It hurts!"

"Oh, you think that hurts?"

The gun seemed to appear in Ralph's hand as if by magic.

Branson came off the Vodrey Heights Bridge exit just in time to see the building on the corner of Eastern and Delaware collapse, throwing up a spectacular fireball. Firefighters scattering appeared in the flash. Pulling up on Eastern, she found herself blocked by a Harbortown cruiser. A uniform came up, his face flashing red in the light of her bubble. Branson held up her badge.

"You Special Investigations?" he asked, sounding a little unsure. It did sound strange to hear someone ask about SI without the note of pity.

"Branson," she said. "My partner Kagan is working the fire."

"Go up half a block and pull over," said the uniform. "Kagan will be over by the fire captain's car. Be careful. We had six firefighters injured when the third and fourth floors collapsed."

"Anyone killed?"

"Haven't found anyone, thank God. That doesn't mean we won't, but the odds get better the longer we don't."

Branson nudged the Pathfinder up to one of the few remaining parking spots along the street. For a moment, she thought she might have to turn south on Delaware, even park on the overpass that merged Delaware and Studebaker.

As she marched toward the fire captain's car, she spotted a young black woman with a baby, who was trying to wrap the infant against the cold. Branson clipped her badge to her jacket and walked up to her. "Did you see it happen?"

The woman tried not to sob. "He told me to pull the alarm. Said the place would be gone. Where are we supposed to go?"

The temperature wasn't much better than the night before. "Miss, why aren't you in a police cruiser or an ambulance."

The woman looked at her like it was the first she'd heard of the idea. "I...I...don't know. That one plainclothes cop told me not to go nowhere, that he wanted to talk to me."

"Motherfuckers," Branson said under her breath. "What's your name, sweetie? Let's go find you a nice warm cruiser."

"I can't believe it was Armand," she said. "He was so nice."

Branson guided her toward the first cruiser she could find. It was driven by Norris and Mendez, the two cops who'd brought in the nearly naked Baggy Anderson earlier. She didn't know Mendez. She did know Norris.

And didn't like him.

"Norris," she barked. "Why in the hell are you letting a witness stand out here in seven-degree weather?"

Norris, who stared at the fire while clutching a styrofoam cup of coffee, slowly turned to Branson. Like the woman, he seemed to be hearing this concept for the first time. The woman had seen her neighbor set her home ablaze and had to be still in shock. Branson didn't know what Norris's problem was. Maybe he had a fire fetish.

"What? We're busy here, Branson."

"Alright, Beavis. Take your eyes off that fire long enough to get this woman into your cruiser. I'm going to get Kagan over here to talk to her. Are you okay, Miss…"

"Chadwick," she said. "Latecia Chadwick." She held up her baby. "This is Mazy. We were staying here while her daddy's overseas."

Bet they bring him home fast, Branson thought. "Wait here. I'm going to get the lead detective." To Norris, she said, "Get her into that cruiser and stop being a walking cliché. I'm gonna go talk to Kagan."

"Aren't you on restricted duty?" said Norris.

"Aren't you on active duty?" Branson turned and headed back toward the fire captain's car, a red sedan with red and white flashers on top. She circled around to the passenger side and knocked on the window. It came down to reveal a grinning Kagan. "Somehow I knew you'd show up. You tell Baker?"

"Fuck Baker," she said. "What's he gonna do? Send me to Special Investigations? You got a witness over there in Norris's car. The dumbass was letting her stand out there so her baby could get frostbite."

Kagan opened his door and climbed out. "Norris? Guy's got shit for brains. If it wasn't for Mendez, he'd shoot himself in the foot. Did he have a donut in his pie hole?"

"Must have eaten them all. Lady said she talked to you earlier. She says Armand Cole did this."

Kagan leaned into the car and said something to the fire captain. "Let's go before Norris starves her on top of freezing her to death."

Walking was already out of the question when Ralph had finished with Fyre. Now, though, it was imperative. One bullet had hit her in the shoulder. The other had cut a deep gash in her side. When the second bullet hit her, she had had enough presence of mind to play dead. He could still shoot her in the head to finish her. The man, though, had worked up such a rage that even chewing her up and spitting her out did nothing to lessen it. Dizzy, in agony, she looked around the room after Ralph left and spotted a ratty pair of painter's coveralls. If she could crawl over to them and get them on, she could escape.

It took ten minutes, during which time she knew she lost a lot of blood. She had to get out in front of the building before she fell unconscious. If she could get out on the sidewalk, she stood a chance of survival.

The trip down the stairwell took another ten minutes, with five more just to reach the main entrance to the building. That was when she spotted it, the MPD cruiser across the street in front of Kosar Stadium. She had to roll over onto her back to push the door open with her legs then work herself out into cold. Once through the door, she crawled out onto the sidewalk. Her strength nearly gone, she took one last deep breath.

And screamed.

The last thing she heard before passing out was a police officer shouting into his shoulder rig, calling for an ambulance.

The construction crews had thoroughly plowed the building site during the day. To Armand, the Walmart almost looked ready for business. Almost. PVC tubing big enough to crawl through lay in snow-covered stacks around the lot, and yellow construction vehicles sat motionless like frozen metal dinosaurs.

Monk waited for them, out in the cold, leaning against Rufus's Escalade and smoking a cigarette. Armand pulled alongside. He got out, and they began walking toward a large dumpster. "Gimme your phone and your gat."

Armand handed him the .45 and the phone. Monk pocketed the gun and tossed the phone into the dumpster. He reached into his overcoat and took out another phone. "We just bought it this afternoon, but Five-Oh's starting to sniff Ralph up good. Be careful. They may have a wire up on him." He took out another gun, a big one like the .45, but somewhat different. "Sig Sauer ten milimeter. Same kick as the magnum, so be careful."

"Not getting Baggy, am I?"

"Baggy will get got soon. Don't worry. Tomorrow, you get Baggy's apartment. You get the Wentworth tower crew. And you getting paid to take out that building. You're on your way, Armand. Play it right, and you'll be just like Rufus in a few years."

That made Armand smile.

"Blue Kia on the other side of the lot. It's registered to a front for Ralph, so it's insured if you get pulled over."

"What about the last job?"

"You sit tight at the safe house. We'll call you when we find Ralph."

"And then?"

Monk pointed his finger at Armand with his thumb up. "Then you do him." He brought his thumb down twice, making a shooting noise as he did so. "He probably won't even expect it."

CHAPTER 19

One could find Ralph Smithers in one of two places. The first everyone knew—The Phoenix Café in Holland Bay. Anyone wanting to do business with Smithers came to the Depression-era dump to meet with him or one of his lieutenants. Even King, the money man, went there once or twice a week to have come-to-Jesus moments with wayward street captains. Marco thought Estrada should do that, have a money man who could lay out the facts of life to their own crews.

As Marco drove down Lake past The Phoenix, he spotted three police cruisers parked along the side. He tried to look through the dirty windows into the dimly lit bar. The light had to be playing tricks with him. Two uniformed cops sat near the front window sipping coffee and scarfing The Phoenix's nasty chicken wings. For once, he felt sorry for a couple of police officers.

But not sorry enough to stop. If the cops had taken over The Phoenix, then Ralph would be gone. He turned around at the entrance to one of the working piers and headed back toward the Musgrave.

Driving over the Hauptmann Bridge into downtown, he looked for his second destination, the Silver Stiletto. Rumor had it Ralph Smithers spent his nights anymore boning a different stripper each night. The whores probably loved it, screwing the boss for a night's cash instead of getting their asses pinched out on the floor or tricking for some hideous old man in the private rooms.

Miguel told him to look for a white Ford Transit van, which he called "the pedo van." It would not have surprised Marco to learn that Ralph's crews called it that, too. The police, however, threatened to ruin that lead as well. An ambulance and an MPD cruiser sat out in front of the Stiletto, EMTs clad in cold-weather gear, working on someone on the sidewalk. A Harbortown patrolman stood nearby, watching and talking into his shoulder rig occasionally. That might or might not have anything to do with Smithers. Marco decided to pull into the print shop next door and wait. Out of curiosity, if not a need to know if he was wasting his time, he went into the print shop and asked the guy at the counter what was happening.

The man, a big black guy in an ink-stained apron, shrugged and said, "Couldn't tell you. One of our guys came in when some woman crawled out of the building next door and started screaming. Said she was a bloody mess. Cop swooped in on her after that and called the ambulance."

"Thanks," said Marco. "Hey, I'm supposed to meet someone, and I don't want to go into that titty bar next door, especially with all those cops out front." He'd only seen one, and that one would probably follow the ambulance to nearby St. Paul's Hospital over by Monticello State. "Mind if I park out front for a bit?"

"Knock yourself out," said the print man. "Haven't had any business all day."

Marco went back out to the car, fired up the motor to keep the heater running, and turned on WTAE to listen to the Cavs game out of Cleveland. So the night wouldn't be a total waste if Smithers didn't show.

The redhead with two bullet wounds came into St. Paul's ER around 7:30 p.m. Medics had her wounds stabilized and plasma going by the time the crash cart made its way to an open operating theater.

Two doctors went to work on her. They already knew she had a serious shoulder wound from a large-caliber weapon and a less serious flesh wound in her side. The orderlies finished stripping the dirty painter's coveralls from her. The EMT's had cut off the top half, which had been soaked in blood by the time the police called for rescue.

"I can't tell," said one of the doctors. "Is she bleeding vaginally or rectally?"

"Someone did a number on her before shooting her," said a nurse.

"Turn her over," said the other doctor. "Gently."

Two orderlies worked the redhead onto her stomach, careful to keep the dressing on her wounds from twisting too much.

The other doctor whistled. "Lot of damage at both ends."

"Do we need informed consent to go in?"

"Does that look consensual to you? We're already bound to treat her for gunshot wounds. I don't think whoever did this to her was chased off by a gunman."

"You haven't met my ex-husband," said a nurse. That produced some weak laughter.

"Let's go in," said the second doctor. "We'll do two rape kits."

"But if we're wrong…"

"She called for help when she spotted a police car," said the second doc. "All evidence points to this being the same assault."

"Do it," said the first doc. "But let's get started on those wounds first. I don't want her bleeding out."

"He had a girl staying with him," said Latecia Chadwick, "maybe seventeen, eighteen years old. I could see the way they acted together that he loved her."

Branson sat in the back of the cruiser with Chadwick and her baby. Kagan sat up front in the driver's seat. Somewhere out in the cold, Norris sulked. Neither Branson nor Kagan particularly gave a shit about Norris. He only had a slot in Holland Bay because Baker had moved Murdoch into plainclothes.

"Have you seen the girl since the fire?" asked Branson.

"No," she said, "but that fat kid who's always on the corner came by and pounded on the door this afternoon. I heard screaming, then nothing. A couple of guys from Comcast or Verizon or something came by later."

Two guys in a van and coveralls, thought Branson, came by. Chadwick had simply assigned the cable or phone company to them in her mind. Screaming, then nothing, then the anonymous utility guys. The "fat kid" was definitely Reginald "Baggy" Anderson, she thought, the kid Murdoch had in custody at the station. Petrocelli had told her Armand Cole had been chasing him down the street with a gun. She caught Kagan's gaze as he looked up from his note-taking. From his look, she knew he'd either reached the same conclusion or something very similar. Someone in Smithers's organization was taking care of Armand Cole. And Baggy Anderson had found himself on the bad side of Ralph Smithers, if not someone else, in Smithers's inner circle.

"Do you know the fat kid's name?" asked Kagan. He knew it was Baggy. Branson knew it was Baggy. But that was deduction. Judges and prosecutors liked personal knowledge, like the statement of a neighbor.

"I heard some of his crew call him 'Baggy,'" said Latecia. "He was a disgusting person. Used to hit on me when he lived in that apartment Armand and the girl moved into. Made me sick just to hear his voice."

Kagan began scribbling furiously. They not only had a lead on Cole, Branson realized, but they could build a shaky but usable case against Baggy Anderson for the murder of the girl. All they needed was her body, which the anonymous utility guys probably spirited away, and Armand Cole to tell them her name.

Someone knocked on Kagan's window. He rolled it down to reveal an impeccably dressed black man, one who would not look out of place in a Holland Island office, if not downtown.

"I'm Rufus King," he said rather sharply to Kagan. "I own this building. You mind telling me when the hell you were going to tell me my tenants were burned out of their homes?" When he spotted Chadwick, he said, "Hello, Latecia. Is there anything I can do to help you?"

The ambulance and the police officer left with the injured woman about fifteen minutes after Marco had settled into his car in front of the print shop. He decided to risk going inside the Silver Stilleto. If he understood the layout of the building, one of the rear entrances had to open into the alley behind the building itself. He could pay his cover fee, wander in, and force his way into the office. Get Smithers right in his office, and be outside and on the road before any of the staff could respond.

He killed the Hyundai's motor and decided to risk it. He had taken two steps when he saw three big men trudge into the parking lot dressed for the cold. One of them had a pipe he beat into his free hand. They headed straight for the Hyundai.

Marco took that as his cue to leave and jumped back into the car. Only now, the Korean piece of shit wouldn't start. He couldn't have flooded the thing. Cars didn't flood anymore.

One of the men smashed his driver's side window and yanked open the door.

A severe beating for Marco followed.

Unlike in most American cities, violent crime seldom happened on Monticello's Martin Luther King Drive. A continuation of Inland Boulevard and the Inland Parkway, the wide avenue cut across the island from the Thurman Reed Bridge out of downtown, bisecting Freedomville and East Holland, the black and white affluent neighborhoods respectively, and ended at Port Jones, formerly a shipyard and now the new Port of Monticello. Violent crime along MLK usually meant a drunk driver taking a swipe at a cop in lieu of blowing into a Breathalyzer.

Tonight, in the offices of King Properties, it meant Goose waiting for Rufus King to show up. He held a gun in his fist, a nice, big .45 with a suppressor on it. Noisy, but not enough for anyone outside to hear it. He sat behind King's desk, a big oak thing once owned by Byron Roosevelt, the city's first modern police commissioner. With the lights off, the only illumination came off the flood-lit high rises across the sound in downtown. Goose could only sit and listen. He'd done it often enough, working for Ralph.

The freight elevator clanged and rumbled to life. At this hour, it could only mean someone who worked for Ralph. Or even Rufus. That nigger had been building his own crew behind Ralph's back for a while. Goose wasn't even sure they could trust Lew Steinberg, Ralph's favorite lawyer.

The elevator came to a stop with a loud clunk. In the silence of the building, Goose could hear its doors open, hear the door to the elevator foyer open into the corridor. Moments later, the alarm beeped as someone tapped in the code to the outside door. He raised his gun and aimed directly at the door to Rufus's inner office. He fired as it swung inward.

The door caught the bullet. He caught sight of Monk's face as he fired again. It was the last thing he saw before Monk's bullet plunged into his forehead.

Heather Leary, formerly known as Fyre, awoke to the smell of rubbing alcohol and the sounds of medical equipment beeping. She felt pain. Ralph had torn her up from both ends. That was nothing compared to the pain in her shoulder. Right now, it was a dull, persistent ache, but she knew she would be in agony as soon as the painkillers wore off.

A nurse came in to check on her, a black lady in her forties. She smiled when she saw that Heather's eyes were open. "You're awake. Good."

"I can't move my arm," said Heather.

"Not surprised. That monster shot you in the shoulder." She handed her a glass of water. "Listen, I heard what happened to you, how you crawled out onto the street. You're very brave."

She didn't feel brave. If she were brave, she would not have been working at the Silver Stiletto for easy money, giving her body to Ralph Smithers in exchange for better shifts and preferential treatment. "I'm not brave."

"You feel like talking to a cop?"

She knew she should, but she couldn't risk it being "Officer Murphy." He was just another user like Ralph. "Is there a female cop around? I'll talk to her."

"I'll go see."

Five minutes later, another black woman, this one slender in a police uniform with a chattering radio mounted on her shoulder, came and sat next to her bed. "Hi, I'm Rosanne." Her nametag said "Ptl. Johnson." She had a Harbortown patch on her sleeve, which meant she came from nearby Settlers Commons. "Looks like you had a rough night."

Well, no shit, Sherlock. "A man raped me for almost an hour, then shot me."

Johnson had her notepad out. "Did they do a rape kit on you?"

"I don't know. I just woke up."

"If you were unconscious, and there was any damage down there, they probably did a kit while they worked on you."

Heather nodded. She only knew they'd done something to her side and her shoulder and that she did not feel right inside down below.

"Do you know who assaulted you?"

Did she? Oh, yes. She was through being used as a blow-up doll. "His name is Ralph Smithers, and he owns the Silver Stiletto."

Johnson looked up from her notebook, her eyes wide. "Did you say 'Ralph Smithers?'"

"Yes. Ralph Smithers."

"I see."

***

The last thing Branson wanted to do was stand out in five-degree weather with a bunch of fire hoses spraying a nearby building. Unfortunately, Chadwick had told her that Armand Cole, gas can in hand, had warned her to get out of the building. If that didn't scream arson, Branson would be damned if she knew what did. So now she and Kagan had to confer with the fire captain on the scene.

The captain, an older guy named Parcells, said his crews had even found the motivation for the fire. One of the lockers in the basement, where the fire started, had somehow remained intact. When the flames had been doused, they found two garbage bags full of crystal meth and a box of baggies full of pot.

"The Estradas making a move on Ralph Smithers?" asked Kagan when Parcells gave him the rundown.

"I thought your witness said the guy was black," said Parcells. "I'm not up on who does what in the drug trade in this city, but aren't the Estradas strictly Mexican?"

"Yeah," said Branson, "but something's happening. Smithers's top enforcer got dumped on Pier Nine this afternoon. A couple hours later, one of the Estrada boys got himself clipped outside a corner store."

"Jesus."

King approached the trio and said, "Well, you guys have any reason why two of my buildings burned down in as many days?"

"And who are you?" said Parcells, clearly not liking a civilian interrupting him.

"Rufus King. I own this building." His gaze settled on the charred hulk where the apartment complex had stood. "Well, owned it. What are you people doing?"

Branson frowned at the mention of the other building behind this one. Oh, she, the fire marshal, and the insurance guys were going to have a field day with this guy tomorrow. "Mr. King, I understand your concern. But remember, this is not exactly the happiest neighborhood. Even with more patrol, we…"

A loud crack interrupted her. She watched as Kagan's leg collapsed under him and spun him around. Another crack sounded and a hole appeared in Parcell's forehead. King flattened himself on the ground as a third shot sounded.

Branson and two uniforms took off running toward the figure across the street as it dropped a rifle. Whoever it was sprinted down an alleyway. Branson reached it first, got into three-point stance, and fired her weapon twice. The man at the end of the alley jerked once and limped around the far corner. She caught sight of his face before he disappeared.

"Smithers." She charged down the alleyway. Before she reached the end, she heard a car door slam and tires squeal. She didn't even need to clear the other side of the alley to know Smithers had gotten away.

"Sonofabitch!"

Her headache from the day before returned as she tried to catch her breath in the cold night air.

Monk groaned. There was no way out of this one. He needed to get to a hospital, assuming he could even call someone. His side burned from where the bullet had hit him. Slowly, he pulled himself to his feet and reached the light switch. When the lights went on, he saw that it was both better and worse. Goose lay in Rufus's chair, part of his skull and brain splattered all over that nice picture window behind the desk.

He pulled his cell phone and hit a speed-dial number. Rufus's phone went to voicemail after five rings. Either that boy was plowing Janiece some more, or something bad had happened to him. He didn't want to think what. Time to dial number two on the emergency list. A groggy female voice answered after two rings. "Hullo?"

"Janiece, it's Monk. I just got shot. Goose is dead. I'm at the office."

"Is Rufus there?" The girl sounded genuinely scared. Maybe she was more than just a gold digger.

"No," he said, struggling to keep from passing out. "Here's what I need you to do. Call this number and ask for Armand." He gave her the phone number. "Tell him where I'm at. Call Steinberg and tell him we got a big mess to clean up at the office. Don't give him details unless he asks. You know the drill. Where you at, baby?"

"Rufus and I were staying at a hotel tonight."

"Smart. Don't even tell me until Ralph's got. Steinberg will know the right people to call. And Janiece?"

"Yes?"

"Armand may need to take me to Pier Nine with Goose."

There was a long pause at the other end. "That bad?"

His vision was going dark now. "That...bad. Tell Rufus... Tell him...I tried."

Everything went black.

CHAPTER 20

Her name was Linda, and she was a cousin to the Estrada boys. Marco had tried to date her a few times, but Linda never dated a colleague. Like Marco, she had become a favorite shooter for the organization. Long and lean, able to pass as black or Anglo if she worked it, she used stealth and surprise to hit her targets. Lately, she had been taking work in other cities for other operations. One of the Five Families had even called her, though she turned it down. Working for the Italians in New York was akin to doing hits for a reality show.

"So," she said, sliding up to him dressed all in black, a pool cue in her hand, "how'd it go?"

Marco looked up from his second Cuervo. "What do you think?"

Linda laughed. "He's a slippery one, that Smithers. Rey put me on him at least four times. He always managed to dodge me long enough for Rey to calm down and call it off."

He downed the rest of his drink and signaled for another. "So I'm wasting my time?"

Linda flashed that sexy smile Marco still dreamed of from time to time. "This isn't a temper tantrum by Rey this time. Miguel wants blood for his big brother. And I hear Johnny B. asked you to take out that weird-looking one that's always hanging around Smithers."

Johnny B., aka Juan Pablo Bosco, had summoned Marco to his

perch in a Huron Junction coffee shop not long after his nephew, Miguel Estrada, had given Marco his marching orders. One did not refuse a summons from Johnny B. The man was a god to most of the Estradas's crews.

"Goose. Ugly motherfucker. Got my ass kicked trying to pick him off at that titty bar."

"They must be desperate. Usually, Ralph Smithers uses another guy, Dmitri. Psycho bastard."

"Isn't that the one they found on the pier?"

"Probably. Smithers has been dumping so many bodies on that pier we could open a funeral home there."

The pier. Pier 9. It had become synonymous with gang murder in Monticello. Marco could not remember the last body to end up there that had a killer attached to it. It was, in fact, an open secret that Harbortown and the Port Police had been sending the bodies off to the morgue without any Homicide detective assigned. People began calling it a "self-cleaning oven." Someone died one week, his or her killer ended up on Pier 9 the next.

"Think any bodies will show up there tonight?" asked Marco.

"You want to get Smithers?"

"Yes."

She made a shooting gesture with her thumb and index finger. "There's an abandoned Big Boy on Pier Ten. Hide out there, and you'll see something on Pier Nine eventually."

The phone rang about nine-thirty. Armand, back at the safe house in Shawnee Heights, was watching reruns of *South Park* when he answered. "Yo."

"Armand, do you know who this is?" The voice was female, familiar.

"Ralph's woman?"

"Used to be. This is Janiece. I'm calling for Monk. He's been hurt. He's at Rufus's office. There's a dead man with him."

On television, Cartman was ripping Kyle for being a Jew. Kyle called him a fat ass.

"Where's Ralph?"

"I'm just relaying a message. Besides, didn't Rufus give you a job to do with Ralph?" Before Armand could answer, she added, "Monk's been shot. He got Goose in the process. Now Ralph is trying to kill Rufus."

Armand didn't say anything. He couldn't.

"I know Rufus wants you to do Ralph tonight. Monk needs you first. Go armed. Take the back way up like you did today. Call Lew Steinberg when you get there so he can send in a cleanup crew. Can you do that for me?"

"How do I know you're not setting me up?"

It was Janiece's turn to be silent.

"I know Monk," he said. "I know Rufus. I even know Ralph. I don't know you, and you telling me Monk is shot."

"Armand, I can't make you trust me. All I can tell you is Monk is hurt and needs you. And Armand?"

"I'm here."

"Monk says you may have to take both him and Goose to Pier Nine."

Damn, thought Armand. *Monk dead?* Goose was hard enough to believe. He was older than Ralph. "Understood."

"Armand?"

"Yeah?"

"If you find Ralph, shoot him twice, one time for me." She hung up.

Armand wondered if he would survive the night. If he did, would Ralph or Mr. King?

Branson watched as they loaded Kagan into an ambulance. Kagan had lost a lot of blood, but he looked up at her, giving her the thumbs-up sign.

"Want me to tell your wife you'll be later than expected?" she said.

Kagan tried to laugh, but no sound came out. Finally, he croaked, "You keep her busy like you been doing, she won't notice." The paramedics slid his stretcher into the ambulance.

"Branson," said a familiar voice, "I thought I told you to go home."

She whirled to see Baker, hands jammed in his pockets, Murdoch at his side, walking toward her. Baker was probably marching, but on his short legs and with his hands in his coat, he looked more like he was waddling. Murdoch wore the gloves from his uniform and clutched a Styrofoam cup in his hands.

"I did go home," she said. "You said nothing about coming back, sir."

"I understand Captain Parcells is gone," said Baker. "Good man. He'll be missed. How is Kagan?"

"I think he seems happier since he took the bullet. Could be the painkillers, though."

Baker grunted. "Landlord still here?"

Branson turned to where Rufus King chatted with a pair of uniforms and a firefighter, most likely Parcells's second-in-command. "Mr. King? Could we see you a moment?"

Mr. King broke off from his group and approached Branson's group alone. "What is this all about?"

For the first time, it occurred to her that King had no entourage. A property owner like him driving an expensive car and wearing expensive clothes would have at least had a driver. For a situation like this, he most certainly would have had his lawyer in tow.

"Mr. King," she said, "this is Captain Baker. He commands the new Holland Bay Squad." Settlers Commons had not officially changed the name of Special Investigations yet, but Branson decided a little rebranding was in order anyway. "You say you know who shot Captain Parcells and Detective Kagan earlier."

"That's right," said King. "Ralph Smithers."

Baker gave a frown Branson knew all too well. "And why would a slum lord such as yourself be in the crosshairs of a fine upstanding citizen like Mr. Smithers?"

"Captain, if you check my record, you will find that I have a less-than-sterling past. The truth is I used to run with one of Smithers's crews when I was younger. Since I got out of prison, I've been working hard. I manage properties. I've bought a number of them. But the nature of real estate in this city means that you often buy in places like this." He turned and gestured toward the remains of his building across the street. "And people like Smithers love to use buildings like mine to do their business. Smithers is angry because I have plans for this property. Big plans. You can't sell dope in those numbers out of a gentrified, rehabbed building full of hipsters. Even that derelict that burned last night could have been rehabbed into a respectable block of condos, perfect for anyone wanting to work out in Gates Park or over on the Island."

As if to illustrate his point, the Monorail slid by, a late-night run out to Glenn-Armstrong Airport.

"But I also have tenants here who can't live anywhere else," King continued. "What about them? If I renovated, they would have had time to move. I can probably rebuild now, and I fully expect you people to work that angle. It is arson after all. But in the meantime, I've got people who had nothing to do with the drug activity on this corner who need a place to stay."

Branson immediately thought of Latecia Chadwick.

Baker started clapping slowly. "Nice speech, Mr. King. Are you the one the *Herald-Star*'s website called 'the Mayor of Holland Bay?'"

King smiled a politician's smile. "Captain, if that's what the people around here want to call me, I can't help it. This is where I grew up. I want to help bring it back to life. Is it true that you inherited a dead-end squad?"

"Hey," said Branson and Murdoch almost in unison.

"And that your job is now to clean this place up?" His cell phone rang. He looked down at the screen. "I have to take this." With the phone up to his ear, he said, "My brother, just talking to the police about my building."

As he walked away, Murdoch said, "I think we've been dismissed."

Baker took Branson by the arm and pulled her away. "Listen, since you won't obey your doctor, let alone your captain, I need you to run over to St. Paul's. There's a rape victim over there. Her attacker shot her twice. Girl crawled out onto the street while bleeding out. EMTs got to her just in time. I want you to talk to her."

"Sir, what about...?"

The rubbery smile reappeared. "Smithers? Glad you asked. Our girl, Heather Leary, regained consciousness and told a Harbortown uniform that Smithers himself did the deed. We have DNA and everything. Happened at the Silver Stiletto."

So Janiece hadn't lied. Armand found Monk on the floor in a puddle of his own blood. Goose lay in Rufus's big high-back chair at a strange angle, blood and brain splattered all over the picture window, marring the view of downtown Monticello and the Thurman Reed Bridge.

Armand knelt down and touched Monk's neck. He had a weak pulse, and Armand could hear faint breathing. He shook him. "Monk? Monk? It's me. Armand."

Monk mumbled something Armand could not hear. He'd have to deal with Monk later. For now...

Yeah, Goose was dead. The funny-looking man stared back at him with a chunk of his head missing. The bullet must have ricocheted off his skull. It had lodged in the window frame, instead of hitting the glass.

Armand wanted to spit on the corpse, but he knew they'd find DNA if he did. Goose's phone rang. Armand grabbed it and saw the last number Ralph had used to call him. "Yo."

There was a roar in the background, like whoever was calling was in a car. He also heard heavy breathing.

"Who this?" The voice sounded ragged but familiar. The dull

background roar told Armand the caller was driving.

"Ralph? This Armand. You looking for Goose?"

"Yeah. How you get this phone? And why ain't you answering yours?"

"Had to ditch mine. Got some bad news, bro. Goose is dead."

Branson badged her way into St. Paul's and made her way to where Heather Leary now rested. The nurse went in ahead and woke her to see if she could talk. Branson chatted with Officer Johnson while she waited.

"She wants to kill that man," said Johnson. "Most people I meet like that, they're scared at first. Someone forced their way inside you, you know?"

Branson nodded but wasn't sure how to respond. She had dealt with few rape victims herself. The closest she had ever come to an assault ended in justifiable homicide. "What about this one?"

"She's pissed. She works at a strip club called the Silver Stiletto, upscale place down by Kosar Stadium. My guess is she's been throwing the higher paying clientele and the boss a little extra attention, and this guy decided he could have all he wanted."

"If you knew what this guy is like, you wouldn't be surprised."

"Smithers, right? Heard the name. Heavy hitter in the dope trade. Right?"

"*The* heavy hitter." And more, she thought to herself. The Great White Whale...

"She'll see you now," said the nurse. "Try not to overtax her. She's still groggy from painkillers and surgery."

The sight of the unfortunate woman made Branson wince. Heather Leary had been the redhead she'd caught with Murdoch earlier. Since then, she had been tortured, no two ways about it. She was probably used to a certain level of abuse or mistreatment, perhaps even considering it an occupational hazard. The eyes, however, told Branson those days were over. There might be an assault charge or two in the coming months if this woman could not find a channel for her rage. Branson had the perfect target.

She took a seat next to the bed. "Good evening, Miss Leary. I'm Detective Branson, Special Investigations. We've taken a singular interest in your case. You and I have a common enemy."

Leary gave Branson the once over. "I doubt it. You look like you eat men for dinner and spit out their bones for breakfast."

That made her feel guilty about Jerry, but she pushed it aside. "Well, I don't take a lot of crap off people. But Ralph Smithers occupies a unique place on our squad's shit list. Sex Crimes would be more than happy to take him down for you. Surgery allowed the doctors to do a rape kit on you, and you gave us a name. For them, that's a slam dunk. Let's just say my captain... Well, all of us, really...have more motivation than most cops in Monticello to take Ralph Smithers down. You should take advantage of that."

"I'd like to kill him," said Leary. "Is it too late to call it self-defense?"

"Unfortunately. Were it me, I wouldn't have told a cop what you just told me." She leaned in a little closer, elbows resting on her knees. She set aside a recorder on the nightstand. "Mind if I record our little chat? Then you tell me what happened in your own words."

"It's my word against his."

"It's his word against yours and the DNA he deposited inside you. You asked for a Plan B pill, didn't you?"

"I'm on the pill. Have to be in our trade."

That was another thing Branson would not have mentioned in Leary's position, but then she wasn't the one who'd been attacked. "If you're good with it, I'd like to begin."

Leary nodded. Branson thumbed the recorder, stated her name, time, and place, and had Leary state her name for the record. Then Leary began.

"A couple of cops came sniffing around the Stiletto this after-noon..."

That would have been her and Murdoch.

"One of them asked specifically for Ralph Smithers."

"Which one?"

"The black one. Murphy."

"What did he look like?" Heather Leary described a tall, slim black man, similar to Murdoch. Branson decided not to correct her. "Then what happened?"

"Ralph slipped out and told me to stall him for a few minutes, that there'd be a few extra bucks in it for me."

"That's when Ralph left?"

"Yeah. Then I realized I could get in trouble for lying to a cop if they were after Ralph. Big deal like that, and I stepped in the way? So, I persuaded Murphy not to tell anyone. I didn't know Ralph was going to come back and try to kill me."

Branson did not like where this was going. "How did you persuade 'Murphy?'"

Leary smiled, but it contained no warmth or humor. She closed her eyes and laughed weakly. "I gave that sonofabitch the best damn blowjob he'd ever had."

That stoked Branson's rage at Murdoch anew. She somehow contained her anger, but her teeth started grinding badly. She was going to have Greg Murdoch's balls when she got back. But first... "Did he demand it?"

"No, I just told him I didn't want to get into trouble and went down on him. He didn't protest."

Branson took out her notepad and thumbed the recorder. "I think maybe I should write this down instead. Do you mind?"

"What's going to happen to Murphy?"

"Never mind what I'm going to do to him. All you need to know is you're not going to face bribing an officer. Let's do a formal statement against Ralph Smithers, shall we?"

"Fine. Detective?"

"Yes."

"I really don't hold it against Murphy. He's no worse than those idiots I dance for in the VIP rooms."

"That's bad enough." She began filling out the formal statement form, writing it up as a complaint for sexual assault and assault with a deadly weapon. "I'll write this up and have you sign it if you're good with what I wrote. Fair enough?"

It was. Heather Leary began outlining the nightmare in earnest.

"I told Ralph the cops were gone," she said. "He told me I could earn a little extra money if I just let him punish me for his bad day. That's when I knew I was in trouble..."

"Wise idea," said Lew Steinberg, "telling Ralph you needed to move the bodies."

Armand recognized Steinberg immediately. He had been Ralph's go-to when one of his crews got into trouble. Apparently, he also worked for Mr. King. The lawyer arrived ten minutes after Armand and Ralph had spoken. During that time, Monk expired. He'd lost too much blood, and there was no way to handle that chest wound anyway without an awkward trip to the ER.

Well, Officer, he liked to clean his gun in the office, but he tripped over an Ottoman and fell on it. Never mind that it was Goose's gun that killed Monk.

Two guys arrived from Ralph's strip club. They usually drove the van. Steinberg did not say a word while they rolled Monk up in an old carpet and wrapped Goose's ruined head in a towel. They would just roll Goose down in the chair.

As soon as they left with Monk's body, Armand said, "Ain't you supposed to stay away from shit like this?"

Steinberg gripped Armand's shoulder. "I like you, Cole. Ralph and Rufus both speak highly of you." He put his arm across Armand's shoulder and gestured widely at the blood-spattered picture window. "You're right. I normally do. It's how I'm part of the inner circle while being able to plead ignorance. But, you see, things have come to a head. As of this moment, you are the most powerful man in Monticello."

Armand stared out at the glittering view of downtown. At nearly 10 p.m. on a weeknight, most of the buildings were no longer floodlit beyond the three towers on Gotham Square. Window lights still burned, and aircraft beacons still winked red, but downtown Monticello had fallen asleep.

Well, Armand knew better. A storm was raging through two, maybe three boroughs tonight.

"You said you would meet Ralph later," said Steinberg. "Correct?"

"After I dump the bodies on the pier," said Armand.

"You have a choice. Rufus King will probably ask you to go to prison for him. There's an APB out on you for trying to kill Baggy Anderson. I'll negotiate that away for you, but you will have to cop to another charge."

"But Rufus said..."

"Rufus says a lot of things. And he usually means them, but this situation is fluid. Rufus will most likely see to it that you get the same education he received and groom you to rise in the organization. Still..."

Armand figured out where Steinberg was going. "Rufus ain't street."

"No, Cole, he's not. He hasn't been for a very long time. If you choose Rufus, you will do time, but you may also find a very different life ahead of you. I'll do what I can to shepherd that along, but the choice is yours. Now, Ralph, on the other hand..."

Ralph. What, exactly, had Ralph ever done to him? Put him under Dmitri? Armand was now Dmitri. "Ralph is street."

"Ralph is street. You'll still do time, and like Rufus, Ralph will appreciate that. You would come out of prison with credibility and the big man's trust. Ralph can promise you big things, just as Rufus can. Ralph, however, knows only the streets. He can't see beyond the Game. The choice is yours, Cole."

The freight elevator clunked to a very loud stop, which meant the two thugs with Monk's body had reached the parking level.

"What about them?" asked Armand.

Steinberg smiled. "They know only that two members of this organization shot each other in Rufus King's office. No more, no less. You will take the bodies to Pier Nine. What you do next is up to you. Think about it, Cole. The future of this organization is in your hands."

As the crew came back to retrieve Goose, Armand wondered if he should call Mr. King after he left.

Branson stormed into the squad room, notepad in hand. "Anyone who gets Smithers, I want him. I'm questioning that motherfucker with a broom handle and a pair of garden shears."

She marched into Baker's office and dropped the notepad in front of him. "Wake a judge. I need a warrant for that sonofabitch. Rape, attempted murder, and assault with a deadly weapon."

Baker picked up the notepad and scanned it. As he read, he nodded with approval. "Nice work, Branson. How's it feel to be a real cop again?"

"Fine. Where's Murdoch?"

"Breakroom. Why?"

She turned and stalked into the break room. Murdoch was stirring creamer into a cup of coffee. She put his hand on her shoulder and spun him around. Her fist connected with his testicles. "You sick sonofabitch. That's for Heather Leary."

"Who?" he grunted, bending over.

"Hope you liked that blowjob she gave you."

When Murdoch finally met Branson's gaze, he looked like a man who knew he was truly screwed.

Marco left his car on Pier 10 as Linda suggested. However, for anything that happened on Pier 9, he would need to get closer. If Smithers showed, he needed to hide almost on top of him. So the car went behind the abandoned Big Boy, out of sight of Lake

Avenue. Marco began the walk over to Pier 9, rifle at his side, away from the road. The walk along Lake would be the most dangerous part. If a police cruiser happened by, just the act of walking between two abandoned piers would be considered suspicious.

Like Pier 10, Pier 9 had its own building, a small garage once used for service vehicles. Chances were, it was unlocked. Homeless people liked to camp out in such buildings in warmer weather. Marco found the door locked with a simple padlock. He drew his pistol and blew the lock open. Like anyone would care about breaking and entering with all the corpses that got dumped on this pier.

Slipping inside, he found an abandoned car part or something like it and shoved it against the door. Pitch black inside, he had to tread carefully. It wouldn't do to trip and break his arm just as he was about to finish off Smithers. He stepped up to the garage door, close enough to see out over the rest of the pier, but far enough back to avoid being seen by anyone who showed up.

CHAPTER 21

Armand recognized the white Ford Transit brought by the two guys from the Stiletto. He'd ridden in it with Dmitri on a few occasions. They used it to pick up meth from the lab on Packard Lane, as well as other substances from Ralph's other connects. He now understood that this vehicle delivered bodies to Pier 9.

Whenever Armand drove the battered sedans he'd either stolen or was given by Monk or Dmitri, he noticed the police eyeballing him. It didn't surprise him. If you were black in Monticello, you had to have a Holland Island vehicle, like an Audi or a Benz. A black guy in a delivery van?

Well, this was Monticello. Police didn't give the working man a second look. Not unless he parked that delivery van outside an elementary school at the wrong time of day. Half an hour after he and the two guys from the Stiletto loaded Goose and Monk's corpses, he swung the Ford Transit onto Pier 9 and drove out to the middle.

As he unrolled Monk from the carpet, Armand felt the weight of Monk's gun in his coat. They'd left Goose's on him since he'd shot Monk. Armand moved the van a few feet, then wheeled Goose in the chair where he had died and dumped him out into the snow. Flipping the chair on its side to keep it from sliding around, he jumped out of the back of the van and slammed the door.

***

Marco watched the van, the infamous "pedo van," push its way through the snow onto the pier. Some kid got out, opened the back, and began dumping two bodies. One of them was hatless. Marco recognized him as Monk, one of Smithers's senior lieutenants.

The kid pushed a second one out into the snow on an office chair. He yanked off the towel that wrapped the corpse's head, then dumped him into the snow. Marco couldn't be sure, but it looked like Goose, Smithers's near-constant companion. Either Smithers was cleaning house, or someone had tried to stage a coup within his operation. The kid threw the chair back into the van, then returned to look over the bodies.

If he couldn't hit Smithers, maybe Marco could send him a message. He raised his rifle, sited the kid, and fired through the glass.

When the gunshot cracked and hit the snow near him, Armand spun and drew Monk's pistol, pelting the garage door with bullets. The shots from inside stopped. He made his way over to the garage and found the door closed but unlocked. He pushed it open, causing something against the door to scrape loudly. No gunfire erupted.

Armand passed a flashlight over the interior of the garage. Near the main overhead door, a man lay bleeding on the concrete. His breathing was shallow. Armand drew Monk's gun from his pocket and fired a round into the man's head. He'd watch the news tomorrow to find out who he was.

The dead man looked vaguely Hispanic, suggesting he was with the Estradas. Armand smiled when he saw the rifle. Then he ran back outside to ditch his own rifle and move the van over to Pier 10.

"What a clusterfuck," said Baker as they all gathered in the breakroom. He looked over at Murdoch. "What's the matter with you? You look like you ate some of Branson's cooking."

Murdoch looked green. "I'm fine, Captain."

"What are you smiling about," Baker said to Branson.

"More like something that ate him," she said with a smirk.

"Okay, here's what I have so far. First off, if you weren't aware of it already, Detective Kagan was shot out at the fire on Eastern." Baker let that sink in for a moment. "He's at University with a leg wound."

"Any idea who shot him?" asked Murdoch.

"Smithers," said Branson. "I managed to shoot him in the leg before he got away."

"Seems he's got a hard-on for the building's landlord," said Baker. "Which would explain two fires in two days quite nicely."

"With all due respect, Captain, but if I see him, restricted duty or no, I'm emptying a magazine into that motherfucker."

The room became very quiet for a moment. Baker cleared his throat. "Anyway, Friedman's on her way in to help out. Now, here's what we have. Taggart's last surviving CI is now in custody going through detox in Norwalk. Kagan told me before he left that his lovely bride will try to get him into Fair Oaks Center in the morning to ride the rest of it out."

"She can try," said Petrocelli. "You know the prosecutor's a major prick."

"All we can ask, then, and lean on the Sheriff to keep him out of the general population. Lt. Kearny's people have picked Packard Lane clean. Looks like they found a few things that tie it directly to either Dmitri Reagan or Ralph Smithers. Murdoch, you got Midtown to confiscate Reagan's computer, and Harbortown's been eyeballing the Silver Stiletto since that stripper crawled out onto the street." He smiled faintly. "I'd like to meet her. That is one tough chick if she can take a bullet and still finger her assailant. Most people just want to curl up and hide."

"A forty-five-caliber slug makes a powerful last straw, Captain," said Branson. "She'd already been used once earlier that day." She gave Murdoch a dirty look.

With a sharp look of his own at Branson, Baker again cleared his throat. "We now have Reginald 'Baggy' Anderson in custody. Mrs. Kagan and a PD are both en route to work out a deal for Mr. Anderson to spill his considerable guts. He doesn't look or sound smart enough to have done it, but he definitely knows who. He's got a tiny little hard-on of his own for Armand Cole. Murdoch?"

Murdoch stretched and managed to regain his composure. "Tera from the IT Department over at Settlers Commons went through the surveillance that came from that gas station out on Amherst Pike. We compared the guy in the video to mug shots and came up with a positive ID on Cole. His last known address was at his mother's on Cumberland. I paid her a visit. She told me he'd moved over to Serievo to Dmitri Reagan's place. Since Reagan was dead, Narcotics and Midtown needed only the manager's permission to enter and search. Dmitri was not the brightest computer user, liked to store passwords for his email. That, in turn, led me and Branson to the Stiletto, where Ms. Leary informed me that Smithers had been there, but had left the building. I suspect she was stalling me."

Branson started chewing her lower lip.

"Two hours later," Murdoch continued, "she crawled down from one of the upstairs offices, all of which are vacant, and out onto the street where the officer watching the place found her."

"All right," said Baker. "What I want to know is this: Do we have anything solid tying Reagan or Smithers to the deaths of the Carciniras or this Doby Clark?"

"Plink's testimony," said Branson. "Maybe Anderson's, if he's reliable and can manage to string a whole sentence together."

"Has anyone seen this Armand Cole?"

Head shakes all around the table.

"Do we agree, though, that if we take down Smithers, we avert a drug war in this town and can probably close the books on these cases after the fact?"

Murdoch drummed his fingers on the table. "You do that, and Carter over in Homicide will probably want to kiss you for it."

"I'll pass," said Baker.

"Would someone tell me why Fox Eighteen's reporter waylaid me outside?" Ana Friedman marched into the break room, looking like she'd stood outside for twenty minutes. "I barely got to my car before that prick shoved a mic in my face."

"You got what?" said Baker. "Why aren't you down on Eastern?"

"Someone tipped off WQIQ that we were working on something big. I just spent twenty minutes trying to no-comment my way out of an interview." Friedman blew into her hands to warm them. "I know there's a lot of shit going down in this city, and I know we're working on most of it, but why is that van out front? Should they be up on Eastern?"

"Murdoch," said Branson. "His wife does traffic for two radio stations and WQIQ. Probably tipped off the newsroom."

All eyes went to Murdoch, who looked down at his shoes. "I'm gonna kill that bitch."

The shots fired at Armand made the beginnings of the perfect picture to leave the police. The Estrada shooter had fired at him as he unrolled Monk, which left bullets all around where Monk lay. He backed the chair out from under Goose so that it would look like he and Monk shot each other after killing the shooter. Goose's gun went into his cold, dead hand.

There was the problem of the snow and the tracks, but Armand wasn't going for realism. He was going for confusion. By the time the medical examiner and CSI team arrived, Armand would be someplace warm and far from the piers. Now, though, he needed to move the van. Even this worked in his favor.

Once the motor started, Armand deliberately slid and spun on his way back to Lake Road. Hanging a right, he drove down to Pier 10 where a closed Big Boy restaurant stood. The Big Boy had moved over to Pier 4 a few years earlier. A car, probably the shooter's, sat behind the building, as well. That worked for Armand. He left the van behind the empty diner, left his phone on the passenger seat to keep it from distracting him, and walked back to Pier 9.

The walk back worried him most. Armand didn't need some bored Port cop pulling over and asking what some random black guy was doing walking along Lake Road late at night in February. He especially did not want to be out in the open when someone found those three bodies. No Port cruiser, or any other cruiser, rolled by. A couple of semis from the active piers did, though, blowing snow in Armand's face and chilling him with their frozen wakes. He pulled his coat around himself tighter. No use fighting the cold, he told himself. He was going to be in it a long time.

As he reentered Pier 9, he looked up at the bridge under construction between Holland Bay and Holland Island. It looked nearly complete, but the lights strung along it were all construction lights. Rufus was right. Connecting I-73 to the Island would change the city forever. The question was whether Ralph or Rufus would rule that future.

He thought of Shandra, snuffed out before she could make something of herself. Sure, the girl was naïve, but Armand loved her. Somewhere between the pier and Oldetown, well beyond the other side of the Musgrave, Baggy Anderson sat in a jail cell. Armand wanted Baggy's head for Shandra's death. He supposed he always would, even if Ralph or Rufus had Baggy killed in prison. He looked back at the scene he'd set for the police to find—Monk and Goose dead with their weapons in their hands, and the Estrada shooter dead with Monk's bullets in him.

Ralph would understand when he arrived. So would Rufus. It might be the last thing the two ever agreed upon.

Armand made his way back to the garage and took up the shooter's rifle. The shooter had brought a blanket with him.

"Well, thanks," he said, wrapping himself in what turned out to be a heavy quilt. "Since you won't be needing this anymore..." He took the shooter's rifle as well. "Or this."

Armand truly was grateful. He might be in that garage for hours. He settled in and watched out the window.

CHAPTER 22

Public Defender Terrie Riley entered Holland Bay Station with Maria Kagan. Maria showed up in a North Face jacket, jeans, and a pair of Puma running shoes that had never seen a morning jog. Riley looked pleat-perfect in her long navy-blue overcoat, hose, and DKNY pumps. The way they dressed, one would never guess they both worked for notoriously stingy Musgrave County.

Branson met them in the station bullpen. She jerked a thumb toward the back. "Your client's in Room Three," she said to Riley. To Maria Kagan, she said, "Come on. Baker's waiting for us."

After the chief's briefing that morning, Room 1 had had to double as a conference room. Until Baker could open up the building's second floor, Special Investigations would have to make do with the break room and one of the interrogation rooms for meetings. They entered to find Baker and Murdoch waiting.

When Baker saw Maria Kagan enter, he rose. "Lovely to see you, Mrs. Kagan, but shouldn't you be at the hospital?"

Maria Kagan pressed her lips thin. "If it's all the same to you, I prefer to take down the sonofabitch who tried to widow me."

Everyone froze as Maria barked her response.

"Terrie and I showed up at the same time," she continued. "She's in a good mood now, but if you've been jerking Anderson's chain, she's going to take it out on you."

"We're cutting him a deal," said Baker. "With your permission, of course."

"Give me what you have."

Branson gave the summary, adding the wounding of Kagan along with the murder of Captain Parcells to the litany of violence that day. Maria Kagan had a difficult time keeping a straight face when Branson related how Baggy had been picked up barefoot in his underwear.

"And how did you convince him he was facing more than an indecent exposure charge?" she asked.

"Obstruction, for one," said Murdoch. "If he did set that fire, arson. If he didn't, lying to a police officer about an ongoing investigation, which can be stepped up to obstruction." He smirked. "Also, his apartment is a crime scene since someone broke in and tried to kill him. No search warrant needed."

"What about Smithers?"

"Victim ID'd him," said Branson. "Since there was vaginal and anal trauma requiring treatment, the doctors did a rape kit under implied consent. We have his DNA."

Maria leaned her head back and blew out her breath. "You're kidding. He raped a woman and didn't expect to leave any evidence? This is Monticello's drug lord?"

"He tried to kill her—shot her twice," said Branson. "Probably thought he could dispose of her body later."

"She was scared when I met her earlier," said Murdoch, drawing a glare from Branson. He fidgeted a bit as he spoke. "Said she was afraid of getting in trouble."

"With the police? Or Smithers?"

"Both."

"Let me go talk to Terrie and her client. Do you think he knows who killed your three victims Sunday and Monday?"

"He probably knows who killed one of the Carciniras," said Branson. "We're betting it was Dmitri Reagan, but we'd like confirmation so they can go black on the board."

"What a mess."

"No one said Holland Bay was going to clean up easy," said Baker. His face lit up. "At least it's never boring."

"I like boring," said Maria. "People don't get killed by boring."

"Really," said Riley, standing in the doorway to the interrogation room with her hands on her hips, "you told him you didn't have to call his lawyer?"

"Unless we charge him," said Murdoch. "And we could have done that at any time up to eight tomorrow night. Besides, the boy claimed someone broke in and tried to kill him. That makes his apartment a crime scene. Guess what Robbery found when we sent over a couple of plainclothes to check it out."

"That's illegal."

Murdoch laughed. "Really? He had scales and baggies of crystal meth, which I heard he was cutting with that crystal kitty litter. Bet Smithers wants his fat ass for breakfast now."

Riley frowned. She'd been handed a worthless client and knew it. Then again, that was par for the course. She looked past Murdoch to Maria Kagan. "He cops to possession of drug paraphernalia. No more. In return, he'll tell you whatever you want to know about Ralph Smithers and Dmitri Reagan."

"Reagan's dead," said Maria, "but if his death clears a lot off our plate, I'll agree to it."

"I'll go tell him."

"Use small words," said Murdoch. "And talk slowly. Remember, he went streaking in his underwear in this weather."

Once Baggy rolled, Baker decided to raid the Silver Stiletto. It was risky, but with Baggy Anderson yammering away under the watchful eye of Terrie Riley, the drug stash removed from his apartment, and the evidence Lt. Kearny's detectives found on Dmitri Reagan's computer, they could put a final nail in Smithers's coffin. First, they had to sell Maria Kagan on the idea.

Then a judge.

"I can probably get Harbortown to supply us with a SWAT

team," said Baker. "Question is: Who do we get to sign off at this hour?"

"Mankie dislikes anything that upsets his routine," said Maria Kagan, referring to Judge Arvin Mankiewicz, a notoriously strict judge who also disliked being called "Mankie" to his face. "How about Boyd?"

"Only if we cross our t's and dot our i's," said Baker. "Boyd is notoriously picky about procedure, probable cause, and rules of evidence."

"Yeah," said Maria, "but every case I've argued before him, win or lose, has never been overturned. Can't say that about Mankie or Daugherty. And they're no slouches, either."

Baker let out a long sigh. "All right, do we agree on charges?"

"We get the girls on prostitution," said Maria. "There's already enough in Heather Leary's rape complaint to investigate it. We work with Vice, maybe Narcotics, just to see if anything pops up. We can shut down the Stiletto tonight. If they're clean, they're back in business tomorrow night, and only the customers' wives and mistresses lose."

"Can you sell this to Boyd with what we have?"

"He's going to think this is a fishing expedition."

"It is. But we deal the girls, get them to roll on Ralph Smithers. Once Plink's had seventy-two hours to detox, he can help us tie the Stiletto to Smithers's operation."

"Let's do it," said Baker. "Quick. Smithers is still loose. I want his ass in County by morning roll. Branson, a word. In my office."

Branson swallowed and fell in step behind Baker.

"I don't want you on the raid," said Baker.

Branson looked up from her desk. "Wait a minute. I earned this. José Carcinira and Doby Clark are my cases."

Baker gestured for Branson to take a seat. "Jess, look, I understand. If I had my way, we'd be wheeling Taggart in as well. But you're on restricted duty, and union rules state that I cannot put you on a raid until a doctor signs-off on it. You're already stretching the rules by working this late, questioning Leary…"

"I'm fine."

"I need a note from your physician to that effect. And frankly, Jess, I'm not through rehabilitating your career. I can't do that if you have a complication from your concussion."

"Rehabilitating…"

Baker put up his hand. "I was supposed to rubber-stamp a guilty ruling on you when you killed Mayor Kozinski's son. I couldn't. Ray Kozinski was a sexual predator, and you did the right thing, shooting him in self-defense. The mayor should have resigned for raising that piece of shit." He spread his hands. "You did four years in this dump. I did four years in Edison, kissing the Sheriff's ass."

"I could at least watch," said Branson. "Maybe question the girls?"

"I know, Jess. I know. I'll tell you what. Why don't you go back to St. Paul's and talk to that Leary woman. Give her the good news."

Branson pushed away from her desk and got to her feet. "I guess. Don't expect me to be at morning roll."

"I expect you to take a couple of well-deserved days off. You earned that much."

Branson went out to her desk and grabbed her purse and her car keys. On her way to the rear parking lot, she met Murdoch.

"Hey, Greg," she said. "You wanna get back on my good side?"

"Do I care?" His look said he did and knew it. "What do you need?"

"Score me a Kevlar vest."

"Why?"

"I gotta run an errand."

CHAPTER 23

Baker never said specifically that there would be a raid at the Silver Stiletto. However, he did mention it might get interesting if Zack Kelly and his cameraman followed the tan 2014 RAV 4 parked in the back lot, which belonged to one of the patrolmen on duty. He also cautioned that it would not be a good idea to start broadcasting until a certain building, one the RAV 4 might park behind, was entered by cops.

The building was entered by a lot of cops. Kelly and his cameraman were allowed to wait in the lot at Bernie Kosar Stadium with a stern warning by the officer in charge not to broadcast until the Stiletto was secured. They could shoot footage of the police going in, but, if a second of footage got on the air before they could surprise everyone on the inside, Baker would charge Kelly and his cameraman with obstruction. If they waited, they would scoop every 5 a.m. newscast in town.

So, when Baker's people began to move, Kelly's cameraman began to record. Soon, three MPD cruisers rolled up on the Stiletto and lit up their flashers, their officers jumping out with guns drawn. Kelly judged that the patrons already knew they were being raided. He looked at his watch. It was almost eleven-thirty when Baker's team took over the club. He was now linked to the newsroom, which would air an update between reruns of *The Middle* and *The King of Queens*.

Sure enough, Kelly heard Jennifer Acosta, the night anchor for

Fox 18, say, "We have a breaking news story for you now. Police have raided a high-end strip club near Kosar Stadium. We go now live to our own Zack Kelly for an update."

When the cameraman pointed at Kelly, he said, "Jennifer, Fox 18 received a news tip that police were planning to raid the Silver Stiletto, a strip club catering to businessmen here in the downtown Monticello area. Earlier tonight, according to a source close to the investigation, a woman was raped and shot in one of the empty offices in the same building as the club. While speaking with police later, she alleged that prostitution runs rampant at the Silver Stiletto…"

Murdoch went in with Petrocelli and Friedman. The three fanned out and made their way to VIP rooms. He looked at his phone and caught a text message from Baker. The captain and Mrs. Kagan had arrived and were across the street in the Kosar Stadium parking lot with the SWAT teams. He sent a two-word reply: "Come in." As soon as he and the others saw Baker paying his cover, all three of them badged the bouncers at the doors to the VIP rooms.

"Say a word," said Murdoch, "and we haul you and your buddies in for interfering with a police investigation. I got a warrant." He pushed his way inside the booth. There was a man with his pants down around his ankles while a naked girl knelt between his legs.

"Hey!" said the girl. "Oh," she added when she saw Murdoch's badge.

Murdoch grinned his best shit-eating grin. "Evening, Councilman. I didn't know you came here, too. I'm afraid I have to place both of you under arrest. What's your name, sweetie? I mean your real name, not your stage name."

Outside, Baker's voice could be heard shouting, "Everybody stay where you are. This is a raid."

The music went quiet as five SWAT team members, followed

by five more Harbortown patrol officers, swarmed the place.

Branson swung into the Kosar Stadium lot. Already, the SWAT team had moved in, with three Harbortown cruisers blocking access to the Silver Stiletto. Once parked, she ran across the street, flashed her badge at one of the uniforms guarding the entrance and went inside.

The scene disgusted her, scantily clad women whose flimsy outfits would come right off if you breathed on them right. Some of the girls were naked. All of them looked angry. She spotted Murdoch with a girl and a very embarrassed looking older man.

"You missed the party," said Murdoch as he approached.

"Baker tried to send me home." She tapped her head. "The concussion and all. I'm supposed to take tomorrow off. It's not like we have a lot of prior work to catch up on."

Murdoch pointed to where two uniforms were escorting a very big black man toward the front door. "One of the girls says that mountainoid they're hauling out has a line on Ralph Smithers. He's not been charged, but he *is* being uncooperative."

"Maybe if I talked to him in his element..."

"Knock yourself out, Branson. You seem to be getting good at that."

She flipped him the bird and marched over to the big guy, intercepting him before the two cops took him out of the building. "Hey, big fella. Detective Branson. They charge you with anything?"

"Watching strippers while black," he said. "What you think?"

She smiled that smile that lured the occasional biker into her bed. "Why don't we sit down somewhere and talk. Maybe you can help me out with something. What's your name?"

"Rock," he said.

"Damon Roque," said one of the cops escorting him. "Calls himself 'Rock,' though he's too ugly to be Dwayne Johnson. Want his priors?"

"Oh, I can read a rap sheet, Patrolman. What I need now is some information that Mr. Roque might have." She winked at Rock. "Might be worth your time to talk to me here instead of someone down at Settlers Commons."

Branson couldn't get over how ugly this guy looked. He wore a perpetually creepy expression that made her feel like she was being sized up for a pit in his basement. "Mr. Roque, Ralph Smithers is going to go down in the next forty-eight hours. If you don't want to be charged tonight with obstruction or pimping out the dancers here, you'd be wise to tell me where he is."

"I ain't no snitch."

"No, but you are a two-time loser. Want to go for three? Hiding him makes you an accomplice to rape. We can throw that into the mix. So what's it going to be, Mr. Roque? Home? Or Mansfield?"

Something was happening behind those weird Charlie Manson eyes of Roque's. Mentioning Mansfield Reformatory made his breathing quicken and his shoulders tense up in a way only ex-cons' did. "Something's gonna happen on Pier Nine, if it ain't already. That's all I know. If he ain't there, you can catch him at The Phoenix Café in Holland Bay."

She looked at the uniform. "Uncuff him." To Rock, she said, "Don't go hiding anywhere. When I come looking for you, whether I get Smithers or not, I own you if you've run off. Got it?"

"Bitch, I ain't got no place to go."

She got up and located Murdoch. "Come on. Let's go. Call the station and see if we got anybody left on patrol."

"What's going on?" said Murdoch.

"I found Smithers. Maybe. We have to run."

If he didn't move much, Armand found he could keep warm under the quilt. That was fine. Working for Dmitri had taught him patience. He once had waited outside a deadbeat's apartment building for four hours. That amazed Dmitri. The enforcer had been such a bundle of rage when he was alive that Armand often feared he would give them away.

But no one corrected Dmitri, not even Ralph. Not that Armand had noticed anyway. No one had corrected Dmitri on his mistakes until today. Armand wasn't even sure why.

Nor was he sure why he was sitting in a frozen shed on an abandoned pier with a rifle in his hand. He only knew that two men had asked him to kill, and each one had told him to kill the other. Already, he was a fugitive. The police would catch him sooner or later, even if he left the city.

More than that, Shandra was dead. Baggy, or one of his crew, had done it. There was no denying that. Ralph had ordered the fat man killed, as had Rufus. But Ralph had done the cleanup. If Armand survived the night, especially if the police caught him, he expected to find himself at the Morgue, identifying Shandra's body. Pin that on Baggy, and the fat man would be doomed. Convicted murderers, particularly if the act looked sexual, went straight into the general population. That much Armand knew about his future home. In the general population, especially at a maximum-security prison, Baggy would be easy prey for whomever Ralph or Rufus hired.

It might even be Armand, if things worked out right.

A pair of headlights swung onto the pier. Armand shifted backward a bit to get out of the light from the streetlamps outside. A small Toyota pushed its way through the snow to where Monk and Goose lay dead. Definitely not cops.

The door opened. Out stepped Ralph Smithers. The man shivered as he looked down at his two dead lieutenants.

CHAPTER 24

They took Branson's Pathfinder back across the river toward Pier 9. Murdoch wrinkled his nose as the heat kicked in. "What is that smell?"

"I confiscated our informant's Rottweiler," said Branson.

"Why?"

"Thought it smelled like a wet dog."

Lucas Avenue cut through downtown and led to the Hauptmann Memorial Bridge. Road salt from the past two days had turned the pavement a dirty white that looked even dirtier under the orange lamps of the bridge.

"Relax," said Murdoch. "Maybe he'll be dead when we get there."

"Fuck that. I'm his executioner."

Armand did not see lights when Rufus King appeared. Someone must have dropped him off at the entrance to the pier. He had a gun in his hand. Ralph had his out, too. The two faced each other at about ten paces, like some wild, wild west thing one of the digital channels showed late at night.

Armand raised his rifle and sited between the two but didn't pick a target. He'd make his decision soon enough. He did not want to go to prison for the wrong motherfucker.

The snow muffled the sound of the nearby Shoreway and the

city itself. Armand worried that Ralph and Rufus could hear him, even though each man had tasked him with killing the other. Then he realized he could hear them, too.

"My brother," said Rufus, looking down at Monk and Goose's corpses. "How did it come to this?"

Ralph watched him, his pistol down at his side. "You call me brother, and that's how I treated you all these years. I take you under my wing. You make your bones working for me, and no one will ever know you and Monk did Pablo Estrada. I put you through school, hand you my wallet, and make you my right hand. You was higher up than Goose, Rufus. Why you do me like this?"

Rufus looked up. "You let your blood boil too fast, Ralph." He looked back down at the corpses. "These two could have handled Dmitri. Quietly. You know when they find them, along with one of us, the police are going to put an end to Pier Nine as a dumping ground."

"One of us, eh?"

Rufus gave a humorless smile. "I know you've been talking to Armand. So have I. That boy has a decision to make." He reached out and put up his hand in the general direction of the garage, which caused Armand's heart to jump into his throat. "One of us is going to be dead. Maybe both of us if Armand thinks neither of us is worth keeping alive. Can't say I blame him. But I want you to know something."

"Janiece," said Ralph.

"She came to me."

"You didn't say no."

"Could you?"

Ralph laughed. "I gotta give you that. She vicious and clever, probably better than either of us, but she fine. If I survive, she dead. But if you live…"

Rufus gave a sad smile. "She's already my partner. You taught her well."

"This is fucked up, Rufus. Finish it?" He raised his gun and aimed at Rufus's chest.

Rufus brought his pistol up. "Finish it."

A pair of headlights appeared at the entrance to the pier.

The guns came up. Armand made his decision. He sited his target and squeezed the trigger. As his target fell to the pavement, a car appeared at the end of the pier. Armand did not even think. Swinging the barrel, he aimed for the headlight and started firing until he saw the lone survivor dive behind some equipment. One of the headlights went dark.

"Oh, no you don't," snarled Branson. She leaped out of the Pathfinder with her weapon drawn and began firing at the garage. Murdoch slid through an open window and started firing as well. Their shots put holes in the garage door, already windowless from return fire and whoever shot the dead men on the pier.

A couple of shots exploded snow around Branson. Another shot clanged off the Pathfinder's rear fender, making her briefly worry about the gas tank. Something slammed into her chest, sending her to the ground, making her cry out.

Armand stopped firing when the woman fell. By then, his benefactor had managed to slip away. Only now some black guy came climbing out the other side of the SUV. The woman had to be dead.

Armand knelt and put the weapon in the dead shooter's hands. It wouldn't convince Five-Oh for long that the dead man was the shooter. Between that and Monk's bullets in his brain, matters would be confused long enough for Armand to cover his tracks.

Moments later, he found out just how cold Lake Erie had become. He had only one chance: Get to the Transit on Pier 10 and fire up the heater. If he didn't, he'd have only two choices: Surrender or freeze to death.

CHAPTER 25

Branson sat up, groaning. Her ribs throbbing underneath the Kevlar. "Oh, God, I forgot how bad that hurts."

Murdoch stood over her, helping her to her feet. "I think we got him."

They looked around and saw three bodies and a bunch of tire tracks on the pier. Murdoch retrieved a flashlight from Branson's car. He shined it on the nearest body.

Ralph Smithers stared back at them with a huge hole in his throat.

Branson began laughing nervously, unable to stop. "He's dead. The sonofabitch is dead."

Murdoch put his arm around her. "So much for your Great White Whale." He looked around. "Wasn't there another guy when we rolled up?"

He shined his flashlight around them and found a set of recent footprints leading to the Pier 8 side. They ended at the edge.

"If he went into the drink..."

Armand climbed a ladder on the side of Pier 10, his body already rebelling against the extreme cold. As he crossed over to the Big Boy, he could feel ice forming in places. The Transit had to start, or he was a dead man. They'd find his cold corpse the next morning.

He had left his cell phone, partly to keep it from distracting him, partly because he thought he might have to swim for it. The keys…

No keys. Not in the ignition, not in his pockets. He sat freezing and wet in the driver's seat, teeth chattering, head pounding. The phone vibrated. It looked like Mr. King's number. He grabbed it.

"Armand," said a woman. "This is Janiece. Look behind you."

Headlights flashed in the rearview mirror.

"Come on," said Janiece. "Let's get you someplace warm."

Armand clicked off the burner, jumped out of the Transit, and charged toward the headlights. An Escalade sat idling alongside the old Big Boy, its lights off. Armand climbed inside, unable to stay in the cold a moment longer. He probably needed to go to the ER. The heat inside felt wonderful.

"Hello, Armand," said Janiece. "There's a blanket back there. Wrap yourself up. We'll get you some clothes."

"Thanks."

Janiece had the van's heater on high. Even in the dark, he could see why both Ralph and Rufus had fallen for her. She reminded him of Shandra.

"What are we waiting for?"

"Rufus," she said. "And patrol cars. Soon as that pier starts swarming with cops, no one's going to look at us until it's too late."

Armand nodded, shaking under the heavy blanket he'd found. Right now, he wanted coffee, maybe a little booze.

Ten minutes later, just as the first ambulance passed the pier entrance, Rufus climbed into the car. He gave Armand a big hug.

"You have no idea what this means to me," said Rufus. "Or to you." He looked up at Janiece. "Let's go, babe. Lights down until we're out on Lake."

Janiece eased the van up the pier to the street entrance then turned right onto Lake toward downtown.

"You did good, Armand," said his Rufus. "Now comes the hard part."

Armand looked over. "Steinberg explained it to me. I wish Shandra could have seen it."

"Me, too, son. You just earned a promotion tonight."

As they passed an oncoming police cruiser, he thought what he'd really like was a way out of the Game. Rufus had told him the only way out was through, but right now, Armand could not even see that.

The flashing lights of the cruiser in the rearview drove that home as it turned onto Pier 9.

Branson and Murdoch flanked Eddie Soroya from Homicide, staring down into the face of Ralph Smithers. Smithers stared back up at them, the back of his head missing. Nearby lay two other bodies, both covered in sheets.

"We found the one who killed Smithers," said Soroya. "He's in the garage. Looks like a guy who hangs out with the Estradas."

Branson and Murdoch looked at each other. "Great," said Murdoch. "A fucking drug war."

Branson pressed her lips together. Her head hurt, mainly from fatigue and too much time in the biting cold. "Maybe it's over for now. Rey Estrada's gone. Ralph Smithers is gone."

"You think this shit ever really ends?"

"No. But maybe we'll get a break while they figure out who fills the void."

They stood looking over the crime scene for a few more moments, mostly staring in disbelief that the Great White Whale known as Ralph Smithers lay dead at their feet. Finally, Murdoch said, "That's what I like about you, Branson. You're an optimist."

"Go to hell, Murdoch."

The kid named Linc arrived at the Walmart construction site in Eastern Shore moments after Armand and Rufus, bearing two sets of dry clothes for them.

"Ralph's gone," said Rufus after he and Armand changed. "So are Monk and Goose. This is my operation now." He jerked a thumb at Armand. "He's my deputy, even though he has to go away for a while."

Linc nodded. "What about when Baggy gets sprung?"

"Baggy's finished. If he shows up at Wentworth or anyplace else we own, I want him capped." His eyes flicked toward the mainland. "We need you to go get the van, get rid of it. Then get word to our new connect. Tell him I want him in my office by ten."

Linc nodded and headed back to where his ride waited.

Armand climbed into the backseat of Rufus's Escalade, now clad in dry clothes and shoes that Linc had brought. "You want someone in your office with all that blood in the carpets?"

"What blood?" said Janiece.

"But…"

"It's been handled," said Rufus. He shifted in his seat to face Armand. "Did Steinberg go over what to say?"

"Dmitri set the first one," said Armand, "then put me up to setting the second one."

"And…?"

"I been laying low since then because I hit someone's car."

"And where's the car?"

"I ditched it in Prussian Meadow."

They rounded the south side of Holland Island. Eastern Shore gave way to Indian Shoals, the island's "downtown." Overhead, the Voinovich Bridge loomed. On this end, it connected to the as-yet-unopened I-73 extension to Port Jones on the north end of the island.

"Steinberg can get you down to five years if you plea-bargain," said Rufus as they came upon the Port Center, the twenty-story twin office towers that defined Holland Island's skyline. "You know what to do once you're in. Since they'll likely send you to Mansfield, our people will get in touch with you after you've been in for a week. When they offer it, you put in for college courses while you're in there."

"I ain't got my GED," said Armand.

"Then do that first. When you go before the parole board, you show remorse. You tell them you're going to school to better yourself. Keep your nose clean. Do what we tell you. You'll be out in two years."

Twenty minutes later, they were back on the mainland and in Holland Bay. Janiece pulled the car over near Holland Bay Station. Armand jumped out and walked the rest of the way. Before opening the front door, he looked at the clock overhead. It read twelve-forty-two. By sunrise, he would be in a jail cell.

"If he screws me over," he said under his breath, "I'll roll on his ass." He went inside and found his way to the duty sergeant. "My name is Armand Cole. You have a warrant out for my arrest?"

The sergeant, a ruddy-faced white guy with red hair to match, looked up, startled. "You're shitting me. After all that's been going down tonight, you walk in off the street?"

"Could I please call my lawyer?"

"Listen," said Murdoch, "about what happened with the Leary woman..."

Branson's hands tightened up on the steering wheel. "Save it. I'll make sure she knows you helped take down Smithers's operation. And I'm not going to tell Jane."

"Screw Jane," said Murdoch. "I kicked her out this morning after we had our fight."

"Over what?"

"You really want to know?"

Branson laughed. "Will it explain why you accepted a blowjob from a stripper?"

"Yeah. Jane's been cheating on me."

"Wow. Greg, I'm sorry about that. So, why'd Channel Eighteen end up on our doorstep?"

"She probably heard about the chief's visit this morning, and decided I was her ticket to a TV news gig."

"Still, you pretty much did abuse your badge with that girl."

Murdoch closed his eyes. "Look, Branson, I was pissed off and hurt. I loved that woman, and she treated me like a house nigger."

"Ouch."

"That's how I felt. Then this stripper, this beautiful stripper, goes down on me without me even asking. Your marriage is over, and you're pissed at your ex. Then a whore throws you some free revenge sex. I should apologize to her then thank her."

"Just apologize. She's in no mood to say, 'You're welcome.'"

Lake emerged from under the Shoreway. Branson turned into the lot for Holland Bay Station and guided the car around back. Before she cut the engine, she turned toward Murdoch. "Look, Greg, first off, I still think that was the worst thing you could have done as a cop. Well, one of the worst. But I know you better than that."

"Gee, thanks." He started to open his door.

"Wait. What I'm trying to say is that I don't approve of what you did, but I understand."

CHAPTER 26

The Silver Stiletto closed indefinitely after the police left with five dancers and five johns in custody. The johns were taken out the back to be driven to Settlers Commons. There, they were released without charge, though a councilman made noises about police funding at the next Finance Committee meeting. Chief Hudepohl, who considered the downfall of Ralph Smithers worth losing sleep over, pulled him into a conference room and explained to him the foolhardiness of retaliating against a department that opted not to end his political career. They did not want the johns. They wanted the girls and only so they could turn them.

After the girls were processed, their lawyers called, and deals made, Hudepohl summoned Baker to his office. "Al, I knew you'd shake things up when I gave you that job. But, Jesus, I thought you'd at least wait until you got the keys to the men's room."

Baker laughed. "Well, you know, I spent the last nine years either investigating my fellow officers or playing gopher for the Sheriff. Just wanted to end the dry spell."

"Yeah, but Ralph Smithers. And on your second day on the job."

"With all due respect, Chief, Smithers took himself out. Homicide and Detectives Branson and Murdoch found Smithers dead on Pier Nine." He leaned forward, resting his elbows on his knees. "With your permission, I want to park a car overnight on that pier from now on. Time we stop letting it be a cemetery."

"You know this isn't over. Smithers is dead. Rey Estrada is dead. You don't think Miguel Estrada isn't going to try and fill the vacuum?"

"What makes you think it's not already filled?" Baker stood up and stretched. "Everything that happened the past two days seems to have been engineered to rattle Ralph Smithers's cage. If that shooter hadn't killed him, we still had him on the rape charge. He got angry, and he got stupid. Even then, Murdoch and Branson found enough on Smithers that we'd have had him in a week. Again, it's almost like someone was leaving us breadcrumbs to follow."

Hudepohl frowned. "Someone set him up? Like, who?"

Branson rushed home after finishing up at Holland Bay Station. She had a Rottweiler who'd had free rein of her apartment all night. Vader needed an emergency 3 a.m. trip to the park. Never mind the scooper. No one was going to care until the snow melted.

She returned home with Vader around 4 a.m., stripped down to her underwear, and collapsed on her bed. She didn't wake up until one that afternoon. Rolling off the bed, she began looking around to see if the dog had taken advantage of his freedom. Unfortunately, he had.

"Oh, no." She knelt down on the floor of her closet and picked up the remains of a pair of expensive high-heels that she loved. "Vader."

The dog came in at the sound of his name spoken so severely.

She held up the destroyed shoes. "You do not eat mommy's fuck-me shoes."

Vader whined and put his head down. That lasted about ten seconds when the doorbell rang.

"Shit." She located her bathrobe and pulled it around herself. When she opened the door... "Hey."

"Hey," said Jerry. "Listen, about last night..."

Branson shut him up by grabbing his neck and covering his mouth with hers. "You want me?" she said when she came up for air.

Jerry looked a little stunned.

"Jerry, I'm asking you. Do you want to be with me?"

"Um... Yes."

She pulled him inside. "Think you can handle me at my worst?"

"I can try."

"Good. 'Cuz if you can, you deserve me at my best." She pulled him inside and guided him toward her bedroom. "Now, show me what we did Sunday night. This time with no vodka."

Armand found himself in Judge Kendra Daugherty's courtroom that afternoon. They had given him an orange jumpsuit and handcuffed him. He sat quietly as though the cuffs and jumpsuit were fashion accessories. When they finally called him his case, Steinberg joined him at the dock.

"The State of Ohio vs. Armand Cole," the bailiff read. "Defendant is charged with one count of aggravated arson."

Daugherty looked over at the prosecution table. "State?"

"Mr. Cole admits setting fire to an occupied apartment complex," said Maria Kagan, now sporting a freshly pressed skirt and jacket, "at the corner of Eastern and Delaware Avenues. No one was injured, but several children did live in the building."

"Counsel, how does your client plead?"

"My client pleads guilty, Your Honor. He is remorseful. He says..."

"I regretted it as soon as I saw that mother in the laundry room," said Armand, much to Steinberg's annoyance. "I didn't want anything bad to happen to her or her baby."

"Mrs. Kagan?"

"Mr. Cole has stated he was prompted to torch the building after a Dmitri Reagan, deceased, put him up to it. He has further agreed to supply the State with information regarding the criminal enterprise which employed him and the late Mr. Reagan. We recommend forty months incarceration with eligibility for parole in twenty-four."

Daugherty looked down to write something and said, "Is that acceptable, Mr. Steinberg?"

"We are satisfied with the State's recommendation."

She looked up. "Mr. Cole, you have pled guilty to arson. I sentence you to thirty-six months at the Mansfield Correctional Institution. You will be eligible for parole in twenty-four months as the State has recommended." She leaned forward, making Armand feel nervous for the first time since he had entered the courtroom. "I'm being far more generous than even the State has been, Mr. Cole. If I see you in this courtroom again, rest assured you will spend much more time in a far more secure facility." She banged the gavel. "Next case."

Deputies came to take Armand to Norwalk, where he would await transport to Mansfield. Steinberg walked alongside him. "Keep your head down, kid. Your friend and mine was standing where you were eight years ago. Now look where he is."

That did not reassure Armand.

Branson and Jerry rolled away from each other, lying on their backs, trying to catch their breath. It had been their third time making love that afternoon. Branson was starting to feel a little loopy.

"God, Jess," said Jerry, his voice hoarse as he tried to slow his breathing. "You're going to kill me."

She turned herself onto her side to face him. Her fingers walked playfully up his chest. "Would that be so bad? You'd die happy."

He laughed. "So, I take it you like what I can do?"

Did she? Branson's usual playmates rippled with muscles. Often, they were big men who could enclose her with their own bodies. Jerry? He had a big, soft body, the body of someone who sat at a desk all day, only to go home and sit on the couch all evening. While Branson never considered herself a beauty queen, she kept herself fit and probably drove Jerry crazy when she took off her clothes. So how did this doughy nerd stack up to the bikers, the marathon runners, and the gym rats Branson had entertained herself with since her divorce?

"I feel loved." She bit him on the chest. "Is that what you wanted to hear?"

"I wanted to hear the truth."

She rolled on top of him and kissed him hard. "What's that tell you? Because that was the truth, baby." She kissed him on the nose. "You're sweet. You came over to take care of me. And you kept your distance when I told you to."

"And do you love me?"

She traced a finger down his cheek. "I trust you. And I care for you."

"But..."

"But nothing. I told you I'm damaged goods. I'm not there yet because I'm not sure I can feel like that yet." Pushing up, she straddled him then leaned back down into his face. "You love me. And I need that right now. So, you need to warm my cold, cold heart. And while you're doing that, I am going to take care of you. I'm going to be the woman you need me to be. Because I'd like to be that woman." She pulled his hand to her chest and pressed it over her heart. "She's in here, trapped. Help me free her."

Jerry's smile made him look like a big, goofy kid, one with a beard. "I suppose I can work with that.

"Do you love me, Jerry?"

"Of course." From the end of the bed, unseen and on the floor, Vader let out a single bark. "And Vader loves you, too. We both love you."

Branson laughed. "And if I asked you to do something for me, would you do it?"

"Name it."

She tickled his chest. "How do I get a photograph onto Instagram without it being traceable to me?"

"Is that all? What's in it for me?"

Branson began stitching kisses down his chest, his belly... She soon had Jerry's eyes rolling back into his head.

That evening, a photo made it from Branson's Android device to a phony Instagram account with a link emailed to Steven Hudepohl, Chief of Police.

And to Branson's old friend Jennifer Acosta at Fox 18 News.

A railroad worker found the burned body of a young black girl on the grounds of the Mittal steel mill. Although Lexy Griffin caught the body, she phoned Jeff Kagan to keep him in the loop. Something, she told him, suggested this was the last chapter in the sad story that had unfolded at Eastern and Delaware. Kagan, in turn, called Branson, then Murdoch, from his hospital room. Branson did not answer. Murdoch promised to update Baker and to meet Griffin at the Morgue.

By late afternoon, Murdoch had Armand Cole brought from Norwalk. The medical examiners were still trying to trace the dead girl's dental records. Murdoch, picking up on Griffin's suspicions, thought that Armand might know who the girl was.

They brought the boy in, looking pathetic in handcuffs and a jumpsuit. Murdoch chatted with him briefly, telling him he knew his mom back in middle school and that he'd look in on her while the boy was in prison. It was half-true. Althea Cole had remembered when Murdoch's father died. The boy had nothing to do with his concern.

Two deputies from the Sheriff's Department escorted Armand into the refrigeration room. The boy shivered, but Murdoch doubted it was from the cold. Slowly, two assistants opened the compartment where the girl had been placed. Some of her face remained intact, enough, Murdoch hoped, for the boy to identify her.

Armand stared down at her for a few moments. Finally, Murdoch asked, "Is that Shandra Rogers?"

Armand nodded silently.

"Are you willing to sign a statement to that effect?"

Armand sniffed once and said, "Yes."

Murdoch nodded to the two deputies, and they escorted Armand out of the room. The boy sobbed as the door closed behind him.

Against the advice of his lawyer, Reginald "Baggy" Anderson, late of the Wentworth Towers Housing Project in Holland Bay, decided to back out of his plea deal and take his chances with the court system. Baggy's keen legal instincts brought him to this decision as Armand Cole wrote his statement to Murdoch and the coroner that the girl found near the city's last steel mill was one Shandra Rogers, also late of Holland Bay. Murdoch doubted that Baggy needed a come-to-Jesus moment, though he mused it wouldn't hurt. No, Baggy needed something much more frightening.

He needed to come to Jessica.

Murdoch and Branson met Maria Kagan at the county holding facility downtown at the Justice Center. Baggy was escorted in with a deputy sheriff and a beleaguered Terrie Riley accompanying him. Riley tried to look stern and professional, but one look in her eyes told Murdoch all he needed to know. Her client was out of control.

"I changed my mind," said Baggy without preamble or prompting. "I ain't testifying against no one. Ralph dead. Dmitri dead. Cole locked up. What you need me for?"

"I see," said Murdoch. He turned to Maria Kagan. "So, Counselor, does this mean we can dump his fat ass into the general population down in Norwalk?"

"I ain't fat!"

Maria ignored him. "No deal. No protection. And with the number of Smithers's people getting arrested this week, no guarantees for your safety. That's not punishment, Mr. Anderson. That's a fact of prison life. I can't even guarantee you won't end up in Mansfield, sharing a cell with Armand Cole."

"But I ain't done nothing." Baggy glared at Murdoch. "That search of my apartment was illegal."

"If he withdraws his earlier statement," said Riley, "that's a valid point. No break-in? No crime scene, which makes it a warrantless search."

Murdoch's mouth curled to one side in a half-grin. "Oh, Mr. Anderson, I'm so pleased you decided to play this game with me today. Because my friend Jess has something she wants to talk to you about that just might change your mind." And then he leaned across the desk into Baggy's face. "One way or another, Reginald, you are going to leave this room as my bitch." He looked up at Riley. "With your attorney making sure I don't abuse the privilege."

Baggy's eyes shifted to Branson. "So, spill it. What you got on me that my lawyer can't get me out of?"

"Shandra Rogers," said Branson.

Baggy's face paled, then darkened. "I didn't kill the bitch."

"How do you know she's dead?"

Baggy sputtered, unable to form a coherent response.

"Her body was found burned in Midtown," said Branson. "But the coroner has already determined she was killed elsewhere. Someone snapped her neck. There were signs of sexual trauma. We might assume she and Mr. Cole liked it rough, but Mr. Cole was missing the morning she died, presumably laying low after your friend, Mr. Reagan, set his last fire. A witness heard screaming the morning Ms. Rogers died. It came from her apartment then stopped suddenly. This same witness saw you outside that same apartment only minutes later." Branson smiled. "I respect your lawyer, Mr. Anderson. I've seen her work before. But with your sheet, your reputation, and the fact you balked on a plea deal, Mrs. Kagan here can have you at Lucasville with three needles sticking in your arm before the current governor's term ends. And he's not been known to commute many death sentences."

"Detective," said Riley, "you can't threaten him with the death penalty. That's for a jury to decide."

"If I get a court order for a DNA sample," said Branson, "what are the chances it will match the semen found inside Ms. Rogers?"

Baggy slammed his hands on the table as though he were about to rise. Riley put a hand on his shoulder.

"The original deal stands," said Riley. "My client will testify as originally planned as long as he is not charged with Ms. Rogers's murder."

Branson grinned. "Lovely. Mr. Anderson, you just got away with murder. With any luck, you and Armand Cole will never meet again."

Murdoch doubted luck would have anything to do with it. If anything, he expected Baggy to be the last-ever body on Pier 9 in three to five years. The boy was just stupid enough to come back to Monticello when he got out.

Deputy Chief of Operations Derek Roberts found himself summoned to the chief's office while Murdoch and Branson explained the facts of life to Baggy Anderson. Meetings with the chief were frequent. He was, after all, responsible for who worked for the Monticello Police, where they worked, and what they did. He also had nominal command of the city's Harbortown Division. Yet the chief often scheduled his meetings in advance. If something urgent came up, the chief came to him. That was Hudepohl's style.

So when the call came requesting Roberts's immediate presence in the chief's office, he assumed it had to do with the recent downfall of one Ralph Smithers. He walked the long hallway down to the opposite end of the corridor where the chiefs of police and fire and the safety director all had their offices. Inside, the secretary, a young redhead who dressed more like a lawyer than a receptionist, looked up and said, "Go right in, sir. They're expecting you."

They? Roberts pushed his way inside the inner office to find a more Spartan version of his own office, this one with a view of the downtown skyline and the Thurman Reed Bridge out to Holland Island.

He also found Chief Hudepohl sitting with Vice Mayor Maly and Safety Director Chalmers around the conference table. All of them scowled.

Hudepohl picked up a tablet and turned the screen out to face Roberts. "Colonel Roberts, do you want to tell me what the hell this is all about?"

The screen displayed a photo of Roberts in civilian clothes, his face inappropriately close to the large breasts of a curvaceous black stripper.

A month later, Branson found herself in Daugherty's courtroom to testify against a former employee of the Silver Stiletto. It was the third day of trial for Damon Roque, the same Damon Roque who had told Branson where she could find Ralph Smithers.

She hated the defense attorney, a smarmy ambulance chaser named Joe Nuñez. She was no lawyer, but she found his frequent objections on the most dubious grounds flimsy at best. She also wanted to throttle him for trying to get Plink disqualified as a witness. The judge listened patiently to his litany of issues, including Plink's unreliability as an unrepentant meth addict.

This morning made Branson's week. Someone had whispered in her ear as everyone shuffled into the courtroom following lunch recess.

"How's our dog?"

Branson nearly jumped in her seat and turned around. Sitting behind her was a man in an Army dress uniform. His nametag read "Wallend," and his stripes indicated the rank of sergeant. She stood up and gave the man a hug. "Plink, how are you?"

Plink returned the embrace. "Much better. Just got out of

rehab, and I'm staying with my sister in Toledo. Under supervision, of course. I don't have to report to Lebanon until next month. I've decided to start working on my degree while I'm there."

"Well, good for you. But the uniform? Is that permitted?"

"I am an honorably discharged soldier. My conviction is for a civilian felony. Can't vote. Can't carry a weapon. But I can sure as hell be proud of my service." He looked her up and down, having never seen her in a dress before. "You clean up pretty well yourself."

Branson stood and did a little turn. "For the first time in years, I'm proud of my job. After Smithers went down, I bought myself a little present. Dress, shoes, a nice bag. Speaking of shoes..."

"Don't tell me Vader chewed up your dress shoes."

She laughed. "How did you guess?"

"Vader was never a drug dog, let alone a drug dealer's dog. He followed me home from Big River Park one day last fall. Good watchdog, which I'm sure you've noticed."

"I have." She frowned. "Plink..."

"Please," he said. "Call me Victor. Plink was a shell of a man."

"Okay. Victor. Tell me I can keep Vader. I've just gotten him and my boyfriend to get along."

Wallend smiled wide. "Detective..."

She put up her hand. "Jessica."

"Jessica, I would be proud to leave Vader with you. You're the first cop he ever trusted, at least while I had him."

The bailiff called out, "All rise."

"Let's have coffee after this is over," she said. "I want to hear how you're doing."

"I'd like that," said Wallend.

Branson turned around as the bailiff announced Judge Daugherty. The last month had made her love being a police officer once more. Seeing Victor Wallend in his dress uniform, clear-eyed and happy, made her prouder than anything else in her career.

ACKNOWLEDGMENTS

No book makes it to publication without help. This one is no exception. For starters, I'd like to thank my sister from another mister, Jennette Heikes, who read a couple of the intermediate drafts and pronounced it readable. Brian Thornton did an initial edit on one of the later drafts and ultimately put this book on Down & Out's radar. Brian also introduced me to his agent, Paula Munier, whose subsequent suggestions brought this a lot closer to the version you're now reading. Then there is Cynthia Bushman, who handed me some sound red ink and had me go find out if "Five-Oh" was still a valid slang term for the police. (It is, and hat tip to retired Officer Josh Hayes for confirming.)

And finally, I have to thank my wife, Candy Jo, who read it shortly after we married and pushed me to get this traditionally published. She's why I do this.

JIM WINTER is the crime fiction byline of author TS Hottle. As Jim he is the creator of the Nick Kepler series, featuring freelance insurance investigator Nick Kepler, and *Road Rules*, a bizarre romp from Cleveland to Savannah, Georgia, involving a classic Coup de Ville and a stolen holy relic. As TS Hottle, he is also the creator of The Compact Universe, a loosely connected series set 500 years in the future. Find out all his doings as Jim Winter at JimWinterBooks.com.